ASIAN PACIFIC AMERICANS
"Keywords", Concepts and History
Third Edition

Joel Franks
San Jose State University

Mc Graw Hill **Custom Publishing**

Boston Burr Ridge, IL Dubuque, IA New York
San Francisco St. Louis Bangkok Bogotá Caracas Kuala Lumpur
Lisbon London Madrid Mexico City Milan Montreal New Delhi

Asian Pacific Americans: "Keywords", Concepts, and History

4 5 6 7 8 9 0 QSR QSR 0 9 8 7

ISBN-13: 978-0-07-353756-6
ISBN-10: 0-07-353756-X

Editor: Julie Kehrwald
Production Editor: Nina Meyer
Printer/Binder: Quebecor World

TABLE OF CONTENTS

PREFACE

This text owes a great deal to a great many people. First, I hope in some ways it reflects the hard work of several San Jose State University faculty members who have taught Asian American Studies 33And 33B since the late 1980s. Among these faculty members are Raymond Lou, Steven Payne, Steven Doi, Robert Fung, Soo-Young Chin, Soo Choi, Alex Yamato, Peter Bacho, Wendy Ng, Hien Duc Do, Robert Kumamoto, Henry Gutierrez, Curtiss Takada Rooks, and Estella Habal. Second, I hope it acknowledges the hard work of the hundreds of students who have taken Asian American Studies 33A and 33B. This text, therefore, is dedicated to my colleagues and students at San Jose State.

INTRODUCTION

For the last several years, those of us who are members of San Jose State University's Asian American Studies Program have developed and taught a pioneering lower division two- semester course--a survey course called Asian Americans and United States History and Political Institutions. This course combines teaching conventional U.S. History and Government with Asian Pacific American History. And we try to teach this course from a comparative racial and ethnic group and interdisciplinary perspectives. Unfortunately, it had been a course burdened with various readers, textbooks, monograph, novels, and autobiographies. To streamline this course, we wanted to put together an accessible textbook combining Asian Pacific American history with a comparative and interdisciplinary analysis of political power, race and ethnicity in the U.S. Because my colleagues were pressed by other important projects, I was honored with the task of putting this textbook together so that it will not only have meaning to our students at San Jose State, but will attract the interest of all sorts of readers concerned with the historical experiences of Asian Pacific Americans from a relatively unique interdisciplinary and comparative framework.

To further streamline the course and allow faculty members more flexibility in organizing their required text, what was once a two volume text has been downsized to one volume. The general American history material has been deleted. Instead, the text is divided into parts. The first deals with concepts and issues that will aid students in their endeavors to master an interdisciplinary perspective to Asian Pacific American and U.S. History. The second part deals with introducing students to key characteristics of Asian Pacific American history. One of these key characteristics of Asian Pacific American history is the Asian Pacific American experiences with changing composition of the People's Club in a society that declares itself based on the will of the people. The second is the perhaps less important but still illuminating Asian Pacific American experiences with the American world of sports—a world which rightly or wrongly reflects America's ability to construct a democratic culture.

A WORD TO READERS

A brief reminder regarding the terminology used in this text to refer to different social groups is necessary. I do not apologize for trying not to offend people. That, after all, is part of being civil, being polite. Still, some terminology I use in this textbook may confuse people more than offend them. The term "oriental" is avoided throughout unless used to describe attitudes toward Asian Pacific people. . Since the earth is fairly rounded it is nonsensical to call people "Orientals" or Easterners, let alone "occidentals" or Westerners. I, therefore, refer to people of Asian Pacific ancestry living in the United States as Asian Pacific Americans. If, more specifically, a person's ancestry is Vietnamese, then I call her a Vietnamese American. Also, this text generally refers to people of European ancestry living in the United States as European Americans. To provide readers with a little variation, I occasionally might use the term white or whites to refer to people of European ancestry. However I prefer European American, because it associates people of European ancestry with a cultural history as opposed to skin color or race, both of which are inadequate ways to objectively categorize people. Similarly, while this text may occasionally refer to Americans of African ancestry as blacks, I prefer, and more often use, the term African American.

PART I
"KEYWORDS" AND CONCEPTS IN SOCIAL, CULTURAL, AND HISTORICAL INQUIRY

I
"KEYWORDS" AND CONCEPTS

Whether we like it or not, we have been defined by what theorist Raymond Williams called "keywords." In America, "keywords" such as race, ethnicity, gender, and class have been crucial. These "keywords" have been used and misused by all sorts of people-- scholars, public policy makers, journalists, lawyers, bureaucrats, educators, market analysts, clerics, coaches, parents and friends. These "keywords" can perhaps help us understand the societies in which we live and why we might vary in terms of beliefs and behaviors within a society. But these keywords have made it far too easy to construct social categories with difficult to transcend boundaries. In the process, we have found it far too hard to understand people who do not seem to fit easily into the categories we have constructed or have been constructed for us by our parents, teachers, clerics, media, employers, coaches, friends, and political leaders. For example, the term Asian Pacific American is a category designed to make sense of the awesome differences and similarities of people who can trace their ancestry to Asia and the Pacific Rim. Yet whether the term does so effectively is open to question. Certainly, none of this is very easy to discuss. But one place to start to understand more fully the social categories distinguishing Asian Pacific Americans from other groups and dividing Americans of Asian Pacific ancestry is to focus on some of the more important theoretical perspectives on social categories in the United States and elsewhere. Perhaps, then, we can get a better view of the boundaries that seemingly set people apart from one another and determine whether we can or should cross those boundaries.

ETHNICITY

Sociologists have argued that members of an ethnic group have to regard themselves as maintaining something in common which distinguishes them as an ethnic group. They have to possess what Shibutani and Kwan called a "common ancestry." And because of their "common ancestry," these people might share similar traditions, historical memories, language, or religion. This identification with a "common ancestry" furnishes them with a sense of "weness." At the same time, people outside of that ethnic group also have to recognize its members' distinctiveness. This imposes upon the group an identity of "theyness." Thus, ethnic groups are not natural phenomena, but products of history.

An immigrant from Italy in the late nineteenth and early twentieth centuries did not necessarily come to the United States thinking that "Yes, now I am going to be a member of an ethnic group. I am going to be an Italian American." This would mean that that the immigrant in question believed that she or he shared much in common with people from all over Italy, regardless of regional, class, or political differences. However, this was not the case as one hundred years or so ago, Italians were similar to many people from generally non-industrial societies. They were kin-oriented and localistic in their loyalties. Their families, villages, and regions of origins often held more meaning to them than their sense of Italian nationality. Moreover, there were bitter divisions among Italians over a variety of issues frequently related to class and region. People from Northern Italy often considered Southern Italians and Sicilians as hopelessly backward. In turn, Southern Italians and Sicilians rarely expressed admiration for Northerners.

While in the United States Italian immigrants learned if not to set aside their differences entirely, then at least to recognize that they shared much more in common with each other than with other immigrant groups and native-born American citizens in terms of history, culture, and language. An ethnic group was, therefore, hammered into existence out of what had been in Italy a set of divergent and sometimes conflicting interests. Italian American ethnicity was expressed through Italian American sponsored and maintained church and mutual aid societies, in addition to political, economic, and athletic organizations. Italian American ethnicity was learned through interactions in the family, places of worship, street, meeting hall, and playground.

While in the past, ethnicity and nationality were seen as similar. It is more helpful to recognize that while related, the terms mean different things. The grandparents of a third generation Chinese American possess a Chinese nationality. They were born in China, spoke Cantonese or Mandarin, and recognize what seems to them a coherent Chinese culture. If they migrated to the United

States, they undoubtedly retain a sense of Chinese nationality but they also became a part of a Chinese American ethnic group—a diverse group that has consisted of American born and Chinese born, U.S. citizens and non-U.S. citizens, native English as well as Cantonese or Mandarin speakers. Thus, a member of an Asian Pacific American ethnic group lives and experiences American life, but lives and experiences that life in a way that is distinctive from someone who can trace his or her ancestry to Italy, Cuba, or West Africa.

RACE

The concept of race, because people have long considered it as scientifically sound, is more complicated and controversial than ethnicity, although the two concepts have been frequently interrelated. We often link race to physical and/or biological characteristics. However, physical anthropologists, those scholars who study the biological impact on human history, frequently argue that there is no such thing as a scientifically proven pure race--that during the thousands of years of human migrations the gene pool has gotten so mixed up that it is quite impossible to determine where one so-called race begins and the other ends.

Race, according to many contemporary scholars, is a social construction. In other words, people's racial identities are history's offspring and not the findings of "objective" science. For example, American citizens typically today do not consider people of Jewish descent as members of a distinctive Jewish race. Yet not so long ago, people of Jewish descent were often considered as possessing distinctive, inherited, and often unflattering physical, moral, and intellectual attributes. Thus, they belonged to a different race. Scholars such as Michael Rogin and Karen Brodkin point out that the genetic make up of Jewish Americans of European origins has not changed, but history has. In the process, Jewish Americans of European ancestry became white.

The political and non-scientific characteristics of the concept of race are underpinned by the historical discrimination experienced by people of mixed racial descent. In the 1940s, Roy Campanella was a great baseball catcher possessing both African American and Italian American backgrounds. Nevertheless, he could not play Major League ball for several years and had to play in the Negro Leagues, because he was socially defined as African American. Why could he not as well have been defined as white just as mid-twentieth century Italian Americans were defined, although

3

sometimes grudgingly, as white? Why could he have not played with and against great Italian American ballplayers such as Joe Dimaggio and Phil Rizzuto before Jackie Robinson donned a Brooklyn Dodger uniform in 1947.

In other words, race, like ethnicity, has a strong subjective component. Racial characteristics are, then, generally socially developed and perceived through art, literature, media, education, sports, and other cultural institutions. Yet one way to distinguish race from ethnicity is to argue that the former is based upon physical and/or biological attributes, **real or imagined**.

Still, just because racial attributes have long and often been based upon flimsy evidence, does not mean that the concept of race is unimportant. Indeed, people act for good or ill on the basis of how they perceive themselves and others racially. However, a person's racial characteristics do not produce a love of Polka music, on the one hand, or Hip-hop music, on the other. There is no Polka gene or Hip-hop gene. If anything one's ethnicity, which is more closely related to a person's social and cultural background, is a more likely explanation of behavior, values, and life styles.

One more thing of note. Not so long ago, intelligent people would earnestly talk about a French race or a Korean race. Today, however, even those scholars who take race seriously as a scientific concept would discredit such talk. National borders have not corresponded to racial borders. There is a Korean nationality, but there is no Korean race.

RACISM AND NATIVISM

Asian Pacific immigrants and their offspring have historically experienced both racism and nativism. While there is any number of ways to define racism, clearly racism entails a belief that a group bears racial characteristics that renders it innately inferior to one or more other groups. Perhaps, it is useful to distinguish racialism from racism. Several years ago, the liberal anthropologist Ashley Montagu argued that races existed--that members of these groups possessed significant innate characteristics that distinguished them from other groups. However, he emphasized that while racial differences were real those differences did not justify a racial hierarchy. On a personal level, someone might remark that Asian Pacific Americans make great engineers. This may be a racialist statement related to a harmful stereotype to boot. However, this person may not mean that Asian Pacific Americans are racially

4

inferior or superior to other groups. He or she might be stupid but not necessarily racist.

Laws aimed at segregating African Americans from whites in the South for decades were racist because they assumed that African Americans were inherently inferior to white people. The internment of 120, 000 Japanese Americans from the American West Coast during World War II was racist because it was based on the assumption that people of Japanese ancestry regardless of nativity were innately untrustworthy.

Nativism is an anti-immigrant ideology. It maintains that in America native born Americans should reign. In America, nativists have argued for immigration restriction and limits on the political power of immigrants. Nativism has often been justified by racism. Those calling for Chinese immigration restriction in the late 1800s often maintained that Chinese people were inherently incapable of contributing to American society. Often nativism has been based on cultural explanations. Some who called for Chinese immigration restriction did not necessarily argue that Chinese people were inherently inferior to whites but that their culture made it too difficult for them to become good Americans. Often nativism uses both racist and cultural justifications. We will examine culture as a concept later in the chapter.

GENDER AND SEXUAL DIFFERENCES

The concept of gender needs discussion, because it connects to historically developed, perceived differences between what is masculine and what is feminine--differences which cut across racial, ethnic, and other socially constructed distinctions. Sexual differences are biologically based. But gender distinctions refer to historically and culturally variable definitions of what constitutes a female, as opposed to a male. One's gender, therefore, is socially constructed. One's sexuality is not.

Historically, human societies developed gender roles across geographical barriers. Yet what would constitute these roles and how they would be valued might vary. For example, in many pre-Columbian Native American societies, women were expected to engage in farming, as well as childcare, while men would engage in hunting and fishing. While distinct, gender roles were apparently valued equally, because corn and healthy children were valued along with meat. In more contemporary European and North

American societies, males were generally considered as the primary cultivators of the soil, while females were to cook, clean, and care for the children's physical needs. Moreover, male gender roles were valued as superior.

In modern American society, distinctive gender roles have prevailed, despite some recent blurring. Many of us, regardless of cultural background, grew up with certain expectations regarding femininity and masculinity--expectations supported at home, in the neighborhood, classroom, workplace, media, church or temple, as well as on the playing field. To a significant degree, male competitiveness and independence get reinforced, as well as female passivity and dependence. That we get gendered in certain ways may or may not be unfortunate. The problem in America and other societies derives from the fact that the "take charge guy" claims greater access to respect and political and economic power than the person expressing the so-called feminine traits associated with sharing and nurturing.

CLASS

Many of us recognize that classes exist in various historical and nearly all contemporary societies. Yet trying to figure out a clear, consistent definition of class seems another matter. According to Raymond Williams, analysts have tended to view class as consisting of both "objective" and "subjective" criteria. For example, some commentators have believed that class is an economic category, defined by income, wealth, property, occupation, or, in Marxist terms, one's relationship to the means of production. Classes, conversely, can have cultural characteristics. Middle and upper class Americans have more likely played tennis and golf in the twentieth century than working class Americans. The problem is how the relationship between objective and subjective criteria interacts historically.

Classes also have political characteristics. In the United States today, a wealthy person is more likely to vote Republican than a person at or below the poverty line. Whether Republican or not, a wealthy American is more likely to vote. Finally, a wealthy American is more likely to have access to public policy makers. Yet how much power wealth has attracted historically in the United States appears open to debate.

The concept of class cannot be underestimated, although when we talk about multicultural societies we often seem to forget how class can divide and unite people across racial, ethnic, and gender lines. Paying more attention to class might allow us to look at perplexing social issues such as gangs, family violence, immigration, or education in a different light. We might determine that the problems associated with these issues grow out of a complex interweaving of class with ethnicity, gender, race, nationality, religion, region, and age.

CAPITALISM

The role of capitalism in American history has been, to say the very least, consequential. Many Americans have understandably regarded themselves as beneficiaries of capitalism. Yet there have always been those Americans who have taken a less charitable stance toward an economic system which they have feared as potentially more oppressive than liberating and more authoritarian than democratic—a breeder of environmental holocausts as well as greed for money and power rather than responsibility, spirituality, and egalitarianism.

How one feels about capitalism will dictate to a significant extent how one defines it. There are certain things, however, about capitalism that generates dynamic economic change, often, but not always, for the better. First, it is based upon private productive property. A society in which the church or the government substantially owns productive property is a society in which capitalism can perhaps exist but not prosper and advance to new and vibrant levels of productivity and consumption. In a capitalist society, the government can, as was the case in Nazi Germany, have a lot to say about how private property is used to benefit a national economy. Ultimately, however, the government will not only allow but protect the private ownership of productive property. Second, the major goal of capitalism is to generate profits for the owners of capital. If everybody breaks even economically, capitalism cannot flourish. Third, free labor is vital to vigorous capitalist growth. Enslaved labor may prove profitable but it will not bring about the kind of profit that capitalism needs to blossom in twentieth century New York, Chicago, or Los Angeles. Free labor is mobile labor. It can go where it is needed. Free labor has some kind of incentive to work harder, for at least in theory free laborers can become bosses. With immensely rare exceptions, the enslaved African American was not going to become the master. Moreover, free labor is free to consume; to constitute an internal market in a capitalist society. Fourth, economic inequality is essential to capitalist growth as well. A robust capitalist economy requires owners and workers, with minimal or no access to ownership of private productive property. Some of these workers might possess high salaries and own extravagant homes and other material possessions. However, a society, envisioned by Jefferson, in which every family owns sufficient private property to produce all they need to live comfortably, although not necessarily luxuriously, is a society that will prove inhospitable to vigorous capitalist development. People in a dynamic capitalist society cannot grow or make their own. They have to work for others to make money in order to buy something that someone else's labor has helped to produce.

There are a number of reasons why capitalism has provoked loyalty, anxiety, and even contempt down through the years. Clearly, capitalism in places like the United States, Western Europe, and Japan has revolutionized humanity's productive capacity. Thanks to capitalism, many might rightly say, humanity's centuries' old fear of scarcity has been overcome. The ability to house, feed, and clothe everyone adequately in modern capitalist societies has been attained through capitalist-inspired improvements in production. Moreover, large numbers of people in modern capitalist societies can enjoy a wide variety of useful and maybe not so useful but enjoyable commodities. Microwave ovens, laptops, flat panel televisions, electric tooth brushes, mini-vans, aluminum baseball bats, talking Elmos, DVDS, and ipods have seemingly enriched countless lives thanks to capitalist-inspired innovations.

Nevertheless, capitalism has elicited opposition, somewhat quieted by the fall of the Soviet empire in the late 1980s. Capitalism, critics lament, nurtures avarice and self-absorption rather than responsibility to others. It places profit above family, community, nation, environment, and spirituality. And it creates

and supports material inequality that leads to political inequality, which, in turn, renders democracy difficult to maintain.

THE INTERNATIONAL MIGRATION PROCESS AND WORK

We often call the United States a "nation of immigrants." More accurately, it is a nation of migrants. It is a nation consisting in large part of people who either themselves of their families moved or were moved to America. It is also a nation consisting in large part of people who either themselves or their ancestors were drawn to the United States or that part of the world that became the United States to meet enduring labor requirements. The movement of people and cultures from one part of the globe to another has constituted a vital part of the human drama. Certainly, we need to understand that movement if we are to make sense of American history in general and Asian Pacific American history in particular.

Not everyone who came to the United States or a part of the world that became the United States has been an immigrant. Immigrants are people who possess some element of choice in whether they migrate out of the countries' of their births or not. They might not want to leave. Yet various social, economic, and political circumstances influence them to leave their native lands. Their freedom or their survival is not immediately threatened. If they choose to stay, their lives might remain harsh or become harsh, but those lives will endure in relative freedom and safety.

Refugees are people who have little or no choice in the matter. War, natural catastrophes, systematic political oppression, and the threat of extermination create refugees who must find asylum in another country in order to survive. The vast majority of Asian Pacific people migrating to the United States have either been immigrants or refugees.

Some Asian Pacific people who migrated to the United States were neither. They were people who were kidnapped or otherwise coerced into labor services in the United States. Accordingly, enslaved Africans, as well as some Asian Pacific people and Europeans, had little or no choice in whether they migrated to America and they certainly did not consider America as an asylum.

There are different kinds of immigrants, refugees, and laborers forced across geographical and legal boundaries. However, some of the ways analysts categorize these people lead to serious misunderstandings relevant to the Asian Pacific American experiences. At the same time, we should develop sensitivity to the global migration process's complexity.

Immigrants have often been labeled as either settlers or sojourners. Settlers go to a country with the general intention of remaining there. Sojourners go to a country temporarily to work and make money. If they cannot make enough money, they will travel to another country. When they make enough money, they will go back to their native lands hoping to remain for the rest of their lives.

Many American analysts have attached a stigma to "sojourning." They believe that those people intending to settle in the United States value its culture, have invariably been European, and typically faced little resentment from native-born American citizens. Thus, as sojourners, Asian Pacific immigrants supposedly have entertained little or no appreciation of American culture and inevitably have aroused resentment, perhaps rightly so, from native-born American citizens.

Admittedly, many Asian Pacific people have come and continue to come to the United States with little desire to settle in America permanently. Many European immigrants however, have also engaged in sojourning. Some Eastern and Southern European immigrants were sojourners in the late nineteenth and early twentieth centuries. Regardless of intention, however, Asian Pacific and many other immigrants trekked to the United States and, despite its faults, learned to love America and settled there permanently.

Exactly who are refugees remains a subject of controversy. Because of its international reputation as a "land of freedom," the United States has long served as a magnet for people migrating here because they cannot abide the governing system in their native countries. In the late 1840s and 1850s, many socialist and Marxist Germans migrated to the United States out of fear for their freedom. During the late nineteenth century, socialists were among the Japanese migrating to the United States. In the 1930s, political dissenters and Jews fled Nazi Germany for American shores, while after World War II political dissenters came to the United States from countries taken over by communist regimes. In the last twenty years, people have sought asylum in the United States from repressive governments headed by communists and non-communists.

One controversy is whether these people's lives and basic freedoms have been truly threatened in the countries from which they migrate. Since World War II, Americans have generally perceived people leaving communist run countries as refugees and have shown a willingness to grant them homes in the United States. Conversely, Americans, in particular members of the U.S. government, have been somewhat less sympathetic to those coming here from countries headed by non-communist dictatorships and have been less willing to grant the possibility that these people have been refugees. In any event, many Asians, especially since World War II, have been considered refugees from communist countries such as China, Vietnam, North Korea, Cambodia, and Laos and have been offered asylum in the United States.

We generally associate the compelled movement of people from their homelands to another society in order to perform difficult, demeaning, or dangerous labor services with the enslavement and forced migration of African people. This association is understandable, but not everyone who was forced to labor in another country was enslaved or possessed African nativity.

Historically, various forms of forced labor existed in America and around the world. It is important to point out that some of those performing difficult, demeaning, or dangerous coerced labor in British colonial North America were people known as indentured servants. Mostly poor people from the British Isles, they frequently came to a North American colony to work for a master or mistress for a specified number of years and they would be released from their labor obligations and hopefully given enough land and cash to get started on their own. Yet some of these English laborers came to the American colonies involuntarily. For example, during the 1600s the English government forced orphans and convicts to work in America.

More pertinent to the experiences of Asian Pacific people was the "coolie" trade, which surfaced during the mid-1800s after European countries like England and France had declared African slavery illegal. European plantation owners in European colonies in the Americas still required labor and looked to Asian Indians and Chinese to supply them with the necessary labor power. Unfortunately, many of these "coolies" were actually victimized by kidnappers of various nationalities, who, Sucheng Chan writes, "spirit<ed> away hapless Chinese youths to hard labor overseas."

While many English and then Chinese laborers were forced into working in the Americas, they were not enslaved. Unlike the Africans who were transported by the millions to the Western Hemisphere, these English and Chinese laborers were not legally bound for the rest of their lives. Nor did their progeny legally inherit their tragic status. Africans and their descendants were not so lucky, if we call an English orphan laborer or a Chinese coolie laborer, lucky.

THE GLOBAL QUEST FOR LABOR AND TRANSPLANTED NETWORKS

What do nearly all of these international migrants have in common? One answer is connected to a global quest for labor that has endured for five centuries and has been based, significantly, on needs perceived to exist in the Americas. Scholars such as the late Eric Wolf have written that the changing requirements of global capitalism has nurtured international migration, forced and unforced, in the last five hundred years. These requirements have consisted of gaining access to inexpensive, reliable, and relatively powerless laborers, many of whom worked on tobacco plantations, railroads, and mines in the United States.

Lesser capitalistic or economically stagnant regions have often surrendered labor to more capitalistic and economically dynamic regions. In the United States, early economic growth in the 1830s drew upon the movement of people from rural areas in New England into industrializing communities such as Lowell, Massachusetts. Young men and women sought wage work in mills and factories significantly because their families needed extra income to pay off or avoid debts in an agricultural setting increasingly dominated by the market economy. If we look carefully, then, we can see a thread running from these New England families to families in Ireland and China—families supplying thousands of workers to nineteenth century, industrializing America.

Therefore, the growth of capitalism in rural regions has aided the growth of capitalism in more urbanized, industrialized regions. It does so by uprooting peasants and rural laborers, who, if they were going to help feed themselves and their families, would have to look to regions that offered jobs—regions that were undergoing capitalist growth. However, the process of getting labor could not always be left to chance. The experiences of enslaved Africans, English servants, and Chinese and Asian Indian coolies prove this, but so too do the experiences of immigrants from various parts of the world, including Asia. In the 1870s, Japanese peasants living in the economically distressed southwestern part of Japan were actively recruited to work for Hawaiian sugar plantations by Hawaiian consul, R.W. Irwin. During the early 1900s, Hawaiian sugar interests placed advertisements in Korean newspapers to entice Korean laborers to Hawai'i. Hawaiian sugar interests also enthusiastically recruited Filipino laborers.

We should note that the voluntary migration across regional and national borders has not typically been an individualistic enterprise. Rather, to an important degree, it has been nurtured by collective networks constructed across regional and national borders. European immigrants were lured across the Atlantic by letters from people they knew and trusted. Such letters and conversations with visiting friends and relatives seemingly promised golden opportunities in the United States. Asian Pacific people have been part of many collective networks. Ronald Takaki mentions that "<w>hen Carlos Patalinghug went back <to the Philippines> for a visit in 1981 after working for ten years, he told his friends, "If you work, you'll get milk and honey in America."

CULTURE

People have thought of culture in a number of ways. There is the elitist notion of culture that argues it belongs to the few, the well bred, and well educated. In the United States, according to this notion of culture, the opera is cultural, while a heavy metal rock concert is not. PBS is cultural, while the Fox television network is not. James Joyce's novels are cultural, while Danielle Steele's novels are not. One major problem with the elitist perception of culture is that it is so elitist. It denies the ability of ordinary people to create meaningful lives and express themselves in meaningful ways. As Raymond Williams pointed out, "culture is ordinary."

The elitist notion of culture runs up against the pioneering work of generations of anthropologists, who have defined culture as a way of life. Anthropologists have involved themselves in the study of human cultures for over one hundred years. Typically, they have done fieldwork, otherwise known as ethnographies, among supposedly preindustrial, premodern cultures in South America, Africa, Asia, the Middle East, and the Pacific Islands. This field work, the anthropologist hopes, will inform her or him of the family and kin relations, economics, art, folklore, diet, and politics of the group of people under study. In other words, the anthropologist tries to learn about the way a certain group of people lives—their culture. A couple of anthropologists, Daniel Bates and Fred Plog, define culture in the following fashion:

> Culture is a system of shared beliefs, values, customs, and behaviors, and artifacts that the members of a society use to cope with their world and with one another, and that are transmitted from generation to

generation through learning. This definition includes not only patterns of thought (shared meanings that the members of a society attach to various phenomena, natural and intellectual, including religions and ideologies) artifacts (tools, pottery, houses, machines, works of art), and the culturally transmitted skills and techniques used to make the artifacts.

This definition of culture is definitely broad and encourages us to consider all humans as cultural beings and to consider all products of human interactions as cultural. However, some cultural analysts have worried that defining culture as a way of life is too broad and that scholars must observe some boundaries between that which is cultural and that which is not cultural. For example, Clifford Geertz has advanced the notion that culture expresses a society's way of life. Geertz has likened culture to a text or a story people use to express their religious beliefs, ideologies, and social relations. Thus, culture is found clearly in a society's rituals, folklore, literature, and art. Less clearly, it is found in, say, a dollar bill on which the picture of George Washington tells a story about American society. The problem for Geertz and cultural analysts following in his footsteps is that a cultural product is open to interpretation. How one person interprets the meaning of the half time show at the Super Bowl may differ from another person.

The distinctions between Bates and Plog, on the one hand, and Geertz, on the other, are important. But these and other scholars agree on several important matters when it comes to characterizing culture. In the first place, they agree that culture significantly shapes and, in turn, is shaped by human behavior. Second, culture is learned. Third, culture is a dynamic process. Fourth, culture is selective. A final, more controversial point is that culture is related to who holds power in a society.

Only a very obtuse cultural analyst would deny the importance of biological inheritance, climate, or geography in influencing human behavior. Yet we are substantially cultural beings, who are influenced by the messages transmitted to us over time, and who, in turn, pass those messages on, often altered, to future generations. That is, every time we hear a story as children we are created and recreated as cultural beings and we have and will do the same with our children and grandchildren.

To say that culture is learned is to say that it is not found in our genes or the wind currents. We learn culture from our families, religions, educators, friends, political leaders, work places, armed

14

services, youth basketball teams, and media. That is, social organizations and individuals socialize us. This does not mean that we learn culture in a consistent, systematic pattern. What we learn to value in one setting such as our family might prove inappropriate or ineffective in another setting such as the military.

We can find the dynamic character of culture in the fact that those practices and institutions that shape culture have changed and continue to change. Anthropologist Renato Rosaldo likens culture to a busy street intersection. For example, people with different cultural backgrounds have encountered one another throughout history and, whether they wanted to or not, have learned from one another. Sometimes, however, they collide with devastating consequences. People, in any event, experience cultural change. Perhaps, relatively pure homogeneous cultures existed at one time in human history, but they are very rare, if not totally extinct, today. To try to defend one's culture as homogeneous, pure, and everlasting is, in many instances, understandable, but absurd—very likely dangerously absurd.

Historically, some cultures have been less selective than others. In oral cultures such as those which existed at one time among many Native American groups, on the one hand, or into the twentieth century, among Laotian Hmong, on the other, the idea was to transmit culture, in its entirety, from one generation to the next. The community elders counted upon their memories to orally teach culture to the community youth. They would attempt to tell stores that they believed needed telling in order to perpetuate their community's traditions and belief systems. To alter the stories or forget them, it was supposed, would damage irreparably the transmission of essential traditions and belief systems. Of course, one could not rely on the flawed and sometimes corrupted character of human memory. Some things were forgotten and sometimes intentionally. Cultural practices were changed in the process.

In more modern, more populated societies, the cause of preserving culture from one generation to another is nearly hopeless and rarely attempted. For us, there is simply too much information out there to pass down entirely through generation after generation. Thus, when we read a book on American history or culture, we do not read all there is to know about American history or culture. Rather, the book's author<s> or publisher select for us those aspects of American history or culture, he, she or they consider important. The outcome of this selection process might vary depending upon the race, gender, politics, and age of those doing the selecting. At one time, American history textbooks taught that slavery was generally a benign institution. Contemporary American history textbooks look upon slavery far more critically.

The issue of selectivity and culture brings up a problem that perhaps more cultural analysts should consider. The problem of who does the selecting and why connects to how culture and power interact. It also connects to how culture is a site of both conflict and agreement among people. Scholars of different political perspectives have recognized that, in the long run, power in a society cannot derive solely from force or threat of force. Those with more power must generally attain the consent of those with less power. Yet how is this consent to domination achieved? Is it acquired through manipulation, sincere persuasion, or a combination of the two?

Other cultural analysts have argued that since the United States is relatively democratic and egalitarian, cultural practices have been generally chosen freely by ordinary Americans, who, in other words, typically know their own minds. They do not read a book or watch a television show or choose a political candidate because they are manipulated by those in power. They do these things, because they like doing them or think that doing these things will benefit them in some way.

To ignore the importance of cultural domination in American history and contemporary society seems naïve. At the same time, to regard Americans as, to quote mid-twentieth century sociologist C. Wright Mills, "cheerful robots" seems insulting to the historical record of ordinary Americans struggling for cultural autonomy and meaningfulness. Instead, we might want to think about culture in the United States and any modern, complex society as like an athletic contest. Sometimes, a team just dominates the opposition, which can either give up or try to put up a losing fight. Sometimes, the contest is close and the outcome remains in doubt. It is, however, important to remember that the opposing sides are not always evenly matched at the start of the contest. The players on the eventual winning side may or may not be smarter or harder working than the eventual losers. Yet the winners have the advantage of being bigger, faster, better coached, and trained in fancier, more modern facilities. Factors such as race, class, and gender assume similar roles in culture. Race, ethnicity, class, gender, and other social categories can and have given certain groups more power to shape culture than other groups. Race, ethnicity, class, gender, and other social categories have, therefore, been used to help certain people acquire and try to preserve a dominant position in society. However, other people have used culture to preserve their freedom from domination and they have often done so effectively. They may not win frequently, but they remain on the field geared for another contest.

Of course, the metaphor of the athletic contest seems only somewhat useful. It does not really help us with the matter of intentions. That is, should we take for granted a conspiratorial theory of American history and society? Are our schools, media, employers, political leaders, military commanders, football coaches, and parents trying to trick us into believing in something for their selfish gain or a narrow political objective? People in authority in the United States and elsewhere have lied to the public and frequently they have done so for not very noble reasons. Yet the truth, as many philosophers constantly point out, is a slippery thing. It can appear hidden from those in power as well as to the rest of us. History can show us that those in power do wrong while believing quite sincerely they are right. Thus, we should take care about ascribing evil intentions to the politicians, media people, corporate heads, and others who claim more authority than the rest of us.

Raymond Williams tried to theorize the dynamic interactions between culture and power. Influenced by an Italian Marxist theorist, Antonio Gramsci, Williams wrote that within societies one could discover a dominant or hegemonic culture—a culture to which most people give consent. This culture may not be a matter of democratic choice, but people are convinced that it is the best cultural alternative available to them or that they have little choice but to accept it. However, no dominant culture can truly sweep aside all alternatives. What Williams called residual cultural practices might remain very important within a society. An example of how residual cultural practices work is that in a highly modern and urbanized society such as the United States, many people find joy and meaning in movies, paintings, and books about rural societies? Moreover, dominant cultures often must contend with what Williams called emergent cultural practices. An example of an emergent cultural practice would be the surfacing of rap music in the later 1970s and early 1980s. The existence of residual and emergent cultural practices can pose problems for the dominant culture if these practices are allowed to develop unchecked. For instance, the hippie movement of the 1960s might conceivably have developed into a genuine oppositional culture in the United States. However, as the hippie movement attracted coverage in *Time* magazine and as some of its leaders received lucrative record and book contracts it no longer posed much of a problem to the dominant culture. We should know, however, that oppositional cultures, as revolutions in the United States, France, Russia, Mexico, and China prove, do develop out of a combustible mixture of residual and emergent cultural practices.

STEREOTYPING AND THE RACIALIZATION PROCESS

Stereotypes have, unfortunately, helped enormously in the cultural construction of hierarchies among people in the United States and globally. They have helped us to perceive that domination is either natural or useful. According to a group of intercultural communication specialists, stereotypes "are preconceptions which are applied to all members of a group or to an individual over a period of time, regardless of individual variations." They are, in other words, overgeneralizations about people, because of, among other things, their race, ethnicity, social class, gender, age, nationality, locality, religion, occupation, physical appearance, and politics.

We use stereotypes, according to some analysts, because we tend to want to avoid ambiguity. The late scholar Robert Heilbroner claimed that stereotypes are used by lazy minds. However, it is important to add that stereotypes are products of history and contain ideological and economic purposes. Stereotypes connect to real historical developments such as wars, social tensions, and economic changes. Their successful transmission can help justify conquest, enslavement, neglect, or extermination of large groups of people. Stereotypes can even make money for those who reproduce them on radio talk shows, movies, and television shows. Stereotypes have not necessarily appeared out of thin air. They may contain a core of truth. Yet this core of truth is often misunderstood. The fact that there were Italian American gangs in the United States should not be translated into the fallacy that Italian Americans are violent, lawless people. The fact that police officers often have to work nights, when they need to be alert and when health food stores are usually closed, does not mean that they possess a donut fancying gene that drive them to police work.

Stereotypes are important helpmates of the racialization process, which is the process of attributing natural characteristics to a group of people. Stereotypes can not only racialize Mexican Americans or Asian Pacific Americans, they can seemingly racialize non-racial groups as well. For example, if I say, "Engineers are socially inept," people can very well interpret my statement as meaning that people who have become engineers lack the innate ability to get along well with others. This may not have been my intention, but by definition stereotypical statements or images do not convey much in the way of detail or modification. They communicate the prevalence of uncrossable borders dividing people in a hierarchical fashion. Yet while stereotypes have stigmatized people across diverse backgrounds, it is important to remember that they have been most harmful to people less positioned to defend themselves than engineers who pull down six figures a year.

Thus, some stereotypes might understandably seem less hurtful than others. And some stereotypes might seem amusing as the writers of the "The Simpsons" well know. Moreover, even when they seem to convey something positive about a people, they contradict an individual's or a group's humanity. Stereotypes deny people their ability to be complicated, ambiguous. Most of us are quite aware of the negative stereotypes that have in the past and continue to circulate about many social groups in the United States Among the examples of these negative stereotypes are: "The Irish drink too much;" "Jews are cheap;" "Southern white Americans are dumb;" "Blondes are dumber;" "Police officers love junk food, especially donuts.." However, we should pay more attention to those stereotypes that seem positive. Among the examples of these are: "African Americans are great athletes;" "Mexicans are happy;" "Californians are laid back;" "Women are nurturing;" "Men are independent." Most of us recognize the need to reject the negative stereotypes even if we occasionally slip up and use them ourselves. It is, nevertheless, more difficult to reject the positive stereotypes despite the potential harm they inspire.

Negative stereotypes can clearly serve to justify doing all sorts of terrible things to one another. But what harm is there is in saying that people of African ancestry have rhythm, that Jews make good lawyers, or that Asians are good in mathematics? Indeed, some people frequently seem proud of others describing them in terms of "positive stereotypes." Yet any time a society allows unchecked, fallacious notions that a group of people possess innate characteristics, however seemingly positive, that society is propagating more harm than it perhaps imagines.

CONCLUSION

Thus, we frequently seek simplistic, one-dimensional explanations for highly complex, contradictory human behaviors. Some people rely upon the explanatory power of race, while others might place equal or even greater emphasis upon gender, class, or some other factor such as nationality, ideology, religion, or diet. Some may even allow stereotypes to reduce humanity to shallow assumptions. However, those of us who accept the importance and contributions of cultural diversity and complexity in American and other societies need to argue that people are products of varied and even conflicting historically developed practices and institutions. In his brilliant statement on the duality of turn-of-the twentieth century African-American consciousness, W.E.B. Dubois wrote nearly one hundred years ago:

> It is a peculiar sensation, this double-consciousness, this sense of always looking at one's self through the eyes of others, of measuring one's soul by the tape of a world that looks on in amused contempt and pity. One ever feels his twoness--an American, a Negro; two souls, two thoughts, two unreconciled strivings, two warring ideals in one dark body, whose dogged strength alone keeps it from being torn asunder.

The point here is not to agree with Dubois, but to see that he went beyond the acceptance of a simple explanation for the African American experience. According to more contemporary intellectuals such as Gloria Anzaldua, Dubois's notion of duality does not go far enough. In *La Frontera/The Borderlands*, the Anzaldua claimed identification with what many of us might consider as multiple and even opposing cultural identifies. While American born of working class parentage, Anzaldua told us that she was partially a product of Mexican history and culture and partially a product of Native American history. Yet the power of gender reminded the late writer that she was not a Chicano and Mestizo, but she was a woman--a Chicana and Mestiza. Moreover, she was a lesbian. The different elements of Anzaldua's multiple consciousnesses might seem hard to reconcile with one another, but she insisted that it endowed her with greater strength and greater insight as she crisscrossed the borders constructed among North Americans.

The concept of cultural citizenship seems to combine Dubois and Anzaldua. Latino/a scholars such as William V. Flores, Rina Benmayor, and Renato Rosaldo have developed the concept of cultural citizenship to explain the experiences of people of Latino/a ancestry in the United States. In the late 1990s, Rosaldo and Flores defined cultural citizenship as "the right to be different (in terms of race, ethnicity, or native languages) with respect to the norms of the dominant national community, without compromising one's right to belong, in the sense of participating in the nation-state's democratic processes." Like Dubois's concept of African American double consciousness, the concept of cultural citizenship embraces a language of duality and even hybridity--that one can and should be allowed to be both different from and similar to other Americans. Like Anzaldua, cultural citizenship theorists point out that cultural identity is a product of varied and conflicting factors.

Finally, the concept of agency refutes easily defined social boundaries separating us into the powerful and less powerful. An inspirational historian, Herbert Gutman, reminded his colleagues twenty-five years ago:

> What <ordinary> men and women experienced (that is, what "one" has done to them") retains interest, but how they interpreted and then dealt with changing patterns of economic, social, and political dependence and inequality becomes our major concern Studying the choices working men and women made and how their behavior affected important historical processes enlarges our understanding of "the condition of being human."

REVIEW

1. Why does the author claim that ethnic groups are a product of history?
2. How are ethnic groups formed?
3. Why do many people claim that race is a social construction?
4. How can we distinguish race from ethnicity?
5. Define racism and nativism?
6. Why does the author say that gender is a social construction?
7. Why is it difficult to figure out a "clear, consistent definition of class"?

8. What are some important characteristics of capitalism?
9. Why has capitalism provoked both "loyalty and contempt"?
10. Why does the author call the United States "a nation of migrants"?
11. What is the difference between an immigrant and a refugee?
12. Why is a slave brought from one land to another not called an immigrant?
13. What are sojourners? And how does sojourning relate to Asian immigration?
14. What has been the "global quest for labor"?
15. What are "transplanted networks"?
16. What are two useful ways to define culture?
17. What are the various characteristics or ingredients of culture?
18. What is the relationship between power and culture?
19. What is a stereotype?
20. Why are stereotypes used?
21. Is there such a thing as a good stereotype?
22. What is the racialization process?
23. What is Dubois notion of "double consciousness"?
24. What did Gloria Anzaldua say about cultural identity?
25. What is the concept of cultural citizenship?
26. What is the concept of agency?

SELECTED BIBLIOGRAPHY

Anzaldua, Glora. *La Frontera/The Borderlands.* (1987).

Appiah, Kwame Anthony. *In My Father's House.* (1992).

Banton, Michael. *The Idea of Race.* (1977).

Barrera, Mario. "Chicano Class Structure," in Ronald Takaki (ed). *From Different Shores.* (1987).

Bhabha, Homi. *Location of Culture.* (1994).

Clifford, James. *The Predicament of Culture.* (1988).

Dubois, W.E.B. *Souls of Black Folk.* (1903).

Fields, Barbara, "Ideology and Race in American History," in J.Morgan Kousser and James M. McPherson, (eds). *Region, Race, and Reconstruction.* (1982).

Flores, William V and Benmayor, Rina. *Latino Cultural Citizenship* (1997).

Gilligan, Carol. *In a Different Voice.* (1982).

Gilroy, Paul. *The Black Atlantic.* (1993).

Goldberg, David Theo. *Racist Culture: Philosophy and the Politics of Meaning.* (1993).

Gossett, Thomas F. *Race: The History of an Idea in America.* (1965).

Gould, Stephen Jay. *The Mismeasure of Man.* (1981).

Gramsci, Antonio. *Selections from the Prison Notebooks.* Quinton Hoare and Geoffrey Nowell-Smith, (eds.) (1971).

Gubar, Susan. *Racechanges.* (1997).

Gutman, Herbert. *Power and Culture.* (1987).

Roediger, David R. *The Wages of Whiteness.* (1991).

Shibutani, T. and Kwan, K.M. *Ethnic Stratification.* (1965).

Sollors, Werner. *Beyond Ethnicity.* (1986).

Williams, Raymond. *Culture and Society, 1780-1950.* (1958).

_____. *Keywords.* (1983).

II
THEORETICAL PERSPECTIVES ON INEQUALITY IN AMERICAN SOCIETY

The raising, maintenance, and lowering of inequitable power relations in the United States have stirred tremendous controversy down through the years. Consequently, intellectuals, politicians, government officials, and social activists have generated different perspectives on why some people in the United States possess more power than others and what can or should be done about it. We need to pay attention to these arguments, because they address the experiences of Asian Pacific Americans, as well as other culturally diverse Americans.

The ability to influence the course of human events locally, nationally, or internationally is political power. Interestingly, Americans do not like to think about political power. They often like to consider themselves as free-floating individuals empowered to construct their own futures. The reality is that American society, historically and today, has been strongly tied to the use and misuse of power, while power has been strongly tied to the raising, maintenance, and lowering of social, economic, and cultural hierarchies.

The following sections will explore some of the important theoretical perspectives on inequality in American society. We should, however, bear in mind that theories, even in the hands of their most careful, sophisticated advocates, are often meant to approximate social reality and not hold a mirror to it. Social Scientists, for example, use theory to organize and analyze data regarding human behavior that might otherwise appear random and meaningless. Of course, human behavior over time reveals contradictions and inconsistencies that a single theory cannot always explain. Yet developing and analyzing thoughtful social and cultural theories helps make that behavior more comprehensible than it would otherwise seem.

Social and cultural theories do not materialize out of thin air. They have histories and their advocates often harbor obvious and not so obvious ideological agendas. This does not make these theories unworthy of consideration. Yet while many theorists describe themselves as objective, none of them can free themselves of history and few from ideology.

NATURE VS. NURTURE

Culture is how we are nurtured by society. It considerably affects and is, in turn, affected by our social, economic, and political experiences. In other words, we are substantially children of history. We should, however, remember that many have in the past and continue now to stress the role of innate and/or natural causes to explain human behavior. These people believe that nature, destiny, or some supreme power can dictate such matters as social roles and power in society. In clearly hierarchical societies, the role of innate differences has often been assumed when political power was perceived as hereditary. Yet in societies presumably founded on egalitarian and democratic principles, those who advocate hierarchical divisions of power as natural or destined often feel the need to root their convictions in scientific or religious foundations.

These advocates of hierarchy can, accordingly, argue that in the United States, the principles of democracy, freedom, and equality are rightly important. However, they can insist that there are people who, perhaps through no fault of their own, are incapable of full and equal participation in public life. Nature has bequeathed them less than equal talents and we must, in turn, treat them as less than equals. These advocates of hierarchical divisions of power might suggest that the public deal with these less than equal people fairly and kindly--as parents ought to deal with their children. Sometimes, however, the public is told that society should exclude and even exterminate the less fit as threats to our democracy, freedom, and equality.

As example of this kind of thinking emerged in the second half of the nineteenth century. This argument favoring the forces of nature over nurture was called Social Darwinism, because it attempted to transfer the biological findings of classical scientist, Charles Darwin, to human society. Darwin maintained that a key to understanding the fall and rise of certain species was "natural selection." Over time, those species survived which proved most adaptive to changing environmental and demographic conditions.

Herbert Spencer was a pioneer of the discipline of sociology. He believed that Darwinian interpretations of the evolution of species were applicable to humanity. In other words, Spencer wrote that nature's laws had commanded a struggle for survival between species and between groups of human beings. The fitter groups would, therefore, emerge from the struggle with wealth and power, while the less fit groups suffered with significantly less wealth and power.

Social Darwinism found many supporters and not surprisingly so. The second half of the nineteenth century was a trying time for those seeking to preserve the status quo in places like the United States. To a greater extent than ever before, people living in the United States were first and second generation immigrants from Europe and Asia. Moreover, these immigrants were perceived by many native born Americans as incapable of becoming useful American citizens, despite or perhaps because of their hunger for expanded participation in American life. American laboring people challenged their employers' authority in the workplace and the political arena. Small, independent farmers and tenant farmers sought greater access to political and economic decision making. Freed African Americans in the South demanded economic independence and the vote. American Indians and people of Mexican descent proved unwilling spectators to westward American expansion. Women proved equally reluctant to quiet their calls for political, social, and economic reform, as well as suffrage rights.

The Social Darwinists were anxious to remind those who wanted to alter the status quo why power was not democratically distributed among all people living in the United States. Nature guided the destinies of societies and nature had decreed, according to the Social Darwinists, that the fit should rule and those who were the most fit should acquire the most political power and wealth. Indeed, Social Darwinists could and did argue that reformers and radicals who supported government intervention on behalf of the poor and the powerless wanted to prop up the weak at the expense of the strong. In so doing, these "do-gooders" supposedly stood in the way of nature's most fundamental laws.

Few people today describe themselves as Social Darwinists and justify complete social neglect of poverty and inequality in Social Darwinian terms. Yet many of the arguments declared by Social Darwinists remain a part of the way some Americans think about social issues. Women, for example, have and continue to hear that biology is destiny and that because of, say, menstruation and menopause they are less fit than men to perform the duties of government leader, corporate head, fighter pilot, or police officer.

ASSIMILATIONIST THEORY

Assimilationist theory is far more respected today by policy makers, social scientists, politicians, educators, and most of the rest of us than views that argue that biology or God dictate social superiority and inferiority. At the same time, assimilationist theory fits nicely the general consensus among Americans that given time and patience the basic American economic and political institutions have and will continue to work for the larger good.

The assimilationist argument is venerable. In the second half of the nineteenth century, for example, many European Americans urged that Native American assimilation into the dominant culture was the most humane answer to the "Indian problem." In other words, they believed that American Indians would or should disappear not through extermination or disease, but by full absorption into European American culture.

These assimilationists have been rightly condemned for their paternalistic and ethnocentric assumption that they knew what was best for American Indians. Yet, to be fair, they and others like them had to hold their ground against influential Americans who insisted that there were just some people who could never change just as zebras could not shed their stripes or leopards their spots. Many of these influential Americans transferred their contemptuous glances from American Indians to European immigrants and expressed dismay at what destiny had brought to the United States. The refuse of Europe, they contended, had washed up on American shores. From Ireland, Germany, and then in the late 1800s, Russia, Poland, Hungary, Italy, Portugal, and Greece these people came, conveying cultures that seemed permanently alien to a good number of native-born Americans.

MELTING POT

A variation on the assimilationist theme, the notion of the melting pot was devised, in part, to counter the arguments of those who declared that significant groups of European immigrants were racially or culturally incapable of assimilating into American society. In its youthful manifestations, the melting pot appeared to have been reserved for whites only.

We can find an early, late eighteenth century expression of America as a "melting pot" in the writings of a French-born resident of New York, Hector St. John de Crèvecoeur. Americans, he wrote during the American Revolution, "are a mixture of English, Scotch, Irish, French, Dutch, German and Swedes. From this promiscuous breed, that race now called Americans have arisen." Crèvecoeur asked, "What, then is the American, this new man? He is either an European or the descendant of an European; hence that strange mixture of blood, which you will find in no other country."

Over one hundred years later, a Jewish immigrant from England, Israel Zangwill wrote a popular play in the early 1900s called "The Melting Pot." In this play, Zangwill depicted the United States as "God's crucible, the great Melting-pot where all the races of Europe are melting and reforming." There was nothing fixed about the character of European immigrants in American society, according to Zangwill. Inevitably, through God's will, they were changing in the United States. They were, in short, becoming new men and women--new-sprung and contributing Americans. But, according to Zangwill, not just immigrants experienced transformation. Also native-born Americans required renovation themselves if they were to embrace American ideals with renewed enthusiasm.

ROBERT PARK AND SOCIOLOGICAL THEORY

Social Science scholarship lent credibility to Zangwill's passionate declaration that nature did not command inequality in the United States—at least among people possessing European ancestry. A journalist turned pioneering sociologist, Robert Park believed that immigrants posed no permanent threat to American society. Unlike Zangwill, however, he was convinced that the promise of assimilation could be redeemed for immigrants of color and native-born Americans of color.

Park's study of racial and ethnic groups in the United States during the first third of the twentieth century compelled him to design what he described as the Race Relations Cycle. He argued that there were four stages to this cycle. The first was the encounter. At this stage, members of an immigrant group met members of the native-born group. The second stage varied in length, but Park conceded that its duration could last generations for immigrants of color and African Americans. Park dubbed this the competition or conflict stage. In the third—accommodation—stage, tensions eased as the groups learned to adjust and begin to accept one another in a new light. In the fourth and final stage, members of the immigrant or outgroup gained complete entrance into the group. Indeed, nothing significantly distinguished the one-time out-group members from long-time in-group members. The out-group members have assimilated.

Social theorists Benjamin Ringer and Elinor Lawless called this theory Park's " 'natural history' of race relations." The description is appropriate. However different from Social Darwinism, Park's race relations cycle went on seemingly unaffected by human intentions and human action. It was inevitable that each group move through this race relations cycle in America and, like natural history, the process was irreversible.

ANGLO-CONFORMITY AND CULTURAL BLENDING

Americans seem to understand the assimilation process from two perspectives. One is based on the "Anglo-conformity" viewpoint. That is, assimilation occurs, sociologist Milton Gordon wrote, with "the complete renunciation of the immigrant's ancestral culture in favor of the behavior and values of the Anglo-Saxon core group." The other perspective relates to Zangwill's notion of the melting pot. According to Gordon, "the 'melting pot" idea envisioned a biological merger of the Anglo-Saxon peoples with other immigrant groups and a blending of their respective cultures into a new indigenous type."

THE IMMIGRANT ANALOGY AND ITS VARIATIONS

The immigrant analogy concurs with assimilationists that there was and remains little fundamentally wrong with American society in the nation's treatment of ethnic and racial groups. It argues as well that the large number of European immigrants to America have successfully assimilated or, at least, achieved upward social and economic mobility. Nevertheless, unlike some pioneering assimilationists such as Robert Park, those who advocate the immigrant analogy claim that ethnic groups succeed through their own strivings not because of some natural process.

Among the major supporters of the immigrant analogy have been important scholars and political thinkers such as Nathan Glazer, Daniel Moynihan, and Irving Kristol, who have written extensively on ethnic and racial relations in the United States. The timing of the emergence of this immigrant analogy was not accidental. It gained importance during the 1960s and 1970s, which was a period in American history when people of color challenged the status quo more effectively and with greater anger than ever before. These anti-racist social movements often argued that America's. social, economic, and political institutions were just, but that some of those placed in leadership were not. However, especially in the late 1960s and early 1970s, they questioned the inherent justice of American. social, economic, and political institutions.

To some extent, the immigrant analogy was meant to assure European Americans that, in reality, the African American underwent experiences not very dissimilar from those faced by many of their parents and grandparents. In other words, according to a title of an Irving Kristol article in the 1960s, "the Negro is Like the Immigrant Yesterday."

The movement of millions of African Americans from the rural, backward south during the twentieth century was, according to the immigrant analogy, similar to the prior movement of peasant European immigrants to the American industrialized north. Both groups arrived poor, formally uneducated, and unskilled. Both groups faced prejudice and discrimination. Both groups had to struggle up the social and economic ladder for success. However, as it turned out, only European immigrants and their offspring apparently succeeded.

Scholarly supporters of the immigrant analogy generally recognized race made the struggle of African Americans at least somewhat more difficult. Legalized racial discrimination was, they argued, a blot on an otherwise admirable historical record of generosity toward diverse ethnic groups in the United States. However, during the post-World War II era, they claimed that the United States removed the legal props of racial discrimination. Consequently, they believed that African Americans could then start acting like European immigrants—work hard, sacrifice, get at least their children formally educated, sober up, and "pull themselves up by the bootstraps."

While generally supportive of the political agenda of most African American civil rights activists in the late 1950s and early 1960s, immigrant analogy supporters shifted their focus during the late 1960s and after. They, then, condemned radical critiques of American race relations by pointing that the American social system has worked fairly with a small amount of adjustment. The proof, they declared, was that if European immigrants, however poor and despised by the native born, could make it, then so could African Americans, Latin Americans, Asian Pacific American Islanders, and American Indians. Moreover, European immigrants made it without asking for help of the U.S. government. Affirmative Action and other government programs designed to specifically aid people of color, consequently, were not only unnecessary, but actually defeated that which all people struggling against racism desired—a color-blind society.

THE HUMAN CAPITAL MODEL

The Human Capital Model makes several of the same arguments made by the immigrant analogy. Led by scholars such as Thomas Sowell and Gary Marx, its advocates address the concern that despite various federal, state, and local programs, poverty persists as a major problem for people of color.

The Human Capital Model argues that the logic of capitalism dictates color blindness. Capitalism rewards those people who attain marketable skills regardless of race, ethnicity, or sex. It would seem irrational to do otherwise and irrationality has little effectiveness in the market place. Accordingly, the human capital model claims members of racial and ethnic minorities ought to acquire human capital—the marketable skills necessary to overcome the initial disadvantage of little or no material capital. By doing so, they would sever substantial link existing between poverty and race.

The kind of human capital needed to overcome impoverished backgrounds includes the following—a dedication to education and relevant vocational training; the willingness to work hard; the desire to put career objectives before personal concerns; the willingness to steer clear of drugs, alcohol, and other unhealthy distractions. However, making these objectives realizable for people of color is a family life that encourages the belief that no goal is impossible for the individual who persistently strives to attain that goal. The ideal here is the poor family headed by honest, heterosexual, and legally married parents who "responsibly" bring into the world two to three children. The father, in particular, is important, because his willingness to sacrifice and work hard offers an essential role model for African American, American Indian, and Latino young males. With his absence, these young males are seemingly cut adrift toward lives of welfare and even worse, violent crime.

The Human Capital Model, then, declares that government programs, however sometimes necessary, will not build the character necessary to take advantage of what the United States offers. The creation of human capital, in the final analysis, is the responsibility of racial and ethnic group members themselves. Just as Jewish American communities supposedly stockpiled human capital in the face of poverty and prejudice, so can poor African Americans, American Indians, and Latinos

MODEL MINORITY THESIS

The Model Minority Thesis is an important variation of the Human Capital Model. Advanced in the mid-1960s by sociologist William Petersen and taken up more recently by Thomas Sowell, the Model Minority thesis argues that Americans of Asian Pacific ancestry have become the model racial minority in the United States. It states that in the United States, Asian Pacific people have successfully overcome racial prejudice through hard work, sacrifice, and valuing education. Japanese, Chinese, Korean, and Vietnamese Americans have, in other words, acquired human capital. In so doing, they have proved the reality of the American Dream and disproved the argument that racism is built into America's political, economic, and social institutions. African Americans, American Indians, and Latinos, therefore, ought to follow the example set by Asian Pacific Americans.

MARXISM AND OTHER CRITICAL THEORIES

Unlike perspectives such as the Human Capital Model, Marxism does not take the generosity of the American social and economic system for granted. The history of Marxism is clearly controversial, highlighted by real insights into some aspects of human social systems over time and tainted by monstrous simplicities. Nevertheless, since its advent in the wake of the writings of Karl Marx and Friedreich Engels during the middle and late 1800s,

Marxism's impact on scholarship has been and remains consequential.

While Marxism has, like other substantial theoretical perspectives, created a highly complex and contradictory body of thought, we can find notable attempts by men and women influenced by Marxism to address puzzling social issues. For Marxists, capitalism has been both friend and enemy of human progress. Marxists have tended to view capitalism more charitably than many traditional conservatives such as the English intellectual Mathew Arnold, who, in the 1800s, blasted capitalism as opposed to civilization. Also in the 1800s, Karl Marx stated that the emergence of capitalism brought humanity a necessary closer step to socialism and the conquest of human inequality. For Arnold, capitalism took humanity a drastic step backward toward barbarism.

In any social system, Marxists generally argue, class is the primary source of inequality. Marxists differ widely over what constitutes a class, but, according to scholar Mario Barrera, traditionally Marxism holds that

> A class is a group of people who have a similar relationship to the process of production in a society. The process of production is that process by which all of the goods and services are produced that people use in their daily lives, such as food, houses, appliances, and so on. Each society has a particular class structure depending on the way in which such goods are produced and on the way in which the work force is organized.

Marxists analyze three primary classes existing in a capitalist social system such as that found in the contemporary America. The first, of course, consists of capitalists. These people own and control an overwhelming proportion of productive property in the United States. Workers compose the second class. As individuals, these workers might claim ownership of cars, computers, stereos, cell phones, and homes, but they own little, if anything, in the way of productive property. Most to all of their income derives from their wages, salaries, and tips. Marxists call a third class the petty bourgeoisie. These people own small amounts of private productive property. They are owners of small businesses or farms.

In recent years people who call themselves Marxists have developed thoughtful insights into the relationships between class, race, ethnicity, and gender. Yet Marxists traditionally have argued that under capitalism, such problems as racism and sexism were by-products of the larger, more important struggle between classes. Once class exploitation was conquered, they declared, then other unequal relationships would disappear. Moreover, formidable Marxists such as Herbert Aptheker and Oliver Cox have asserted that racism acted as a powerful tool in the hands of capitalists trying to divide and conquer the American working class. Without racial divisions this working class might otherwise have led the United States effectively and democratically toward socialism.

SPLIT LABOR MARKET THEORY

The Split Labor Market Theory offers an interesting variation on traditional Marxist perspectives on race and ethnicity. Like Marxism, it focuses on capitalist development and argues that racial and ethnic distinctions benefit capitalists. Sociologist Edna Bonacich is considered a major pioneer in developing this theory. Certainly, Bonacich has done substantial work in studying racial and ethnic relations in the United States. She performs, in particular, a great deal of important research on the historical and contemporary labor market experiences of Asian Pacific Americans.

Bonacich argues that capitalism in the United States has exploited a labor market split disproportionately between European American and non-European American workers. European Americans have very likely been found in the labor market sector constituted by higher status, higher paid jobs. People of color have disproportionately been found in the labor market sector constituted by lower status, lower paid jobs. This labor market split benefits capitalism, according to Bonacich, because it relegates low paying and often dangerous, demeaning, and just plain boring jobs to people widely identified as racially despised and lacking the full citizenship rights available to European Americans. This split labor market also serves capitalism by keeping potentially antagonistic workers divided by race. Workers, consequently, learn to identify other workers as enemies rather than allies against capitalism. The popularity of anti-Asian Pacific politics among white workers, according to Bonacich, can be explained significantly by the split labor market theory.

RACIAL OPPRESSION THEORISTS

Theorists who focus on the importance of racial oppression radically challenge the generosity of American economic, social, and political institutions. We can link the history of this perspective to the social ferment in the United States and the world during the 1950s, 1960s, and 1970s. Out of this social ferment the internal colonial model emerged as a coherent, although contentious, analysis of race in the United States.

By the mid-1960s, the effectiveness of the Civil Rights movement was wearing thin. It occurred to some black leaders and intellectuals that for African Americans the Civil Rights movement's objective of racial integration into the mainstream of American life was neither possible nor a particularly worthy goal. Violence committed by government law enforcement agencies and individual white citizens against African Americans convinced many one-time Civil Rights activists that racism in the United States was too tough for peaceful marches and voter registration drives to tame. These activists saw a social movement of militant African Americans aimed at self-determination for people of African descent in the United States as necessary.

For these militant activists, Malcolm X ranked as both a leading spokesperson and later a martyred hero. Like Malcolm X, they claimed a similarity in the struggle of African Americans in the United States with the anti-colonial movements of people in Africa, Asia, the Middle East, and Latin America. Like these people, African Americans were historically colonized by whites. Forced into a colonial relationship, their labor was exploited and their cultures suppressed. The Internal Colonial Model emerged to meet developing theoretical needs.

Some advocates of the internal colonial model condemned capitalism and its alliance with imperialism. Generally, however, the internal colonial model argued that racial oppression, not capitalism, was the primary source of inequality in the United States. The model's supporters admitted that European immigrant workers suffered some form of exploitation and discrimination. Still, they contended that the experiences of European Americans, regardless of ethnicity and class, were qualitatively more positive than the experiences of non-white people.

Internal colonial theorists essentially declared that people of color in the United States formed nations within a nation. Such an argument received scholarly support in the 1970s from sociologist Robert Blauner and anthropologist Joseph. G. Jorgensen, as well as Chicano scholars Rudolpho Acuña, Mario Barrera, and Carlos Muñoz. Many Chicano and Native American activists and scholars became particularly taken with the internal colonial model. Their sense of distinctive nationalities was rooted in the land from which they felt European Americans displaced them. They maintained that isolated in barrios and reservations on the lands over which they once ruled, people of Mexican descent and Native Americans became a source of exploitable labor and targets of racial violence and neglect.

Not too many theorists describe themselves today as supporters of the internal colonial model. Nevertheless, many theorists persist in arguing that there is no more important feature of American society than institutional racism. Institutional racism means that American political and economic institutions have bred racism deeply into American society and nothing less than a substantial, even revolutionary, change in the United States can end racial oppression. Theorists such as Michael Omi and Howard Winant, for example, write about "racial formation" as a powerful process though which American institutions shape race into a primary way for Americans to categorize themselves and others in a hierarchical manner. Omi and Winant have written:

> We define *racial formation* as the sociohistorical process by which social categories are created, inhabited, transformed and destroyed. ...<W>e argue that racial formation is a process of historically situated *projects* in which human bodies and social structures are represented and organized...<W>e link racial formation to the evolution of hegemony, the way in which society is organized and ruled.

FEMINISM

The feminist critique has added another dimension to the problem of how hierarchies have been raised, particularly in America, a presumably democratic society. People who identify themselves as feminists vary in ideology and politics. Liberal feminists argue that men exclude women from achieving the necessary human capital to success in the United States. The system does work. But wise legislation and judicial decisions, as well as changes in male and female behavior can make the system work better for women and, in the long run, men. Radical feminists maintain that sexism is not so easily overcome. It is embedded in all patriarchal—male dominated, societies. Radical transformations of gender roles are demanded. These transformations, perhaps, take into account other forms of inequality based on race, ethnicity, and class, but do demand that gender issues receive equal, if not, prime attention. Socialist feminists maintain that it is important to note the relationship between capitalism and patriarchy. Class exploitation under capitalism cannot be ended without doing away with patriarchal oppression.

A critical variation of feminism has been offered by bell hooks, Angela Davis, Audre Lode, and Patricia Zavella, among others. This perspective claims that feminism has ignored the power of racial and ethnic, as well as class, hierarchies. It points out that any kind of useful feminism must see the interrelationship of multiple sources of raised hierarchies.

POSTMODERNISM

Like racial oppression theorists and feminism, postmodern theory emanated from the scholarly battles fought in the 1960s and 1970s. Postmodern thinkers have been called many things and they have varied in terms of how much they can contribute to our understanding how societies have operated over time. They have tended to reject the idea that the effective application of science, whether physical, biological, or human, can make much sense out of how we live. Historical or sociological research into race relations or immigration, postmodernists contend, are so burdened by subjective factors such as ideology, class, race, ethnicity, gender, religion, and age that unlike the character in the television series, "X-Files," they doubt if "the truth is out there" or anywhere, for that matter.

Postmodernists, therefore, tend to believe that modern human beings should stop depending upon science and technology to bring about or disclose order. There is little in the way of order. Yet postmodernists find it interesting and perhaps paradoxically useful to do research and write papers and books. They even find it necessary to denounce social injustice. In doing so, they may lose their nihilist edge while becoming scholars and writers that we need to hear even if we disagree with much of their methodology.

Postmodernists stress less the facts than how people, events, and developments are represented. They tend to assert that the Civil War is a text open to interpretation as to its real meaning. Critics charge that postmodernists would argue that the only thing important about the American Civil War is its textural nature.

Perhaps, that is true of some of the more eccentric postmodernists. But the more in-touch postmodern theorists concede that the American Civil War started and ended at a certain period in human history for a variety of reasons and had enormous consequences in terms of lives changed and, of course, lives lost. In other words, postmodernists generally do not doubt that there is an objective reality. They do, however, quibble with those who believe that all one needs to know is the facts. Facts held to the postmodernist light may not be all they are cracked up to be. What is a fact to one group of interpreters may be a fabrication to another.

By exposing us to the possibility that much of what we take for granted as objective reality is a product of very subjective human constructions, postmodernists do a service to critical scholarship. For example, postmodern thinking has helped encourage more and more scholars to think about race as a social construction rather than an objective, proven scientific reality. It has come up with provocative analyses of key literary texts and cultural performances, from Shakespeare to American soap operas.

Postmodernists have provoked considerable opposition, much of it warranted. For one thing, if a reader thinks this text is hard to understand, he or she should thank God I am not a postmodernist. Otherwise, she or he would not get past this sentence without taking a water break. Second, postmodernists may be rightly taken to task for an excessively egalitarian approach to social inquiry. By focusing so much on interpreting texts, they leave the impression that such serious issues as poverty and unemployment really do not matter all that much. In the postmodernist world everything might easily appear equal in importance—soap operas. Elvis, the Super Bowl, genocidal wars in Eastern Europe and Africa, terrorist bombings, an American Indian reservation without running water might seem all pretty much the same.

INFLUENTIAL THEORIES OF SOCIAL CHANGE

We cannot understand Asian Pacific American experiences unless we get a handle on why people migrate from one region of the world to another. And we cannot get a handle on why people migrate from one region of the world to another unless we figure out social change from a global perspective. Three major classical theorists have attempted to shed light on why societies change. They are Adam Smith, Karl Marx, and Max Weber. And they have inspired thoughtful and not so thoughtful scholarship down through the years.

Adam Smith is known as the theoretical father of modern capitalism. In *Wealth of Nations*, published in 1776. Smith argued that the "invisible hand" of the market would economically transform a nation for the better. It was crucial, however, to remove most institutional fetters on the market economy. An Englishman well acquainted with how the government can intrude on the market economy, Smith believed that a society's political-legal system or state had better things to do than dictate to shop keepers and manufacturers what they should do with their private productive property. The primary law an economy should respect, according to Smith, was the law of "supply and demand." To do so would enrich the individual who would wisely adhere to the law of supply and demand, but would enrich a nation governed by a state that knew that its major obligation was to protect private property.

Smith also acknowledged that in many societies powerful religious organizations posed a serious obstacle to economic growth. For one thing, churches accumulated substantial control over land. Moreover, state churches or churches sanctioned by the state were able to accumulate revenue through taxes—revenue that entrepreneurs might otherwise use to enhance a society's commercial potential.

To Smith's followers capitalism, if given a free hand by the state, would generate positive social change. While unfettered capitalism does not guarantee nor desire an even distribution of wealth, it would create conditions for truly productive members of society to own their homes, wear decent clothes, and usually find their refrigerators full. As for those who are deemed not truly productive, their fate is their responsibility and certainly not society's, although society has to cough up money to pay for the consequences—police, prisons, hospitals, and perhaps a bit of welfare.

We have already discussed Marx. Needless to say, Marx was far less optimistic than Smith when it came to how much progress capitalism could inspire. Marx was certain that if left unfettered capitalism would ultimately foster its own executioners—an efficiently organized industrial working class or proletariat that would overthrow capitalist rule. How this would take place is not easy to explain. Marx was a great thinker but not a great writer.

And the dozens of English translations of his work rarely help matters.

It does seem clear, however, that Marx agreed with Smith that capitalism bore the potential of eliminating much of the world's most venerable misery—scarcity. It would fill stomachs, warm bodies, and build homes for all but society's most poor and least productive members—a group which Marx identified as the lumpenproletariat. However, it would not produce that which people crave as well—justice and power to determine their futures.

Brought together in factories and cities industrial capitalists who along with their finance capitalist allies have achieved ownership of nearly all of society's productive property, workers would come to acknowledge the relative misery of their condition. They would recognize that their labor was exploited in order to accumulate prodigious levels of profit. They would also understand that there is potential strength in numbers. However, they will have to organize in order to overcome capitalist control of the repressive powers of the state.

Marx also wrote about another dangerous contradiction in the way modern capitalism developed. While the productive power of capitalism becomes increasingly awesome, capitalists face a dilemma. Advances in industrial technology renders more and more workers superfluous. They join the ranks of the underemployed and the unemployed, and their earnings fall accordingly. However, industrial capitalists count upon people to buy the products their factories make. And capitalists who supply industrialists with financial support and raw material also count upon a healthy consumer market. If people cannot consume as they once did because of erratic or non-existent employment, factories shut down, costly machinery stands unused, and profits plummet. Economists influenced by Adam Smith and his followers believed that this situation was self-correcting—that things would work out in the long run. Marxist economists were more pessimistic and perhaps better understood that people do not always live in the long run—they have families to feed in the short run and that resentment of their condition might lead them into labor militancy and radical political activism.

Thus, Marx and generations of Marxists believed that societies progress through class conflict. Many Marxists and Marx himself were convinced that socialism, about which we will talk in a future chapter, could best develop in an industrialized society. Such a society would possess a small class of bourgeoisie or large-scale capitalists and a large proletariat class. Because of its size, the proletariat could effect a relatively democratic and peaceful revolution. Because the new socialist state would command an industrialized economy, it need not worry about the problem of scarcity plaguing the people. And because other industrialized societies would undoubtedly undergo similar revolutions, no socialist state would have to fear isolation for very long.

Ironically, however, revolutions claiming socialist credentials have taken place in relatively non-industrialized societies such as Russia, China, and Cuba. In order to modernize their economies, the Communist leadership in these societies believed it necessary to brutally discipline workers and peasants. And because these communist societies took place in comparative geographic and ideological isolation, leaders such as Stalin, Mao, and Castro have thought themselves justified in using repressive measures in order to protect the progress of the socialist state. It is unlikely that Marx, ornery and eccentric rebel that he was, would have approved.

Moreover, Marx and many twentieth century Marxists underestimated capitalism's capacity to not only survive but thrive in places like the United States. Perhaps capitalism's inherent contradictions will ultimately force its destruction. In the meantime, it will happily find and cultivate new markets and new technologies to master and prolong its existence.

Max Weber was, like Marx, a German. And like Marx he used powerful interdisciplinary skills to analyze daunting social and economic problems. Yet while both Smith and Marx exhibited optimism in humanity's future, Weber was a tough minded skeptic when it came to either capitalism or socialism.

Regardless of whether they were run by capitalists or communists, societies undergoing modernization, according to Weber, required the "iron cage" of bureaucracy to sustain themselves. Order and efficiency were needed in industrializing and modernizing societies and only vast bureaucracies, private and public, could maintain that order. Consequently, Weber feared that modern societies had to be less concerned about social justice and democratic processes than making sure the trains run on time.

Weber's work has spawned modernization theory. That is, modern societies have undergone key changes. First, modernization means secularization. Religion and ritual becomes notably less important. Second, equality is accepted as a virtue in modern societies, which praise "equality before the law" or "equal opportunity." Third, modern societies experience intense bureaucratization. The Social Security Administration and the Defense Department are bureaucratic as well as our insurance companies and Little League. People in modern societies are less likely to be "jacks of all trades." They have rather become specialists. Indeed, the New England Patriots of the National Football League pay an obscene salary to a man who specializes as a place kicker. Fourth, modern societies encourage rationalization—the application of science and technology to public and private problems such as curing cancer or hitting golf balls further. Quantification is essential in modern societies. Modern people need to know how many calories are in a Krispy Kreme donut or how many home runs does Barry Bonds need to break Henry Aaron's record. Yet whether these changes are good or bad, depends upon the theorist's perspective. Weber and his scholarly followers did not much fancy societies based upon religion and magic. But he was not sure if modern societies were much of an improvement.

RICH NATION/POOR NATION

Why some nations become rich and powerful and other nations fall into or languish in poverty and powerlessness has stirred scholarly controversy across disciplinary lines. This controversy links to the historical debate among those influenced by Smith, Marx, and Weber and links to why people, including Asian Pacific people, seek jobs, educational opportunities, and freedom by migrating to places like Hawai'i, California, and New York.

Market-friendly economists and economic historians claim that economic development has been hindered most by states incapable of understanding that their proper role is to protect private property and not regulate it or even worse misappropriate it in the name of the proletariat. The United States has prospered, they argue, because its political-legal system has generally been sympathetic to the idea of letting the law of supply and demand work. Less fortunate nations have been governed by sometimes well meaning egalitarian policies that only manage to place impossible to overcome restraints on capitalist development and thereby hurt in the long run the people those short-sighted policies were implemented to help.

To people who call themselves socialist, populist, progressive, or liberal, a market-oriented society might at first glance appear inhumane. However, its worshippers assert that the law of supply and demand, if unfettered, will eliminate eventually from the market place dishonest manufacturers and merchants, as well as cruel employers and despoilers of the environment. Poverty is the price, they claim, for excessive restraints imposed on the market economy.

Immigration is largely explained and frequently supported in market-oriented terms. People leave countries where their skills and knowledge are not needed and their ambition goes substantially unrewarded. That is, they emigrate from countries where the market economy is not so free for a country like the United States which has a well developed market economy. In the United States, people will gain access to a marketplace that rewards skill, knowledge, and ambition.

Unsurprisingly, economists and economic historians writing in the Marxist tradition disagree. They also, however, disagree with one another as to the source of inequality between nations and why people might journey from less developed to more developed nations. One tendency within Marxist economic thinking says that internal class dynamics are most essential to dooming one nation to poverty and raising another to prosperity. Why have most socialist revolutions failed to lift their countries out of poverty? These Marxist would respond that the failure of the socialist states to allow capitalism to modernize their countries' economic bases was at fault. If nothing else, capitalism knows how to beat scarcity—to push a society toward and beyond industrialism. Socialism can build upon capitalism's achievements by leveling the economic and political playing field for all members' of society. Thus, these Marxists agree that only capitalism can achieve economic prosperity but only socialism can bring about a truly just society. They add, however, that emigration from lesser developed countries to more developed countries like the United States is often a function of internal class dynamics. The imposition of capitalism on a society uproots peasants and diminishes the life chances of artisans and small-scale shop keepers. These people often seek themselves or through their children opportunities in other countries for economic independence. The premature imposition of capitalism, these Marxists argue, can also push people out of a country. Such an imposition is inevitably too regimented—small-scale farmers and business people are forced marched into an increasingly unlikely socialist future. These immigrants would rather work under the banner of Uncle Sam than some Communist Party commissar.

Other economists and economic historians, influenced by Marxism, are the world-systems theorists. They place less stress on internal class dynamics and more on global structuring of inequities by a world capitalist system, which, they contend, has been active since about the sixteenth century. Led by economic theorists such as Immanuel Wallerstein and Andre Gunder Frank, they assert that capitalism on a global scale has divided the world into highly developed, wealthy metropolises and lesser developed satellites. The latter serves the former by provisioning it with raw material, food, cheaply made consumer goods, and inexpensive unskilled and semi-skilled labor. The capitalist metropolis directs the flow of capital and labor and disproportionately profits from their use.

In order for world capitalism to exist, these theorists point out, some countries have to be metropolises and others have to be satellites. Some countries have to be exploiters and other countries have to be exploited. If all nations were economic equals, some other kind of economic system would have to be in charge because capitalism would have been long gone. Thus, these theorists analyze in detail the role of capitalist inspired imperialism, emanating originally in sixteenth century Western Europe but finding new blood among capitalists and their political allies in North America and Japan by the early twentieth century. And they point out that immigration from lesser developed or, what Wallerstein has called, "peripheral" countries has largely been the product of the way "core countries" have underdeveloped the periphery.

Weberian influenced theory has argued not always justifiably that Marxist and pro-capitalist theorists have been too obsessed with economic change. It claims that we need to look at cultural, ideological, and even psychological factors too. In a classic and often misunderstood study, *The Protestant Ethic and the Spirit of Capitalism* (1904-1905), Weber claimed that countries that imbibed the protestant work ethic—that working hard at one's calling honored God—were better able than other countries to foster a dynamic, wealth producing capitalism. While Weber clearly did not worship the emergence of modern capitalist nations, he maintained that capitalism most effectively developed in Great Britain, the United States, and Germany—places where Protestantism most effectively took hold. Roman Catholic and non-Christian dominated countries were falling behind the English, Americans, and Germans, Weber insisted.

Weberians, a good number of whom have been more enamored with capitalism than the great German social thinker, have focused on a society's need to develop an attitude more receptive to modern capitalism. People need to modernize—become more individualistic, hard working, sober, thrifty, and materialistic. If they do so, they and their countries need not fear poverty. At the same time, modernized societies would not have to fear many of its more ambitious members heading off to find work in America. Their ambitions would be met in the countries of their birth. More skeptical Weberians would argue that they still would have plenty of other things to fear, such as oppressive bureaucracies and the diminishment of their spiritual lives.

CONCLUSION

It is easy and hopefully necessary to ultimately dismiss Social Darwinism. Yet we need to confront it and other similar perspectives, because they ask us to consider to what extent we are blank slates when we come into this world. Moreover, it is foolish to deny out of hand nature's role in determining who we are. The overwhelming problem is that when people start asking about innate differences between, for example, men and women, as well as Asian Pacific and non-Asian Pacific Americans, a crude and dangerous notion of science is usually lurking about.

The fact is that much of the discussion about innate differences turns on self-fulfilling prophecies and denials of history. People gain possession of power for a variety of reasons. Once in power, it is not unusual for people to justify their status in reference to their natural fitness when they could have just as easily, but probably more reluctantly referred to their good fortune and ruthlessness. Indeed, many scientists point out that one problem with classical evolution theory is that it did not adequately account for dumb luck in why some species survive while others disappear.

As for the other perspectives mentioned, it is important to note that they do not exhaust all of the useful conceptualizations of how and whether hierarchies are raised. However, these perspectives do allow us a peek at the divergent range of arguments expressed by generally thoughtful people. All of these perspectives have important, if not always widespread, support. They direct our attention to useful ways of looking at cultural diversity in the United States and around the world, even if they possess serious shortcoming. In particular, they focus our attention on the issue of power.

Often very sensible people talk or write about the experiences of Asian Pacific Americans and other racial and ethnic groups as if the issue of political power has not or does not exist. If we attend enough intercultural communication classes or eat enough "ethnic foods," we will move beyond the barriers separating people in the United States and elsewhere. We will empathize with the "others" and learn to celebrate diversity.

The problem is that despite our good intentions and the many fine efforts on the part of Americans to encourage cross-cultural understanding, we need as well to understand better why boundaries exist between social groups. History is an important place to look for why hierarchies are raised. It is also an important place to find hope, for it reveals the often courageous struggles of ordinary people and famous people to see more clearly and transcend what were supposedly eternally constructed barriers between supposedly unequal people. History reveals diverse Americans empowering themselves and democratizing their society against very long odds.

STUDY QUESTIONS

1. What is Social Darwinism? How might it determine social policy?
2. What is the melting pot theory? Does it explain racial and ethnic relations in the United States adequately?
3. What was Robert Park's race relations cycle? Does it adequately explain racial and ethnic relations in the United States?
4. What is the immigrant analogy? Does it adequately explain racial and ethnic relations in the United States?
5. What is the Human Capital Model? How might it determine social policy in today's America?
6. What is the Model Minority Thesis? How might it determine social policy and attitudes toward Asian Pacific Americans?
7. What is Marxism? How does it explain the relationship between class and racial and ethnic relations?
8. What is the Split Labor Market Theory? How does it explain the relationship between class and racial and ethnic relations?
9. What is the Internal Colonial Model? How is it an example of a racial oppression theory?

10. According to Omi and Winant, what is a racial formation?
11. What are the various kinds of feminism? How does each explain sexual discrimination?
12. What is postmodernist theory? What might make it useful and not so useful to the scholar?
13. Who are the three major theorists of social change? How do they differ? How are they the same?
14. Why, according to Marxist theorists, is there economic inequality between nations?
15. Why, according to pro-capitalist theorists, is their economic inequality between nations?
16. Why, according to the Weberian theorists, is their economic inequality between nations?
17. Why are theories useful to the scholar doing historical and social inquiry?

SELECTED BIBLIOGRAPHY

Acuña, Rodolfo. *Occupied America.* 2nd ed. (1981).

Blauner, Robert. *Racial Oppression in America.* (1972).

Bonacich, Edna, "A Theory of Ethnic Antagonism: The Split Labor Market," in Ronald Takaki, (ed). *From Different Shores.* (1987).

Carmichael, Stokely and Hamilton, Charles. *Black Power.* (1967).

Cox, Oliver C. *Class, Caste, and Race.* (1967).

Davis, Angela. *Women, Race, and Class.* (1981).

Frank, Andre. Capitalism and Underdevelopment in Latin America. (1967).

Glazer, Nathan and Moynihan, Daniel M. *Beyond the Melting Pot.* (1970).

Gordon, Milton M. *Assimilation in American Life.* (1964).

Hofstadter, Richard. *Social Darwinism in American Thought.* (1970).

hooks, bell, *Feminist Theory: From Margins to Center.* (1984).

Jagger, Alisom M. and Rothernberg, Paula S. *Feminist Frameworks.* (1984).

Jorgensen, Joseph G. "A Century of Political Economic Effects on American Indian Society, 1880-1900," *The Journal of Ethnic Studies.* (1978).

Kristol, Irving. "The Negro is Like the Immigrant Yesterday," *New York Times Magazine,* September 11, 1966.

Omi, Michael and Winant, Howard. *Racial Formation in the United States.* 2nd Ed. (1994).

Park, Robert E. *Race and Culture.* (1950).

Ringer, Benjamin B. and Lawless, Elinor. *Race-Ethnicity and Society*. (1989).

Sowell, Thomas. *The Economics and Politics of Race*. (1983).

Wallerstein, Immanuel. *The Modern World System*. Vol. 1, (1974).

Weber, Max. *The Protestant Ethic and the Spirit of Capitalism*. (1958).

Wiebe, Robert. *Self-Rule* (1995).

Wolf, Eric. *Europe and the People With History*. (1982).

Winant, Howard. *The World is a Ghetto*. (2001).

Zavella, Patricia. *Women's Work & Chicano Families*. (1987).

III
POLITICAL POWER IN THE UNITED STATES

An easy way to think about political power is that it relates to the ability of individuals and groups to shape political decision-making in their societies. It is much harder to figure out why certain individuals and groups possess more of this power and why others possess less. It is most difficult to determine what should be done about the hierarchies raised in the United States and other countries.

In discussing political power, it is useful to consider some possible meanings of relevant terms such as democracy, freedom, and equality. In the United States, citizens and potential citizens generally agree that democracy, freedom, and equality are important and good. But Americans have not always agreed on the meaning of these words. Given the heterogeneity of those calling themselves Americans down through the years and given America's relative youth, Americans should probably take some comfort in understanding each other as well as they have. However, the lack of deep-seated agreement on the meaning of the keywords and concepts we will explore in this chapter has contributed to long-standing and frequently bitter political controversies, many of which have ensnared Americans of Asian Pacific ancestry. Perhaps, too, they have contributed to the cultural divide which contemporary pundits declare exists in the United States in the early 2000s.

DEMOCRACY, FREEDOM, AND EQUALITY

We often refer to the United States as a democracy. Depending upon one's definition of democracy, this reference may make sense. Then again, it may not. Moreover, historically as a concept, democracy has stirred as much fear among Americans as admiration.

When the United States was established in 1776, relatively few political leaders entertained positive views of democracy. Many agreed with twelfth century philosopher, St. Thomas Aquinas that democracy meant the unjust, irrational rule of the majority over the minority. However, alternate, more positive perceptions of democracy were available to the political leaders of the new country in 1776. For example, the first American political constitution to mention democracy was written in the then colony of Rhode Island. In 1641, that constitution maintained that democracy was a "popular government; that is to say it is in the power of the body of freemen orderly assembled, or a major part of them, to make or constitute just Lawes, by which they will be regulated and to <choose> from among themselves such ministers as shall see them faithfully executed between man and man." The Rhode Island constitution exemplified what English philosopher Jeremy Bentham described as "direct democracy." In other words, the people "or a major part of them" made the laws.

Conversely, the great American political leader Alexander Hamilton confronted the notion of representative or indirect democracy as he declared, "When the deliberative or judicial powers are vested wholly or partly in the people, you must expect error, confusion, and instability." However, he stated that a "representative democracy, where the right of election is well regulated, and the exercise of the legislative, executive, and judicial authorities is vested in selected persons" would be more responsible.

Direct democracy asserts a faith in the people to consistently make wise decisions. Indirect democracy exudes a greater distrust in the ability of the people to consistently make intelligent political choices. The few then should make decisions on behalf of the people. Confusing matters greatly, however, is the problem of who are the people in political-legal terms—those who are eligible for citizenship and political participation within a community or a state. In 1776, there was plenty of disagreement among American.

political leaders over who were the people. Simultaneously, they agreed substantially about those who were not the people.

The people ought to consist of property-holders, according to most American political leaders in the late 1700s. Whether they should consist of artisans and small-scale farmers and merchants was debated by the early American political elite. For Alexander Hamilton, one needed sufficient property to qualify for responsible political participation. For Thomas Jefferson, small-scale property holders were very able to make responsible political decisions. However, both Hamilton and Jefferson excluded the property less from the people's domain, as well as women and the people they identified as non-white. Since 1776, the people's domain has become more accessible to greater numbers of Americans. Yet how it has become more accessible and whether it is adequately accessible today remains worthy of consideration.

What then is a democracy? Lincoln has offered Americans some kind of working definition when he said in the Gettysburg Address that a democracy is a "government of the people, by the people, and for the people." In other words, the people rule in a democracy. Contemporary political scientists Edward Greenberg and Benjamin Page argue that three major principles comprise a democracy. It must be based on popular sovereignty. In other words, the political system derives from the "consent of the governed." Second, a democracy must reflect political equality. My vote, for example, should not possess ten times more worth than your vote. And a third major element of a democracy is political liberty. People must freely discuss political alternatives and the press must freely and fully inform the people.

Americans have always seemed to cherish freedom more than democracy, although they generally believe that the one cannot thrive without the other. Yet freedom, too, is a word that possesses different meanings to different Americans.

For many Americans, freedom has tended to mean the absence of restraints. In other words, one enjoys freedom **from** something such as government or any other person or collections of persons representing authority. To some extent, this is what those who supported the American struggle for independence from Great Britain or wrote the Bill of Rights meant by freedom. They feared tyrannical governments. That is, they believed that a people's freedom required preservation from governments that no longer respected the people's "unalienable rights."

Many Americans have also emphasized a more proactive meaning of freedom—the freedom to do something, the freedom to participate. Thus, the first amendment to the U.S. Constitution was not just written to guarantee certain freedoms from a tyrannical central government. It was written as well to guarantee the freedom to participate in decision-making processes in the United States. Similarly, when Civil Rights activists such as Martin Luther King referred to freedom in the 1950s and 1960s, they sought a freedom to participate fully in American life as well as a freedom from oppression.

A third emphasis associates freedom with freedom of choice or freedom of consumption and, perhaps, with a lack of responsibility. Living in a free society for the people who buy into this definition of freedom is a bit like living in a shopping mall. They celebrate the freedom to buy a certain brand of clothing or cup of coffee. These people, admittedly, do not always seem curious as to how various products get to the mall or whether the differences between them are all that great. If the labels differ, then they are satisfied that they are exercising their freedom of choice. Thus, many Americans contentedly associate having the ability to choose between a Republican Party candidate or a Democratic Party candidate as an incontestable part of a free and democratic society, even if a Libertarian or Green Party candidate better represents their views.

Americans probably value equality less than democracy or freedom. It is perhaps no coincidence that while President George W. Bush has hailed America's effort to spread democracy and freedom to the Middle East, he has pointedly omitted the need for Iraq and Iran to cherish equality. Nevertheless, equality is still widely admired in the United States. Americans have long maintained different meanings regarding equality, depending upon whether these meanings stress equality of opportunity, equality of outcome, or equality before the law.

Equality has always provoked a substantial amount of controversy in the United States. Many early American political leaders, such as Alexander Hamilton and George Washington, expressed little interest in supporting equality among the people living in the United States. They were convinced that such equality did not exist except perhaps in a narrow, but significant, legal sense. However, as we all know, Thomas Jefferson emphasized in the Declaration of Independence that "all men are created equal" and, thus, helped establish equality as a major component of American political thinking.

What Jefferson meant is debatable since he was a slaveholder, harbored racist attitudes toward people of African ancestry generally, and believed women should stay out of politics and commerce. Perhaps, as some of us would argue, he meant that we are all created with an equal start in life and whatever happens to us should flow from our character and luck and not from what some government does to help or hinder us. In other words, Jefferson was an early advocate of equality of opportunity. Perhaps, as also some of us would argue, Jefferson meant that our birth alone should afford us equal consideration before the law. We should stand as equal before the law despite whether some of us are rich and some of us are poor, some of us possess lighter skins and some of us possess darker skins, some of us are men and some of us are women. Very likely, Jefferson was not interested in interpreting equality as equality of condition. He did not believe that people should live roughly the same way on roughly the same income. Nevertheless, Jefferson favored an American society that produced only a relatively small gap between the wealthiest citizens and the poorest. These different variations on equality that might have influenced Jefferson have also affected other Americans through the years. In the United State, these varied interpretations have at times provoked momentous and often virulent political debates.

POLITICAL IDEOLOGIES

There are two ways we can look at ideologies—one in a less negative light than the other. Often ideology means to theorists a political philosophy and some ideologies are more accurate, more useful than others. At other times, theorists will describe ideologies as belief systems that are inherently false and irrational. In this text, we will use the former, more generous notion of ideology.

To some extent, then, we all have ideologies. The ideologies that we maintain might not seem clearly and consistently thought out. Yet our ideologies do attempt to describe who holds political power in our societies, how they came to hold political power, how they make use of political power, and what, if anything, we should do about them. This section of the chapter will analyze various ideologies that historically helped shape the American political system. In the process, we should bear in mind that the people who subscribed to these ideologies might differ from one another in many consequential details. We should also bear in mind that these ideologies are not hermetically sealed off from one another. They can embrace overlapping beliefs and practices.

COLLECTIVISM

Hundreds of years ago, North American Indian groups and Native Hawaiians were political people, retaining political philosophies about the use of power and the fundamental basis of a beneficial governing system. Like many other preindustrial, premodern people, they followed the notion that the group, the collective, was the fundamental unit in their societies and that their governing systems should emerge out of and reinforce reciprocal relations among group members. These governing systems might appear relatively hierarchical, leading outsiders to describe them as "chiefdoms" or they could appear relatively open-ended and democratic.

In fact, the belief that the individual stood in a reciprocal relationship of obligation to other group members, whether high or low in status, permeated much of the thinking of European, African, Latin American, and Asian Pacific migrants to the United States into the twentieth century. Native-born American observers noted that these migrants valued family and kin to an extraordinary extent and that, as individuals, they subordinated their individuality to the needs of the group. Even today, some cultural analysts claim that Asian Pacific people value collective societies, as opposed to the individualism honored among many European Americans. Whether these analysts are determined to exaggerate intercultural differences or not, the United States, despite its strong individualistic leanings, has not entirely abandoned the collectivism on which American Indians, New England Puritans, and many Polish, Mexican, and Southeast Asian migrants might find something of a common ground.

One possible problem with collectivist ideology is that it does tend to deny the importance of individual autonomy and, therefore, the need to value individual rights. Moreover, collectivist ideology generally devalues dissent and organized protest against those in power. Collectivist ideology can conversely encourage people to feel a sense of responsibility to one another and discourage selfishness and greed. Emerging from this sense of responsibility to one another is the notion that "an injury to one is an injury to all"—a notion that seemingly has supported collective protest against injustice. Historian E.P. Thompson and political scientist James C. Scott have claimed that premodern people, whether in eighteenth century England or twentieth century Southeast Asia, have honored a "moral economy." This "moral economy" offers ideological justification for collective protest against those in power who place personal gain over their public obligations.

REPUBLICANISM

Republicanism was an ideology that claimed European roots, but grew well in North American soil about the time of the American Revolutionary War. In the 1500s, an Italian political philosopher, Machiavelli, advocated that republics, governments attempting to represent the will of the people, prospered when citizens embraced civic virtue. For Machiavelli, civic virtue translated into active participation in the fate of the republic. A virtuous citizen did not let personal needs get in the way of public involvement. A virtuous citizen became informed on key issues, voted and held office when allowed, and defended the republic through military service when called upon. While recognizing the importance of the individual, Republicanism contained a strong residual measure of premodern collectivism as it faced the advent of modern society.

In the United States of two hundred years ago, political leaders and political philosophers maintained a strong belief in republicanism despite their many deeply felt differences. They were justly proud of the creation of the United States and that they had forged in the new country, republican forms of government nationally and in the individual states. Some European observers predicted the quick collapse of representative government in the United States. These Europeans believed that American political institutions faced destruction by mob rule or despotism. However, if U.S. citizens practiced their civic virtues the new republic would survive and prosper, according to American Republicanism.

Not the possession of any particular political party then or now, the ideology of Republicanism helped furnish much that was vital and creative about the new United States. It helped many American citizens to realize that they could reconcile the public good with individual liberty. It generated the widespread belief in the importance of an informed citizenry. In other words, the ideology of Republicanism expressed faith in a thoughtful and freedom-loving citizenry, independent enough to engage in responsible political dissent and patriotic enough to defend the United States from tyranny. Many, but not all, advocates of republicanism supported the advancement of democracy and equality in the United States at a time when American leaders like George Washington and Alexander Hamilton associated democracy and equality with social disorder and subversion of vital American institutions.

However, American republicanism also tended to reinforce racial, ethnic, gender, and class distinctions within the United States, as well as a patriotism that too easily grew arrogant. While American citizens expressed an understandable pride in their young country's accomplishments in the late 1700s and early 1800s, some tended to view people of other countries as inherently or culturally incapable of supporting republican institutions. Republicanism seemed to give some Americans the excuse to look from continent to continent, nation to nation, and see little but tyrants and people bowing down to tyranny. American Indians, for example, were often regarded as childlike, tyrannized by their savage emotions and too dependent upon despotic chiefs or white people for guidance. American Indians were, thus, unfit for U.S. citizenry, according to many supporters of republicanism.

The notion of manliness played a strong role in the development of American republicanism. Supposedly, the most useful U.S. citizens were assertive, cool under pressure, "stout hearted", and independent—characteristics that were connected to manliness. Accordingly, republicanism tended to exclude women from a central place in American public life as women were often represented and perceived as dependent upon men as providers, political leaders, and soldiers. However, republicanism also claimed that women, middle and upper class European American women that is, might help out as homebound cultivators of cleanliness, full stomachs, and good morals.

Supporters of republicanism did not always agree as to what kind of person made a suitable American. citizen. Some might, for instance, express prejudice for or against the wealthy. Yet they tended to agree that that the useful American citizen was independent in status and mind, rational, mature, and courageous—characteristics not only associated with men, but associated with men identified as white. Thus, republicanism in trying to find a way to unite white American citizens ideologically, sought to exclude or limit the importance of most of the people living in the United States and the rest of North America, since most of these people were female or defined as non-white.

In the late 1800s, early Asian Pacific immigrants to the United States found a country in which the ideology of republicanism remained influential. Regardless of sex and age, Asian Pacific immigrants were often described by European Americans as servile, dependent, passive, childlike, and unmanly. While

European Americans might disagree as to whether these characteristics were innate or not, too few of them regarded early Asian Pacific immigrants as capable of useful American citizenship.

CLASSICAL LIBERALISM

Classical liberalism arose as a potent ideology in the late 1700s. It emerged largely from Great Britain, where philosophers such as John Locke in the 1600s and Adam Smith in the 1700s significantly contributed to classical liberalism's vitality. Classical liberalism, moreover, contributed much to the thinking of early American political leaders such as Thomas Jefferson. Finally, it helped pull American republicanism from collectivism toward recognizing the importance of the individual and individual private property.

In contrast to the collectivism, then, classical liberalism argued that the individual stood as the primary unit of society and it was the role of government to do little but protect the individual's natural rights. For Locke, this meant the protection of an individual's "life, liberty, and property." For Jefferson, these natural rights were "life, liberty, and the pursuit of happiness."

Classical liberalism and republicanism combined in a historically temporary marriage. In so doing, they philosophically underwrote noteworthy and even revolutionary social, cultural, and economic movements in Europe and North America from the 1600s through the 1800s. For both, the enemy was tyranny as practiced by those retaining undeserved, inherited wealth and power—kings, queens, and aristocrats in general.

John Locke and then the American revolutionary leaders argued against the "Divine Right of Kings." Those who supported the "Divine Right of Kings" believed that God had designated certain individuals to represent him in various countries such as England and France. One could not, consequently, rebel against these monarchs, however corrupt, cruel, and inept, because that would seem like rebelling against God. John Locke in England offered ideological cover for a bloody civil war against the monarchy in the mid-1600s. He stated that God did not create governments. The people combined as individuals created governments to protect their individual lives, liberties, and property. They combined, that is, to draw up a social contract. The terms of this social contract were that the people would agree to abide by the laws instituted by government and the government would agree to protect the natural rights of each individual member of the people. If the government failed to carry out its obligation, then the people had a right to combine again into a revolutionary force. The people had a right, in other words, to expel the old government and institute a new form of government.

Similarly, American revolutionaries complained that their protests against the rule of Great Britain's King George III were not protests against God. A recent English emigré to Pennsylvania, Thomas Paine, pointed out in his very influential pamphlet *Common Sense* (1776) that King George was nothing but "the royal brute of England." Writing to excite American colonists to fight for independence from the British Empire, Paine also showed his republican influences by calling for the institution of a republican form of government in the former British colonies along the Atlantic Coast of North America.

Thomas Jefferson, the primary author of the Declaration of Independence (1776), also combined classical liberalism with republicanism. The Declaration of Independence was clearly influenced by philosophers such as Locke. Jefferson not only argued in the Declaration that American colonists had a right to engage in a revolution, but later in his long career maintained that every twenty-five years or so the United States should experience a revolution. In part, Jefferson shared with Adam Smith and other classical liberals the belief that government had the important, but limited, role of protecting individual liberties. From that point, he declared that a government too long in power would inevitably grow tyrannical and destructive of individual freedom.

Classical liberalism tended to argue that individual private property rights were sacred. It declared that government had no business interfering with the conduct of private property owners even if that conduct seemed injurious to labor, consumers, and other property owners. Classical liberalism tended to believe as well that, in the long run, government interference, even if well intentioned, would prove ultimately harmful to society. Instead, the marketplace, which Adam Smith called "the invisible hand," ought to determine what private property should or should not do. However, republican advocates as different as Jefferson and Alexander Hamilton feared unlimited veneration and unrestricted use of private property. They believed that the laws of supply and demand needed discipline from civic virtue.

For classical liberals, the marketplace and a host of personal and political freedoms such as freedom of speech and thought blended well with one another. Classical liberalism claimed it wanted to protect freedoms of speech and thought, as well as a free marketplace. Many classical liberals extended the metaphor of the marketplace to the world of political ideas and dialogue. Just as in the marketplace, buyers and sellers should face few restrictions so should ideas freely circulate. Consequently, the most satisfying products and the most satisfying ideas would achieve the most success. Generally, however, classical liberals were more adamant about protecting the free marketplace than protecting personal and political liberties.

Even many of its most earnest critics realize that classical liberalism helped unleash dynamic political, cultural, and economic forces in Europe and North America. Likewise, its legacy of taking seriously the individual's rights has aided profound changes throughout the world. However, its stress upon individualism, according to critics, has often produced selfishness and materialism at the expense of time-honored traditions or collective institutions such as the family.

Like republicanism, classical liberalism has promoted a mixed bag of positives and negatives for culturally diverse Americans. Seemingly, classical liberalism would have little use for racism and any other form of bigotry. If the most important unit in society is the individual, then classical liberalism would apparently encourage the judgment of people based on their personal characteristics and not their group affiliation. In the 1800s, some classical liberals spoke out against the enslavement of Africans as an obstacle to capitalist expansion. They stated that the law of supply and demand required free, not enslaved, labor. Some classical liberals, as well, expressed a dislike for immigration restriction, including proposed laws to limit the movement of Asian Pacific immigrants into the United States. They argued that immigrants were potentially productive workers and the unrestrained migration of labor from one region or one country to another was beneficial in the long run for the country. For these classical liberals, the issue of social or racial justice was, perhaps, important. Many such as the nineteenth century English philosopher, John Stuart Mill, became passionate advocates of social justice. However, the overriding factor for many classical liberals was that slavery and immigration restriction posed barriers to the development of economic freedom which they associated with capitalism.

At the same time, classical liberalism could lead to troubling implications for people like American Indians and immigrants to the United States. The collectivist orientation of native peoples and, to some extent, immigrants bothered classical liberals, who often complained that American Indians or Irish immigrants or Chinese immigrants would not amount to much unless they freed themselves of collectivism and became individualistic. Just as some classical liberals spoke out against racial and ethnic bigotry in the name of freedom, others supported ethnocentric measures against American Indians or immigrants in the name of freedom.

Classical liberalism's venerable distaste for government could also prove problematic. People of color and immigrants have historically required some kind of government support to help them through economic travails and overt discrimination. When given a choice, classical liberalism has viewed social policy aimed at protecting society's most vulnerable people as antagonistic to economic freedom.

CLASSICAL CONSERVATISM

Classical conservatism was a powerful response to some of the changes called for by republicanism and classical liberalism. Since republicanism and classical liberalism generally sought more power for non-aristocratic people and even relatively poor people, classical conservatives in Europe and the Americas fought to preserve the advantages and disadvantages of birth. In the process, classical conservatism probably lacked the influence of more democratic and egalitarian ideologies by the 1800s. Classical conservatism simply was too pessimistic and elitist for many Americans, despite the fact that it contributed greatly to the establishment of U.S. political institutions.

Classical conservatism was well represented by thinkers such as the English politician and philosopher, Edmund Burke. In the late 1700s, Burke condemned a bitter revolution taking place in France. In the name of "liberty, equality, and fraternity" and guided intellectually in part by Thomas Paine and Thomas Jefferson, this revolution had succeeded, according to Burke, in fragmenting an organically created French society. For Burke, the preservation of an organic society was vital, because it was bonded together by very human and, in the long run, very humane relations between the rich and powerful and the not so rich and powerful. Democracy and equality, therefore, empowered people who did not deserve power, who would abuse power and destroy what had taken centuries of thoughtful courage to build.

In the 1800s, classical conservatism turned much of its attention on the abuses of industrialization and developing capitalism. Classical conservatives were not so concerned with the fact that laborers were often ruthlessly exploited. Rather, they faulted the industrial revolution for destroying long cherished traditions and the spiritual basis of community. The industrial revolution, moreover, was condemned by classical conservatives for empowering people who presumably did not deserve power— capitalists who honored greed more than nobility. Indeed, the most influential critics of capitalism in places like the British Isles and North America were not anti-capitalist socialists, but classical conservatives.

What many American might see as progress in terms of democracy or economic growth, other Americans saw as potentially destructive of valued and traditional, although hierarchical, bonds between humans. We can find traces or even more than traces of classical conservative thinking among some of America's "founding fathers." Alexander Hamilton, James Madison, and John Adams feared the consequences of empowering ordinary American farmers and laboring people. Thomas Jefferson was more optimistic, but he favored the preservation of rural communities over the development of manufacturing and mercantile-based capitalism in the United States.

The legacy of classical conservatism when it comes to multicultural issues in the United States is more mixed than many of us might think. Clearly, if classical conservatives would not want to see native-born European Americans of ordinary means have much of a say in government, they were unlikely to favor extending democracy to immigrants or people of color. Moreover, American classical conservatism tended to become highly anti-immigrant. It often argued that immigrants, except perhaps those of Anglo or upper class backgrounds, undermined American institutions and traditions. However, classical conservatives were often very critical of anti-African American and anti-Asian Pacific American violence in the United States. Much of this violence was perpetuated by lower class European Americans and, as far as classical conservatives were concerned, proved the irrationality of lower class people, regardless of race and ethnicity.

PRODUCERISM TO POPULISM

In many respects, producerism in the United States linked ordinary people to republicanism. During the late 1700s and early 1800s, the market revolution became more apparent in the United States. The early stirrings of the market revolution encompassed industrialization, urbanization, the continued commercialization of American agriculture, the expansion of transportation and communication systems, and the creation of more and more wage workers and tenant farmers. To a good number of ordinary Americans, the market revolution also seemed to breed and enlarge class differences. Many of those who labored as artisans, industrial workers, small-time merchants, and small-scale farmers believed that the economic changes they experienced in the 1800s threatened their livelihoods and their ways of life. Moreover, they held a group of people they often condemned as monopolists accountable, because presumably this group's monopoly of economic and political power deprived ordinary people of the fruits of their hard work.

Producerism was largely based upon something economists call a labor theory of value. Supporters of producerism, therefore, believed that wealth was produced by labor, not capital. They tended to divide Americans into non-producers and producers. The former consisted of monopolists and other people castigated as parasites by producerists. These "parasitic" people included groups such as landlords, speculators in land or stock, financiers, Southern plantation owners and slaveholders, and most lawyers. These people were called parasites because while they might have made money, they supposedly did not earn it through hard work, but made money by taking advantage of the labor of others. The producers were typically small farmers and artisans, who seemingly possessed the characteristics of good republicans. In other words, they were independent, owned property or a skill, trusted in the dignity of labor, participated in civic affairs, believed in manliness, and so up to a point believed in democracy and egalitarianism.

Producerism helped democratize the American political system during the first half of the nineteenth century. For example, voting rights were extended to non-property holding white adult male citizens. Producerism inspired the early labor movement in the United States. The trade unions formed during much of the 1800s were organized to protect highly skilled, male workers from industrialization. Producerism also helped support the Free Soil Movement before the Civil War. Free Soilers sought to keep America's western territories free to ordinary white people and out of the reach of Southern slaveholders.

Producersim, however, was soiled by racism, nativism, and sexism. Taking its cue from republicanism, producerism generally considered people of color as unmanly servants of the "monopolists." Producerism fed into nativist suspicions of immigrants, especially if they were non-Protestants. Many advocates of producerism regarded Catholicism and Judaism, for example, as religions that were antithetical to American republican institutions. Producerism also left little doubt that women's work was subordinate to men's work in importance to American society. Producerism lay at the heart of early outcries against Chinese immigration to the United States during the second half of the 1800s. Chinese immigrants often found that their most outspoken critics were European American working people, who condemned them as "toiling machines" used to enrich the wealthy few at the expense of white laboring people.

During the late 1800s, producerism furnished a foundation for the rise of a potent populist movement in the United States. In the 1890s, populists created a political party called the Populist Party and threatened, for a while, the dominance of the Republican and especially Democratic parties. More than that, one historian, Lawrence Goodwyn, has referred to late nineteenth century populism as the last powerfully democratic movement in American history. For a variety of reasons, the "populist moment," as Goodwyn called it, lost its luster, but it has not disappeared.

Populism, reinforced by producerism, continues to shake American political institutions and practices well into the twenty first century. For instance, it helped to create support for significant reforms in American political and economic institutions—reforms which, often erratically, benefited Americans across racial and ethnic barriers. The Social Security Act passed into law during the 1930s, is one example. Indeed, populism generated widespread backing in the twentieth century for the development of an American welfare system, because populism has long demanded that government should help out needy, hard working people.

Perhaps paradoxically, populism has also played a role in influencing attacks upon the welfare system developing in the late twentieth century. One reason is that populism also expresses the claim that some people are not deserving of welfare and that welfare recipients are not sufficiently hard-working. Another reason to consider is that populist arguments in recent years shifted from condemning big business to attacking big government. Despite the tremendous growth of corporate power in the late twentieth century, many ordinary American citizens regard big government as the greater enemy. To many of these American citizens, the welfare system and the taxes that finance the welfare system represent big government gone haywire at the expense of ordinary, hard-working, tax-paying Americans.

Since the late 1800s, populism has carried on producerist tendencies to reinforce racial and ethnic barriers among Americans. Largely supported in the late nineteenth century by native-born Protestants, rural Americans, populism generated a great deal of distrust toward immigrants. Some, but certainly not all populists, were bigoted against Jewish people. They claimed that Jewish people controlled financial capitalism on a global level and were at the root of the financial problems facing ordinary Americans. The fact that a vast number of Jewish immigrants were relatively impoverished seemed not to impress many populist anti-Semites.

Anti-immigrant and, more to the point, anti-Asian Pacific immigrant advocates were inspired by populist sentiments into the 1900s. In the late twentieth century and today, Asian Pacific immigrants to America. have been accused of taking jobs and business opportunities away from hard-working native-born American citizens. They have done so, because Asian Pacific people supposedly possess a lower standard of living than native-born Americans and receive undeserved help from the American. government. Immigrants from non-Asian Pacific countries also have heard similar criticisms.

Populist political rhetoric has long flirted with xenophobic—anti-foreign sentiments—in the United States. In recent years a great deal of populist rhetoric articulated by very different politicians such as Pat Buchanan and Richard Gephart argues that foreign business concerns threaten the livelihoods of ordinary American citizens. This xenophobic populism also maintains that working and lower-middle class economic security can become significantly guaranteed if the United States stopped importing cars and computer parts from Asia. Indeed, Japan and China, as well as other Asian countries appeared as the major enemies of xenophobic populists during the last generation. While Japanese, Chinese, and other Asian political and economic elites certainly have their faults, much of this xenophobic rhetoric has encouraged racism and discouraged reasonable dialogue about international trade policies.

Populism has long maintained a mixed record when it comes to racial issues. Many rural Southern African Americans supported the populist movement in the late 1800s. Similarly, populistic beliefs inspired Mexican Americans in New Mexico to engage in rural protests in the 1880s. Called the White Caps or Las Gorras

Blancas, these Mexican American farmers declared: "Our purpose is to protect the rights of the people in general and especially those of the helpless classes."

While some European American populists elicited and appreciated the support of non-whites, others did not. In the South, populism could not overcome the region's tragic history of race relations. Some white populists even used racism as a way of gaining white support. Georgia's Tom Watson during the late 1890s and early 1900s, Mississippi's Theodore Bilbo during the 1930s and 1940s, and, most recently, Alabama's George Wallace during the 1960s and 1970s have convinced many supporters that racial segregation was beneficial to ordinary white people. Even now, racial bigotry infiltrates populist political rhetoric. Even now, some politicians will suggest or state openly that ordinary European Americans will suffer if people of color get better jobs, housing, education, as well as more political power.

SOCIALISM

Socialism emerged in Europe during the first half of the nineteenth century. At this time, European nations such as France and England experienced powerful economic, political, social, and cultural changes. Early socialists were convinced that the industrial revolution had created permanent and unjust class divisions and that capitalism fed off the impoverishment of the laboring classes. What European socialists intended to do about this situation varied and led to bitter and frequently pointless and trite debates among socialists. Raymond Williams wrote, "<T>he resulting controversy between many groups and tendencies all calling themselves socialist, has long been intricate and bitter. Each main tendency has found alternative, often derogatory terms for the other." Indeed, for decades, socialists have seemed to spend more time harassing other socialists than non-socialists or even anti-socialists.

This is too bad, because socialism, like many other ideologies we have discussed, deserves serious consideration. What grew at the heart of the socialist tradition is a linkage made between capitalism, class divisions, and the exploitation of working people. To break the link, according to socialism, working people must gain control of the economy from capitalists and gain control of the government from politicians allied with capitalists. How this ought to happen has separated the various tendencies within socialism.

Socialism, like producerism and populism, has responded in a mixed way to racial and ethnic problems in the United States. In theory, socialism has presented itself as color-blind and prejudiced-free. This claim was one of socialism's greatest assets in the United States, but it was also one of its greatest weaknesses. Generally, socialism has argued that capitalism and class exploitation were humanity's primary enemies. Once workers, consisting of men and women of all races and nationalities, vanquished capitalism and class exploitation then other problems such as racial and sexual discrimination would disappear. Moreover, socialists have often been in the forefront of specific struggles against racism and have helped people of color, such as Filipino and Mexican farm workers in the 1930s, to organize against injustice.

Yet many people of color, as well as others, have argued that racial and ethnic problems retain sufficient importance on their own. They state that racism requires concern just as much if not more than capitalist exploitation. Hence, they assert that American socialism has frequently failed to address significant issues facing diverse racial and ethnic groups. Indeed, many people of color will insist that capitalism can help eliminate racial and ethnic barriers if personal bigotry is eliminated.

More seriously, socialists have at times reinforced racial and ethnic barriers. For example, Frank Roney was one of the more important labor leaders in San Francisco during the late 1870s and 1880s. An Irish immigrant, Roney was also a socialist, who had little stomach for the anti-Chinese beliefs then popular among San Francisco's workers. Yet he supported the anti-Chinese movement, because it was a good way to attract white workers to trade unionism.

PROGRESSIVISM

Many American historians have called the time period of 1900 to 1918 the Progressive Age. Other, more recent, historians have questioned whether progressivism was coherent and consistent enough to dominate two decades of American history. It is true that people who called themselves or were called progressives differed quite a bit from one another on very important issues. Some progressives were very close to socialists and populists when it came to seeing the need for more democratization of American political and economic institutions. Other progressives were much more elitist than democratic. Some progressives wanted to see big business tamed by government. Other progressives wanted to see government help big business. Some progressives believed that the United States could become a "melting pot" for immigrants. Others were convinced that immigrants, in particular, Asian Pacific immigrants, were unmeltable and unwelcomed in the United States. Some fought against racial discrimination. Others were unapologetic racists. Some were Republicans. Others were Democrats.

What seemed to hold these diverse people together was simply a belief in progress. They may have differed greatly on how to achieve that progress, but they all seemed to think that something seriously had gone wrong with the United States after the Civil War. One way or another, they argued, America had to change for the better.

In fact, under the prodding of progressives, substantial reforms occurred during the first decades of the twentieth century. Progressive politicians were elected to many state and national offices. Republican Theodore Roosevelt, who was President from 1901 to 1909 and Democrat Woodrow Wilson, who was President from 1913 to 1921, were both associated with progressivism. Numerous progressive-minded men were elected as state governors. Among the most notable were Wisconsin's Robert LaFollette and California's Hiram Johnson. Thanks to these and other progressives such as social reformers and social critics, Jane Addams and Upton Sinclair, many Americans became convinced that America could eliminate political corruption and corporate abuses of laborers and consumers. They believed that government and the private sector could ally for a better America.

If we just look at California during the first two decades of the twentieth century, we can see some interesting, but ambiguous things happening. Many politically and socially concerned Californians were upset by what was occurring in the Golden State by the turn-of-the-century. Corporations such as the Southern Pacific Railroad Company had seemingly amassed an enormous amount of economic and political power in California; so much power that it could dominate the state government as well as numerous local governments. In cities such as San Francisco, highly organized political machines were apparently corrupting the political process as well, while illegally enriching their leaders. Labor unrest was rampant, especially in San Francisco. Immigration, particularly Asian Pacific immigration, was seen as a disturbing political, economic, and social problem. The existence of gambling, prostitution, substance abuse, and "blood sports" such as prize fighting, distressed many Californians, who connected these "vices" with lower class, immigrant cultures.

Progressives such as Hiram Johnson represented the dissatisfaction expressed by many well education, European American middle and upper class Californians. Neither a socialist nor a populist, Johnson was able to forge an alliance with trade unions in California and convince many working class Californians that he was something of a hero. He persuaded them that he and other California progressives were going to clean up government and big business corruption and make California more responsive to the desires of all Californians—at least all white Californians.

In California, as in several other states, voter propositions were introduced as a means of eliminating the power of corrupt politicians and corporations. If the state government failed to enact laws voters wanted, then voters could initiate and pass laws on their own. In theory, at least, California's progressives sought to introduce direct democracy into the Golden State's political system.

However, many of California's progressives were deeply involved in orchestrating a vicious anti-Asian Pacific movement in the Golden State during the first two decades of the twentieth century. This reflected a tendency within American progressivism to see cultural homogeneity as a key to progress. Immigrants who came from places outside of Western and Northern Europe, as well as native born people of color, confused and even frightened a good number of American progressives. In California, much of this confusion and fear was targeted at Asian Pacific people, who were viewed as a troublesome source of criminality, decadence, and labor unrest. In addition, for progressive politicians anti-Asian Pacific rhetoric was a good way to get votes in California.

Interestingly, in light of many Americans aversion to labels such as "socialist" and "left wing," leftist political activists in recent years have taken on the label of progressive as a way of separating themselves from contemporary liberal and neo-liberal politicians and policies. Modern progressives might, for example, associate themselves more willingly with the Green Party than the Democrat Party and certainly the Republican Party.

FEMINISM

Those of us who lack historical perspective like to think that feminism is a relatively new phenomenon. This is not true. Indeed, nineteenth century feminism arose out of republicanism. While stressing the values of manliness, republicanism argued that women could enact important roles in the American republic. Thomas Jefferson, for example, maintained that women were morally superior to men. Logically, then, women should become spiritual and moral guides in the United States. They should steer young Americans toward what was right and away from what was wrong. Men, according to the father of the Declaration of Independence, should stick to what they presumably did better than women—politics, business, diplomacy, and warfare. In so doing, men would spare women from involvement in matters that often demanded dishonesty and violence. Men, so to speak, would risk their own souls and save women from eternal damnation.

Some historians have referred to the development of something called the cult of domesticity to explain what was happening in the late 1700s and early 1800s. Both middle and upper class men and women could agree that females were morally superior to men and that they should command American domestic life. That is, women should command the household. Men, however, should command the public sphere of American life—politics, economics, foreign relations, and warfare. In part, this cult of domesticity was a product of economic changes as the market revolution during the early 1800s meant that less work for pay was done in and around the home and more work for pay was done in factories, shops, and offices away from the home. Hence, the notion of men "bringing home the bread" while women stayed home and performed housework made sense to many Americans.

Yet this cult of domesticity became something of a double-edged sword. In other words, if women were perceived as morally superior some American women wondered why they were confined to the household when men were making a mess of public life. Because they possessed the time and energy, many middle and upper class women participated in various reform movements that blossomed during the first decades of the nineteenth century. The temperance movement aimed at eliminating alcohol abuse, if not alcohol, was one of these movements that attracted considerable support from women. Women also got involved in prison reform, education reform, and, in the 1830s and 1840s, the most serious movement of all to change American society—the abolitionist movement.

While American women struggled against slavery in the 1830s and 1840s, it occurred to some early feminists such as Angeline Grimke, Elizabeth Cady Stanton, Susan B. Anthony, and Lucy Stone that women, regardless of race, ethnicity, and class, also required liberation. In 1848, America's first national women's rights convention was held in Seneca Falls, New York. This convention issued a document modeled on the Declaration of Independence—a document that declared that "all men and women are created equal."

In the mid-1800s, the campaign against slavery became more paramount than the struggle for women's rights. However, after the Civil War, the crusade for female suffrage in the United States. animated a strong feminist spirit. Still, it was not until 1920 that "suffragettes" were able to get an amendment to the U.S. Constitution enacted that furnished a federal guarantee of the right to vote to women. Those men and women who expected that giving women the right to vote would cause feminism to disappear were disappointed. Women continued to insist that their contributions to American society should exceed those of housewives and occasional voters.

While feminism has clearly enlarged the possibilities for American women, it has provoked severe criticism. Some Americans, including conservative women, claim that feminism has "gone too far." They declare it has supposedly endangered American family values by encouraging women to work outside of the home. Indeed, many critics complain that feminism has become a major destroyer of American morality.

The relationship between feminism and people of color has long been problematic. Women of color have often been inspired by feminism's call for equal rights across gender boundaries and have acted upon that inspiration. Nevertheless, women of Asian Pacific ancestry and other women of color often have viewed feminism as a creation of white, middle and upper class women who entertain an inadequate understanding of the dynamics of race and class.

NATIONALISM

Political scientist Benedict Anderson describes nationalism as an effort to construct "imagined communities" among people who will rarely if ever have a chance to meet one another across geographic and time barriers. Nationalism can stem from a variety of concepts, including ethnicity. Within the United States, nationalism has generated complex responses. On Independence Day and other celebrations of nationhood, Americans have been reminded that they are or ought to be one people. Yet groups identified in racial and ethnic terms within the United States have given birth to varied kinds of ethnic nationalism, which creates the image of the United States as a nation of nations.

In the early 1800s, Tenskwatawa and Tecumseh sought to forge a Native American nation in North America that transcended local and tribal differences. These Shawnee brothers were unsuccessful, but helped inspire subsequent efforts to unify American Indians into a nation. For example, in the late 1960s and early 1970s, a Native American organization called the American Indian Movement pushed militantly for a separate Native American nation within the United States.

When thousands of Irish immigrants poured into the United States before the Civil War, many continued to cling to an Irish nationality, as they became U.S. citizens, voters, soldiers, and office holders. These Irish immigrants and their offspring often portrayed Ireland as under the thumb of cruel British colonizers and themselves as exiles in a country that was much too unappreciative of them.

Ethnic group members can be characterized by a dual nationality. An Italian American or a Mexican American might truly believe that there is an Italian nation or a Mexican nation that transcends the borders constructed by governments. Nevertheless, both might passionately celebrate American Independence Day and sing the "Star Spangled Banner" with sincere gusto.

One serious problem with nationalism is that its most fervent promoters often overrate the homogeneity of those they identify as belonging to one nationality or another. Class, regional, religious, gender, and political variations exist among all nationalities. To poor Irish immigrants in the United States struggling for survival for themselves and their families in the nineteenth century, St. Patrick's Day may have seemed a very meaningful symbol of Irish nationalism. But St. Patrick's Day did not get them jobs or fill their stomachs or achieve much in the way of meaningful political power.

"Patriotism," according to the eighteenth century English literary giant, Samuel Johnson, "is the last refuge of scoundrels." If we substitute the word nationalism for patriotism, we will see both sides of Johnson's remarks. Nationalists in denying significant distinctions within a nation often neglect and even sustain the raising of hierarchies. Yet nationalism has also inspired important movements of people against exploitation and oppression.

Asian Pacific Americans have experienced both the best and the worst of nationalism. The Americans who supported exclusive legislation against Asian Pacific immigrants in the nineteenth often did so in the name of a perceived homogeneous American nationality. Yet when Asian Pacific Americans struggled against discrimination they often appealed to an inclusive American nationality based on open-ended readings of the Declaration of Independence, the Gettysburg Address, and the 14th Amendment to the U.S. Constitution.

Asian Pacific American communities have not always been hotbeds of ethnic nationalism. Still, ethnic nationalism has not left these communities untouched. During the early 1900s, as China struggled toward achieving a more democratic nationhood, many Chinese Americans took the time and spent the money to support the movement led by Sun Yat Sen to modernize and democratize China. Asian Indian and Korean struggles against colonialism also encouraged an ethnic nationalism among East Indian and Korean Americans. Given the historical experiences of Asian Pacific American communities, ethnic nationalism among them makes sense. But the question remains has ethnic nationalism diverted people from more important tasks.

MODERN LIBERALISM AND CONSERVATISM

Given what we know about classical liberalism and conservatism, it is hard to figure out why anyone would have the nerve to use "liberal" or "conservative" to describe themselves or others. But I will leave my senses for awhile and wonder about the mysterious world of contemporary liberals and conservatives. What tends to set contemporary liberals and conservatives apart is the role of government in American society. As they would not do in the 1800s, both groups claim they believe in progress, democracy, capitalism, political freedom for all, and equal opportunity for all.

A brief examination of the history of the Republican Party, which is now considered a repository of contemporary conservatism, might illuminate the differences between conservatives and liberals of the late twentieth and early twenty-first centuries. During the first half of the twentieth century, there were Republican Party leaders such as Wisconsin's Robert La Follete, Sr. and Robert La Follette Jr., Nebraska's George Norris, and California's Earl Warren who were not so terribly different from contemporary liberals. Indeed, the La Follettes and Norris were probably much more sympathetic to a socialist perspective on public policy than either of the Clintons or John Kerry. At the same time, men who are now considered idols of American conservatism, Republicans Herbert Hoover and Robert Taft, often described themselves as nineteenth century liberals. What happened?

Politicians and political reformers established the Republican Party in the 1850s to half the spread of slavery. Some early Republicans were Jeffersonian in that they sought a limited role of the national government in economic development. Other early Republicans, such as Abraham Lincoln, believed that the national government was an important ally and generator of capitalist growth. Some early Republicans were very anti-immigrant. Others, like Lincoln, were not. Some early Republicans supported equal rights for African Americans. Others, like Lincoln, did not. Some early Republicans believed that Chinese immigrants should be treated as fairly as any other immigrants. Other Republicans, especially California Republicans, generally argued that Chinese immigrant labor was good for business but that Chinese were racially inferior. And ultimately a Republican James Blaine would lead the congressional fight for Chinese Exclusion in 1882, because he mistakenly hoped that doing so would win him the White House.

After the Civil War, a strong pro-business element of the Republican Party emerged. One could, with some misgivings, characterize this element as conservative in that it claimed that the chief task of government was the protection of private property. Yet from whom did private property require protection? According to these Republicans, the labor movement dominated by immigrants and their children posed a major threat since it demanded that the government strip the private property owner of the right to do whatever he or she wanted to with her or his property. Thus, these Republicans supported government efforts to militarily suppress labor protests and, for that matter, American Indian uprisings against privately owned railroad companies in the West. Other Republicans, such as Theodore Roosevelt, did not necessarily see labor as an enduring enemy and supported an alliance between business and labor. Moreover, Roosevelt believed that that big business was capable of abusing its power and that the national government should be able to regulate big business in order to keep populists and socialists out of power.

Events such as the communist take over of Russia in 1917, the Great Depression, the emergence of the Democratic Party dominated New Deal as a result of the Great Depression, World War II, the Cold War, and the Civil Rights Movement all helped to shake up Republican Party ideologies considerably. The progressive wing of the Republican Party remained a force into the 1960s. It allied with Democrats such as President Franklin D. Roosevelt to devise and implement government programs to alleviate social and economic problems during the Great Depression and after. Indeed, some progressive Republicans were far more supportive of civil rights for people of color and the labor movement than the typical Democrat.

At the same time, a contemporary conservative wing also remained powerful. This wing became staunchly, in a few cases hysterically, anti-Communist, often opposed government social programs as "stalking communism" and tended to claim that race relations were matters of personal taste and government should not legislate racial democracy. Since the 1960s, this wing has become dominant in the Republican Party, in part because its members seemed to care more passionately about key issues than more "moderate" Republicans.

Some members of this wing such as journalist William F. Buckley and California's present governor, Arnold Schwarzenegger, appeal to the libertarian side of contemporary conservatism. They might believe that government has a role in investigating terrorists and subversives in the United States. They, however, believe that the government should stay out of an American's personal life as much as possible. And they definitely believe that government should encourage capitalist development by eliminating what they consider as onerous regulations and taxes. Other contemporary conservatives appeal to what is called the "moral majority." Often evangelical Christians, these contemporary conservatives share a hatred of "godless" communism and extreme Islamic terrorism, but they also tend to distrust libertarian politics. They express a deeply felt belief that contemporary liberalism lies at the heart of very serious problems in American life—the dissolution of the nuclear family, crime, drug abuse, pre-marital sex, gay and lesbian sex, economic downturns, and bloated government budgets. In recent years, contemporary conservatives, especially those like Ronald Reagan who could bridge the differences among contemporary conservatives, have achieved impressive electoral victories. These victories have frightened many Democrats away from describing themselves as liberals even when such labels have been appropriate, although there is good reason to believe that successful Democrats such as Bill Clinton transcend the conservative/liberal dichotomy.

Since the 1930s, contemporary liberalism has generally found a home in the Democratic Party, where Presidents Franklin D. Roosevelt and John F. Kennedy have reigned as political heroes. Contemporary liberalism shares with progressivism a belief that government ought to get involved in generating economic growth, as well as in regulating business and supporting social programs. Since the 1930s, African Americans, once generally Republican in tribute to Lincoln, have become generally Democratic in tribute to Franklin D. Roosevelt and the Civil Rights legislation introduced and enacted under the Kennedy-Johnson presidential administrations. Mexican Americans have gravitated toward the Democrats as well because they generally consider Democrats more responsive to their concerns. European-based ethnic groups such as Irish and Jewish Americans have also found Democrats more receptive and have historically voted Democrat. Other racial and ethnic groups, including some Asian Pacific ethnic groups, seem more divided.

There is good reason for lack of solid support for either contemporary liberal Democrats or contemporary conservative Republicans from many Asian Pacific American communities. Contemporary conservative Republican appeal to the anti-Communist, pro-law and order, pro-business side of the Asian Pacific American experience. However, contemporary liberal Democrats appeal to the pro-civil rights, pro-social legislation, and pro-immigration side of the Asian Pacific American experience.

WHO ARE THE PEOPLE?

If the United States is a land of freedom, democracy, and equality, many people have asked, why do racial and ethnic, class, and gender divisions persist in American society? Moreover, what have American political institutions contributed to breaking down or reinforcing these divisions? Over the years, political scientists and other scholars have come up with different answers to these questions. For example, during the 1950s, 1960s, and 1970s many scholars debated over the extent to which American political institutions embraced democracy

Yet how do varied perspectives on politics, democracy, equality, and freedom in the United States relate to real people with real experiences? Many of the people living in the United States look at other societies and understandably feel grateful that they have been granted so much democracy, equality, and freedom. Americans, indeed, often view documents such as the Declaration of Independence and the U.S. Constitution as sacred. They have faith that the "founding fathers" with the help of Abe Lincoln have done their jobs. They believe that they can safely go on with the business of doing their jobs and voting every once in a while. At the same time, many Americans should consider more carefully the words of two thoughtful American leaders.

Thomas Jefferson wrote, "The cost of liberty is eternal vigilance." If they agree, Americans who value their freedoms in the United States have to remain ever watchful for those who might wish to seize those freedoms away from them. Americans cannot take their freedoms for granted. Many believe that the Bill of Rights cannot be eliminated or altered. But the Bill of Rights is but the first ten amendments to the U.S. Constitution. Future amendments can expand, but also limit the scope of those first ten amendments. Future amendments can render the Bill of Rights into a figurative pile of dust.

African American civil rights leader and trade union activist A. Philip Randolph once said, "Freedom isn't granted, it's fought for." Randolph believed that people who possess economic and political power do not generally wish to share that power even in a relatively democratic society such as the United States. They do not surrender power or rights easily to the rest of the people or allow them to vote or keep their children in school rather than send them to factories. Rather, people have to fight for what they consider as withheld rights in whatever ways they can. They may, moreover, have to work hard at protecting those rights for future generations.

The United States did not begin in a very democratic fashion. It, moreover, began at a time when equality and freedom seemed most enjoyed by those with substantial wealth, the proper skin color, and the right sexual organs. Some would say things have not changed much since 1776. Others would say things have dramatically changed for the better. In either event, changes have taken place. Yet many of these changes have revealed the ambivalent character of American political experiences. These political experiences have expressed conflict, compromise, generosity, bigotry, brilliance, ignorance, courage, and cowardice. Americans of Asian Pacific ancestry have been unfortunate and fortunate enough to play a part in many of these experiences.

PLURALIST AND ELITIST POLITICAL THEORIES

Scholars have linked pluralism to the political thinking of James Madison, as well as the work of Alexis De Tocqueville, a French intellectual who toured the United States in 1830s. James Madison, as most of us know was the fourth President of the United States, but fewer of us know that he was probably the most important intellectual contributor to the original U.S. Constitution, in addition to the Bill of Rights. For Madison at the time the Constitution was written in the late 1780s, the young United States consisted of a plurality of political interest groups or what he called "factions." He hoped that these varied interest groups would come to share a commitment to the basic welfare of American society and would compete peacefully and fairly for political advantage. De Tocqueville wrote a famous book called *Democracy in America*. He believed that at least white middle class Americans shared a commitment to private property and individualism and through organizations like political parties, voluntary associations, and religious institutions were able to maintain a relatively responsible democratic society.

After World War II, pluralism became a dominant perspective among American political scientists who wanted to know why the United States did not suffer from totalitarianism and the violent social upheavals plaguing other countries. These political scientists such as David Truman and Robert Dahl argued that politically the United States could be divided into various interest groups—big business, labor, farmers, ethnic groups, war veterans, small business, lawyers, educators, building contractors, and doctors among others. Each interest group, to at least some extent, wants political power. In other words, an interest group wants the ability to sway local, state, or federal governments to help it out. Interest group members would form organizations such as the American Medical Association and hire lobbyists to give them greater influence over public policy decisions.

For pluralist political theorists, the existence of these various interest groups is good as long as each group agrees upon the basic benefits of the American political and economic system and as long as each competes for political power fairly. These interest groups would, therefore, check and balance each other in the long run. In the process, they would keep the United States democratic, but moderate in political tone.

Elitist political theory can trace some of its heritage to theorists such as Karl Marx and Max Weber. Marx argued that in a capitalist society a numerically small capitalist class of very rich owners of private property ruled economically, politically, and culturally. Political decisions in a capitalist society would roughly approximate the needs of that capitalist class. Weber argued in the early decades of the 1900s that social development would lead urbanized and industrialized societies, whether capitalist or socialist, to establish private and government bureaucracies. These bureaucracies would serve a relatively small group of centralized decision-makers, who would generally ignore democratic processes.

In the 1950s, an American sociologist named C. Wright Mills took on pluralist political theory by writing an influential book called *The Power Elite*. Blending Marx with Weber, Mills stated that the United States was not a democratic society, but was ruled by an elite, comprised of powerful members of government, the military, and big business. There was little to check these highly influential powerbrokers, as American citizens, according to Mills, had become "cheerful robots," thanks to the ability of the power elite to control and manipulate public opinion.

RACE AND POLITICAL-LEGAL THEORY

While they are significant ways of looking at American political institutions and practices, pluralist and elitist political theories have generally ignored what Swedish social scientist, Gunner Myrdal, called "the American dilemma." During World War II, Myrdal wrote an influential book about American race relations called *The American Dilemma*. This book detailed a great irony in American society—that while most Americans treasured democracy and equality, they seemed relatively untroubled by the fact that millions of their countrymen and countrywomen suffered from racial discrimination and, therefore, were denied the fruits of democracy and equality.

One noteworthy attempt to interrelate political power and race in the United States has been made by sociologist Benjamin Ringer. Ringer's book, *"We the People" and Others*, was published in the early 1980s. The title of this book is significant because it refers to the first three words of the U.S. Constitution. But who were the People then and throughout American history? And who are the people now? Ringer's book seeks to resolve the issue by arguing that from a political-legal standpoint, American race relations has been marked by a duality.

Ringer wrote about something he called "the People's Domain:" "Within the Domain of the People, universalistic, egalitarian, achievement-oriented and democratic norms and values were to be the ideals.... Membership in this People's Domain, though, was confined...to whites." Conversely, there is the "Domain of the Others." In this domain, the others have encountered racism that was institutionalized—that is, built into the political-legal structures of British colonial American society and then of the United States. The struggle to extend the People's Domain beyond European Americans has comprised one of the central themes of American history, according to Ringer.

In the 1980s and 1990s, legal scholars such as Derrick Bell, Patricia Williams, Richard Delgaldo, Ian Haney Lopez, Marie Matsuda, and Angelo Ancheta have argued that racism has been the rule rather than the exception in terms of the development and interpretation of the U.S. legal system. These scholars have been crucial in creating a perspective called Critical Race Theory. They have tended to contend that only a radical reconstruction of the American legal-political system would achieve true equality and democracy.

CONCLUSION

We should try to keep these theoretical and ideological perspectives on the American political system in mind as we discuss some of the key developments in American political institutions and practices and how they have related to Asian Pacific Americans. We probably can apply each theory and ideology to Asian Pacific American political history in some ways, but each theory and ideology might leave some very important matters unexplained.

REVIEW

1. What are the various ways in which democracy can be defined?
2. Have American political leaders always supported democracy? Explain.
3. What are the various ways in which freedom can be defined?

4. What are the various ways in which equality can be defined?
5. Describe and analyze collectivism.
6. Describe and analyze republicanism.
7. Describe and analyze classical liberalism.
8. Describe and analyze classical conservatism.
9. Describe and analyze producerism and how does it relate to populism?
10. Define and analyze socialism.
11. Describe and analyze progressivism.
12. Describe and analyze feminism.
13. Describe and analyze nationalism.
14. Describe and analyze contemporary liberalism.
15. Describe and analyze contemporary conservatism.
16. Define the People and relate it to class, gender, race, and ethnicity.
17. What are the issues raised by Thomas Jefferson and A. Philip Randolph?
18. Compare and contrast pluralist and elitist political theories.
19. What is Benjamin Ringer's perspective on race and power in the United States?
20. What is Critical Race Theory?

SELECTED BIBLIOGRAPHY

Almaguer, Tomas. *Racial Faultlines*. (1994).
Ancheta, Angelo N. *Race, Rights, and the Asian American Experience*. (2000).
Anderson, Benedict. *Imagined Communities*. (1983).
Barber, Benjamin. *Strong Democracy*. (1984).
Bell, Derrick. *Faces at the Bottom of the Well*. (1992).
Chan, Sucheng. *Asian Americans*. (1990).
Dahl, Robert. *Who Governs?* (1961).
_____. *On Democracy*. (1998).
Delgaldo, Richard (ed). *Critical Race Theory*. (1995).
De Tocqueville, Alexis. *Democracy in America*. George Lawrence (ed). (1969).
Dionne, E.J., Jr. *Why Americans Hate Politics*. (1991).
Drinnon, Richard. *Facing West*. (1981).
Epstein, Cynthia Fuchs. *Deceptive Distinctions*. (1988).
Foner, Eric. *Free Soil, Free Labor Free Men*. (1970).
_____. *Tom Paine and Revolutionary America*. (1976).

Gerth, H.H. and Mills, C. Wright (eds). *From Max Weber.* (1946).

Goodwyn, Lawrence. *Democratic Promise.* (1976).

Green, David. *Shaping Political Consciousness.* (1987).

Greenberg, Edward S. and Page, Benjamin I. *The Struggle for Democracy.* 6th Edition. (2003).

Hartz, Louis. *The Liberal Tradition in America.* (1955).

Heizer, Robert F. and Almquist, Alan F. *The Other Californians.* (1971).

Hing, Bill Ong. *Making and Remaking Asian American Through Immigration Policy, 1850-1990.* (1993).

Hofstadter, Richard. *The Paranoid Style of American Politics.* (1967).

Jacobson, Mathew. *Whiteness of a Different Color.* (1998).

Kerber, Linda. *Women of the Republic.* (1980).

Lopez, Ian F. Haney. *White By Law.* (1996).

McClain,Charles. *In Search of Equality.* (1994).

Mills, C. Wright. *The Power Elite.* (1956).

Pells, Richard. *The Liberal Mind in a Conservative Age.* (1985).

Ricci, David M. *The Tragedy of Political Science.* (1984).

Ringer, Benjamin. *We The People and Others.* (1983).

Roediger, David R. *The Wages of Whiteness.* (1991).

Salyer, Lucy. *Laws Harsh as Tigers.* (1995).

Saxton, Alexander. *The Rise and Fall of the White Republic.* (1990).

Scott, James, C. *The Moral Economy of the Peasant.* (1976).

Smith, Rogers M. *Civic Ideals.* (1997).

Thompson, Edward P. *Customs in Common Culture.* (1991).

Yung, Judy. *Unbound Feet.* (1995).

IV
DOING HISTORY

American educators, public officials, political activists, and journalists have long complained that Americans simply do not know much about history and seem very content in not knowing much about history--even American history. Regardless of their ideology, these educators, public officials, and journalists are convinced that Americans need to learn history better--that the cornerstone of a democratic society consists of an informed citizenry which understands the historical experiences of their communities, nation, and world. To understand why folks do the things they do, we need to put their behavior in historical perspective. Even if history cannot teach us how to end a war or avoid a depression, it humbles us because through history we know that our actions have often unfortunate and even tragic consequences and it emboldens us because we know that our actions can make our community, nation, and world better.

However, heated controversies erupted in the 1990s over the kinds of history books Americans read and the kinds of things Americans learned in their history classes. While running for President in 1996, Republican candidates Robert Dole and Pat Buchanan lamented that American students learned the wrong things in most history classes. That is, they learned too much about the bad things that have happened in the American past-- slavery, the Ku Klux Klan, Indian removal, poverty, and political persecutions. Instead, American students, according to Dole and Buchanan, needed to learn to celebrate American History--the glories of the U.S. Constitution, the creativity of American inventors, and the bravery of Americans in the armed services. At fault, they claimed, were cynical academics who always saw the dark side of things as well as the zealous advocates of multiculturalism who would rather protest racism than teach about great white men such as Paul Revere or Thomas Edison.

Much of this was and remains, of course, a matter of politics— the simplification of complicated issues in order to get votes. Yet thoughtful people continue to worry about whether the way history is presented in many books, scholarly journals, and classrooms diverts young Americans from finding a sense of commonality that transcends social and cultural divisions. It is hard, indeed, to disagree with the point that young Americans should discover common symbols around which to rally. It is just as hard to disagree with the argument that young Americans should gain a respectful knowledge of the words and deeds of Thomas Jefferson, Abraham Lincoln, and Douglas MacArthur--people who have had a great impact on American history.

The other side of the matter is that the study and teaching of history should provide students with culturally diverse role models. How can young women and young women and men of color gain inspiration from Paul Revere and Thomas Edison--two very dead white men. As for Jefferson, Lincoln, and MacArthur, they were a slaveholder, a racist, and a warmonger respectively. What kind of figures are they to celebrate as role models? Therefore, our students need to learn more about the positive contributions of women and people of color in American history.

To be sure, the desire for a consistently inclusive history of the American people merits respect. An American history course that fails to explore the struggles and triumphs of culturally diverse Americans is incomplete. The point is not that historians should shove Jefferson and Lincoln off the stage. The point is that these historical figures should share the stage with not so famous, not so male, and not so white people.

HISTORY AND OBJECTIVITY

History has been called the "political" science. The reason is not too hard to figure out. If we really think about it, we should recognize that the writing and teaching of history have long comprised contested ground for individuals and groups struggling for political power. This does not mean that our history teachers have been biased foot soldiers for some political party or cause. They have generally been well-intentioned folks seriously aiming at fairness. However, as anthropologist Renato Rosaldo points out, scholars are "positioned" within the societies in which they research, write, and teach. They cannot easily transcend those societies. Their age, religion, sex, ethnic identity, social class, religion, and political ideology interweave in fascinating ways to both limit and expand their search for truth.

For many of us, objectivity means to acknowledge that truth exists outside of our own subjective experiences. We do not have to meet Marilyn Monroe to know that at one time she was alive and was a popular movie star. The next step is a bit trickier. Some of us will argue that truth is revealed to those scholars who look for it without biases. If so, then it would seem difficult for anyone to claim complete objectivity. If we think of objectivity, however, as an open-minded and open-ended search for truth, then more of us can attain it.

In other words, few historians or any scholars begin research on a topic without assumptions about what they will find. For example, when I started research on my dissertation on boot and shoe workers in late nineteenth century San Francisco, I assumed that as in other urbanizing northern and western communities in the United States, my subjects would generally consist of European American males and females. I soon discovered, however, that a good number of the people making shoes in San Francisco were Chinese immigrants. A second assumption was that while significant tensions would develop between European American and Chinese American workers, they at least occasionally managed to overcome racial and ethnic barriers to organize effectively against their bosses. Yet I was stunned and admittedly deeply disappointed to discover that evidence of interracial cooperation of any kind was lacking between San Francisco's Chinese and European American boot and shoe workers. Finally, I assumed that people of Asian Pacific ancestry faced relatively little racial discrimination in the United States outside of Japanese American experiences during World War II. I was, nevertheless, at least somewhat surprised to find that the nineteenth century discloses a long and painful history of racial discrimination against people of Asian Pacific ancestry. The only thing I could do was as sadly and accurately as possible report in my dissertation on what I discovered. I would like to think that, if nothing else, my dissertation was objective and that I was fair enough to not allow my prior assumptions hinder exposure of what seemed then and now to be the truth.

Many of us who research, write, and teach about the past, nevertheless, are plagued with excessive skepticism and relativism. In other words, our skepticism forces us to deny the existence of truths that transcend time and cultural barriers. And whatever truths we do believe exist are relative to our time and culture-- unique to us but not necessarily to our grandchildren or those people culturally diverse from us.

Truth is, indeed, a slippery devil and we should entertain great care and critical awareness when we hear voices who insist they have found the truth and that it is both grand and everlasting. Some fine historians, Joyce Appleby, Lynn Hunt, and Margaret Jacob advise: "A practice of history...encourages skepticism about dominant views, but at the same time trusts in the reality of the past and its knowability... An openness to the interplay between certainty and doubt keeps faith with the expansive quality of democracy."

Appleby, Hunt, and Jacob also point out the provisional quality of historical truth. We should, in other words, prepare ourselves to listen to versions of history distinct from our own. We should prepare ourselves to attend with analytical respect to what different historical perspectives say about an issue and just as important what they fail to say.

DIFFERENT VOICES, DIFFERENT HISTORIES

The writing and telling of American History has varied over time depending greatly on historical context. No matter how eloquent and perceptive the historian, the diverse and often contrasting political agendas of his or her time shadow the kind of history he or she produces. In this section, we will examine how historical context interacts with historical scholarship in American society.

BANCROFT AND PARKMAN

The first half of the nineteenth century witnessed a great deal of nationalistic fervor in Europe and the Americas. During this time, American intellectuals wanted to fashion a national culture in the new country. As of the 1820s and 1820s, they argued that American cultural institutions and practices were too derivative of European cultural institutions and practices. It was time, they declared, that the United States nurtured its own culture. This meant as well that the United States should stress the writing and teaching of its own history rather than English or French or Ancient Roman history. George Bancroft and Francis Parkman were very important in developing and transmitting this national history.

To Bancroft and Parkman, the study of American history disclosed the visible hand of human progress. In the United States before the Civil War, they claimed to have seen the almost inevitable destruction of savagery (American Indians) and the rise of the rule of civilization. If nothing else, Bancroft and Parkman could tell stories well. Parkman, for example, quite eloquently dismissed American Indians: "For the most part, a civilized white man can discover very few points of sympathy between his own nature and that of the Indian. With every disposition to do justice to their good qualities, he must be conscious of an impassable gap between him and his red brethren." Parkman, in particular, was an historian who used Manifest Destiny as a justification for the western expansion of the United States.

Bancroft was deeply involved in the politics of pre-Civil War U.S. America. A Democratic Party activist, Bancroft served as James Polk's Secretary of War and Secretary of Navy. According to historian Alexander Saxton, Bancroft "detailed arrangements for the seizure of California and the invasion of Mexico." Bancroft's interpretations of American history corresponded well to his politics. He declared that American history fulfilled destiny's desire. For Bancroft, that history followed in the light cast by the ancient struggles of Greek and Roman Republicans, as well as early Christians and the New England Puritans of the 1600s.

THE RISE OF SCIENTIFIC HISTORY AND PROFESSIONALISM

Bancroft and Parkman remained popular among readers of American history well into the twentieth century. Nevertheless, historical scholars insisted after the Civil War that the kind of history produced by Bancroft and Parkman was insufficiently scientific. Post-Civil War America. was a site of substantial industrialization and urbanization. Moreover, it inspired intellectual responses calling for more systematic production of knowledge to correspond to the more systematic production of commodities and professional services. An historian, therefore, could not just tell a good story vividly. An historian had to learn to document his or her findings. The historian had to, furthermore, become an objective professional. Among other things, this meant basing one's research upon primary sources such as diaries, letters, and government surveys. It also meant not worrying about how one's findings connected to human destiny.

Much of the research done in American history during the late nineteenth and early twentieth centuries inspires admiration today. This research was often quite careful and continues to reveal important glimpses into the American past. Yet by basing their findings upon written documents, historians of this time often reflected the perspectives of the men and occasionally women who wrote and gathered those documents. Ulrich B. Philips, for example, taught many subsequent generations of scholars significant things about the slave South. Yet his version of history grew out of the documents created by slaveholders and supporters of the slaveholders. Economic and labor historian John S. Commons scrutinized weighty documents in labor relations before and after the American Revolution. To his credit, he studied not only the documents created by owners of capital but also the documents created by labor organizations. Thus, when examining the late nineteenth century anti-Chinese movement in California, Commons lost sight of the perspectives possessed by Chinese immigrants. Commons, therefore, could write: "The anti-Chinese agitation in California, culminating as it did in the Exclusion Law of 1882, doubtless was the most important single factor in the history of American labor, for without it the entire country might have been overrun by Mongolian labor, and the labor movement might have become a conflict of races instead of classes."

Careful historical research, however, could overcome cultural biases and political ideologies. For example, Edith Abbott effectively documented the historical experiences of women workers in the early 1900s. During the late 1890s, W.E.B. Dubois wrote a well researched, yet powerful and still influential work on the African slave trade.

PROGRESSIVE HISTORIANS

During the early 1900s, the cry for objective historical scholarship was somewhat challenged by the so-called progressive historians in the United States. One of these historians, Carl Becker, claimed that each generation writes its own history. Thus, according to Becker, historians cannot claim they are value-free. Rather, they share the concerns and values of the times and places in which they live.

Maturing at a time when the United States experienced difficult periods of social unrest based on socio-economic divisions, the progressive historians tended to look for socio-economic explanations of key events in American history. For example, in 1913, Charles Beard's *An Economic Interpretation of the Constitution of the United States* was published. Beard maintained that the U.S. Constitution was the product of its time and the political agendas of its framers, who were property-holding men writing the Constitution in such a way as to benefit Americans socially and economically like themselves.

Progressive history seemed also to encourage historical scholarship to break away from merely analyzing elite Americans, but also ordinary Americans. At one time, that is, history was written and taught as little more than past politics. Yet historical scholarship nurtured during the Progressive Era sought to represent the lives of ordinary workingwomen, rural farmers, and urban immigrants. The historical work done by Constance Rourke and Arthur M. Schlesinger, Sr. exemplified the growing influence of social history during the early decades of the twentieth century. Some of the best history written at this time, moreover, connected the study of American literature to the study of American history. Vernon L. Parrington, for example tried to demonstrate how literature reflected and reinforced ideological conflicts.

Shadowing much of this historical scholarship were Marxist and non-Marxist scholarship in the social sciences such as sociology, anthropology, political science, and economics. This scholarship, while highly varied, tended to argue that social relationships determined events and ideas. In other words, an individual, no matter how great, could not rise above the social world in which she or he was born. Historians, influenced by Marxism, furthermore tended to look upon American history as driven by socio-economic differences and conflicts.

Perhaps one of the more powerful products of progressive history is W.E.B. Dubois's *Black Reconstruction.* Published originally in 1935, *Black Reconstruction* sought to refute the prevailing scholarship on America's Reconstruction period (1865-1877). Generally, students in American history classes at the time and for many years thereafter heard and read that the formerly enslaved African Americans and their white Northern allies were the villains of the era. For decades, historians often presented freed African Americans as unready for the responsibilities of freedom and their white Northern allies as politically ambitious hypocrites and white Southerners, even those enrolled in the Ku Klux Klan, were simply trying to defend themselves against unprincipled Northerners and unruly African Americans. Dubois paints a very different picture.

> The most magnificent drama in the last thousand years of human history is the transportation of ten million beings out of the dark beauty of their mother continent into the new found El Dorado of the West. They descended into Hell; and then in the third century they arose from the dead, in the finest effort to

achieve democracy for the working millions which this world had ever seen. <The Reconstruction Era> was a tragedy that beggared the Greeks; it was an upheaval of humanity like the Reformation and the French Revolution.

By the time Dubois wrote *Black Reconstruction,* he considered himself a Marxist. But Dubois was an unusual Marxist for his time and for other times as well in that he recognized the interaction of class and race and documented that interaction with skill. Dubois, moreover, considered the ultimate failure of Reconstruction as a tragedy not just for African Americans, but also for European American workers. Indeed, he considered Reconstruction's demise a tragedy for the cause of democracy in general in the United States.

While progressive historians were influential before World War II, those historians who still sang the praises of value-free scholarship remained influential as well. For example, *Black Reconstruction* received little support from professional historians in the United States. One reason, of course, was that Dubois's book attacked long held racial stereotypes in the United States. Another reason was that it was viewed widely as unprofessional and excessively indebted to Marxism. The fact that its author was black did not improve the book's reputation in the minds of too many white historians.

COLD WAR HISTORY

World War II and the onset of the Cold War plunged American historians and other scholars into an intellectual crisis of sorts. To a significant extent, American historians embraced the belief that an underlying cause of both World War II and the Cold War was ideological passion. In other words, many American historians in the 1940s and 1950s believed that America's archenemies--fascism and communism--were bred by ideological passion. They also believed that what kept the United States free of fascism and communism was that Americans were not ideological and basically agreed with one another on fundamental issues. Other historians regretted, as did sociologist C. Wright Mills, Americans' blind commitment to capitalism and militarism.

Richard Hofstadter was one of the most important of Cold War historians. Hofstadter critically examined American political traditions and social movements. He claimed that political ideals largely masked their advocates' ambitions, fears, and prejudices. Hofstadter and many of the "consensus" historians of the 1950s generally examined American political history from an elitist perspective in that the protesting voices of lower middle class, working class and poor Americans struck them as too often filled with irrational anger. Hofstadter, for instance, thought the populists were largely inspired by a rural-bred idiocy.

Nevertheless, other historians scrutinized the experiences of non-elite Americans. For instance, the 1940s and especially the 1950s witnessed important reappraisals of the then dominant "Gone with the Wind" school of history--the historical interpretation of American slavery as an essentially misguided but benevolent institution. Highly influenced by Dubois, Marxist historian Herbert Aptheker published *Negro Slave Revolts* in 1943. Kenneth Stampp's *Peculiar Institution* (1956) is much better known as a powerful argument against the notion that American slavery was a kinder, gentler form of slavery. A few years later, Stanley Elkin's *Slavery* was published. Elkins's controversial book depicted American slavery as comparable to the German death camps during World War II and depicted enslaved African Americans as "Sambos," who quietly acquiesced in their own oppression. In 1961, John Hope Franklin's *Reconstruction: After the Civil War* was published. An inspirational African American scholar, Franklin offered a more accessible and less ideological version of Dubois's earlier work.

While not a professional historian, Carey McWilliams was a lawyer and journalist who put together provocative analyses of race and ethnicity in California and Western American history. In the 1930s, McWilliams wrote *Factories in the Field*, which remains highly relevant to anyone who wants to understand the history of migratory labor in California. Significantly, it details the experiences of farm workers of Mexican and Asian Pacific ancestries. In the 1940s, McWilliams's *North from Mexico* was published. If one wished before 1970 to get a relatively fair picture of Mexican American history, *North from Mexico* was a good place to start.

While countless children eagerly played cowboys and Indians in the 1950s, D'Arcy McNickle's *They Came Here First* acquired relatively little attention from historians. Intending to describe the American Indian side of American history, McNickle wrote this book in the 1940s. However, it was not until the 1970s that *They Came Here First* earned its due credit.

Oscar Handlin and John Higham eloquently described some of the historical experiences of European immigrants. Published in 1951, Handlin's *The Uprooted* received a great deal of critical and popular success and Handlin became known as America's leading scholar of immigration history. Just as powerful, if not as well known, John Higham's *Strangers in the Land* was published in the early 1970s. This book vividly depicts anti-immigrant politics in the United States during the late 1800s and early 1900s.

There were other important non-consensus historians during the 1940s, 1950s, and early 1960s. C. Vann Woodward opened up many readers' eyes to the experiences of the post-Reconstruction South. Meanwhile, Marxist historian Philip Foner began his multi-volume and highly detailed narrative of American labor history.

HISTORICAL SCHOLARSHIP IN THE LATE 1900S AND TODAY

During the mid to late 1960s, "consensus" historians such as Hofstadter found their work under attack from a group that was labeled then as "New Left" historians. These younger scholars were motivated by a wide variety of factors. For one thing, many scholars had become disillusioned with American foreign policy during the 1960s, especially as the Vietnam War heated up. For another, many had also become convinced that deep-seated racial, class, and gender divisions seriously fragmented Americans; that the consensus was breaking down, if, in fact, it ever existed.

These historians were generally highly critical of American institutions and society and favored radical transformations in the way Americans lived and were governed. Nevertheless, they generally distanced themselves from older generations of communists and socialists. They thought of themselves as connected to a political radicalism that favored democratic forms of socialism and culture. They considered themselves as part of a movement to establish a "New Left" in the United States and elsewhere.

William Appleman Williams was an architect of this "New Left" history. Generally concerned about American foreign policy, Williams argued that socio-economic interests drove that policy and were key factors in the development of American history. Williams was critical of Marxism as excessively dogmatic, but believed that American scholars needed to understand and appreciate Marx's writings better.

One of the most important legacies of the "New Left" history was that its advocates called upon historians to write history "from the bottom up." In part, these "New Left" historians were inspired by the struggles for social justice engaged in by culturally diverse people all over the world during the 1950s and 1960s. They were also inspired by the scholarship of English and French historians such as E.P. Thompson, Eric Hobsbawm, Christopher Hill, Marc Bloch, and Albert Soboul--historians who had demonstrated that it was possible to write with intelligence and sensitivity about people at the bottom of the social ladder.

Herbert Gutman became a key American pioneer among those writing history "from the bottom up." He focused a great deal of attention on American working people in the nineteenth century and early twentieth century. Moreover, he wrote a book about African American slave families in the 1970s that endures as a classic. For Gutman, non-elite, often poor Americans were not just victims of industrialization or slavery. They were fully capable of making history themselves—of acting as their own historical agents. In 1980, Gutman wrote:

> What <ordinary> men and women experienced (that is, what "one" has done to them) retains interest, but how they interpreted and then dealt with changing patterns of economic, social, and political dependence and inequality becomes our major concern. Studying the choices working men and women made and how their behavior affected important historical processes enlarges our understanding of "the condition of being human."

Gutman reminded students and readers of his work that it was important to reconstruct the historical experiences of culturally diverse Americans. In some cases, however, then young historians Albert Carmarillo, Ronald Takaki, Eric Foner, and Vincent Harding did not need much reminding as they powerfully delved into the historical experiences of Mexican Americans, American Indians, Asian Pacific Americans, and European immigrants with skill and passion. Meanwhile, historians such as Mary Norton, Linda Kerber, Linda Gordon, Alice Kessler-Harris, Sara Evans, and Paula Giddings provided powerful studies of American women across class, ethnic and racial lines.

Such historical scholarship, however, generated controversy. Some historians such as Eugene Genovese worried in the 1970s that so much attention was lavished on ordinary people that scholars were forgetting about the powerful. One did not need to sympathize with the powerful to realize that what they did was very important and worth the attention of historians.

In the last several years, however, more pointed and, often unfair, critiques have developed. Frequently, these critiques contend that the effort to reconstruct the histories of culturally diverse Americans has politicized the teaching and writing of history--that really what a number of modern historians have been doing is trying to carry out some left wing agenda to destroy the confidence of students in the American way of life. In other words, historians ought to encourage students to celebrate Columbus, Washington, Jefferson, and Lincoln as role models. Apparently, to some of these critics, enslaved African Americans struggling for freedom and European immigrants struggling for dignity seem inadequate role models.

Underlying these critiques is the complaint, cynically or sincerely asserted, that at one time American historical scholarship was objective in the sense that it was free of political bias. At the same time, to demand that historians encourage an uncritical celebration of the American past is to encourage them to become right wing propagandists. Accordingly, criticisms of the way American history is taught today are often merited. But critics cannot have it both ways. If they want historians to be more objective, then they have to forego wanting historians to become propagandists for any political agenda--even a patriotic political agenda that bleeds red, white, and blue.

ASIAN PACIFIC AMERICAN HISTORY

Despite the assertions that historians were more objective in the past, it is hard to imagine that anyone would find much comfort in the way Asian Pacific American history was represented or, more to the point, misrepresented or ignored for many years. A part of the problem was that historians, even if free of racial and ethnic biases, taught and wrote American history from an East Coast perspective. They, thus, might have regarded the experiences of African Americans or European immigrants worth discussing since the Atlantic Coast regions possessed significant numbers of African Americans and European immigrants. However, the experiences of people of color and European ethnic groups in the West and Hawai'i were often viewed as marginal.

This East Coast-centricism is quite understandable, even if regrettable. From the perspective of people living along the Atlantic seaboard in 1870, the key issues facing the United States were largely unconcerned with the very visible population of people of Chinese ancestry living in California. The matter of Chinese immigration concerned Easterners, but hardly as much as it did white Californians. When Easterners discussed racial issues they generally referred to African Americans and, maybe, Irish Americans, as well. When Californians discussed racial issues they generally referred to Chinese immigrants. By the same token, the people who fought most vigorously against racial discrimination in the East were African Americans. In California, Chinese immigrants stood in the vanguard of those struggling for "color blind" laws. Thus, to write a history of the United States in the 1860s and 1870s from the perspective of the East Coast selects out the experiences, good and bad, of substantial numbers of Chinese immigrants. A more inclusive history would not necessarily move from the East towards the West, but, according to historian Patricia Limerick, move in multiple geographical directions.

Sadly, for decades much of the history American students learned about their society was, at the very least, ethnocentric, if not downright racist. To be fair, the people who wrote and taught this history were generally intelligent and good people who considered themselves just and open-minded. Some of these historians were, indeed, splendid scholars and teachers. But as we will no doubt leave an ambivalent legacy to future generations of teachers and students, they left an ambivalent legacy to us.

Generally, then, U.S. history did not take Asian Pacific American history seriously for years. For example, U.S. history textbooks habitually ignored Asian Pacific Americans. And even somewhat recent textbooks limited Asian Pacific Americans to the margins. For example, Edward Rozwenc's *The Making of American Society* (1973) had comparatively little to say about Asian Pacific Americans. What it did say related to anti-Asian Pacific politics in the United States. How Asian Pacific Americans lived in the United States was left to readers' imaginations. *An American Portrait* (1985) by David Burner, *et. al.* resembled Rozwenc's approach. It did discuss Southeast Asian immigrants in terms of President Ford's generosity in setting the United States up as an asylum for Southeast Asian refugees. Howard Zinn's text *A People's History of the United States*, while abhorrent to the political rights, has precious little to say about Asian Pacific Americans or Mexican Americans, for that matter. While these textbooks were written as informative guides to American history, they essentially made nearly invisible the lives of hundreds of thousands of Americans. What might students have learned from these textbooks was that Asian Pacific Americans have been and remain unimportant in American society. Asian Pacific American students might have discovered the reality described by poet Adrienne Rich, who asked what happens "when someone with the authority of a teacher" teaches history and "you're not in it?" It would be as if "you looked into a mirror and saw nothing."

That textbooks have focused on anti-Asian Pacific politics is not surprising given that most specific research on Asian Pacific American history generally dealt with what was done to Asian Pacific immigrants and why. Gunther Barth, a fine University of California, Berkeley, professor for many years, generated an important interpretation of the anti-Chinese movement in late nineteenth century America. In *Bitter Strength,* Barth articulated his now controversial "sojourners' thesis." Barth was not at all sympathetic to the bigotry underlying anti-Chinese politics, but he argued that Chinese immigrants typically asked for trouble by not coming to the United States armed with a settler's mentality. Because they were sojourners, Barth declared, Chinese immigrants unwittingly aided the anti-Chinese movement. Chinese immigrants should have declared their intentions of becoming good Americans. In so doing, Barth maintained, Chinese immigrants would have weakened their opponents who complained that Chinese immigrants did not want to settle down as Americans. In other words, Chinese immigrants were substantially responsible for the anti-Chinese movement. Racism and nativism, accordingly, played relatively negligible roles in Chinese immigrant experiences.

Historians Roger Daniels and Alexander Saxton have offered different perspectives on anti-Asian Pacific politics in the United States. They both have maintained that anti-Asian immigration movements contained a logic that furnished Asian Pacific immigrants and their offspring little opportunity to represent themselves as good Americans. For Daniels and Saxton, anti-Asian Pacific politics helped advocates to claim and maintain political power. Indeed, anti-Asian Pacific politics embraced an irony that was not lost on either Daniels or Saxton. Daniels wrote in the preface to *The Politics of Prejudice* that his "study clearly reveals that the generators of much of California's antidemocratic energy were those very groups supposedly dedicated to democracy: the labor unions, the progressives, and other left groups."

95

In *The Indispensable Enemy*, Saxton focused on the European American dominated labor movement's responsibility in the development of anti-Asian Pacific politics in California. For Saxton, Chinese and then Japanese immigrants in California became handy organizing tools for white trade union leaders and politicians who professed sympathy for white workers. The leaders of the anti-Asian Pacific movement recognized and exploited the fact that the one thing the different segments of California's white working class agreed upon was that the Chinese and then the Japanese "must go."

While important, *The Politics of Prejudice* and *The Indispensable Enemy* gave readers little sense of who were Chinese Americans and Japanese Americans at the turn of the twentieth century. These people had voices, but few historians were listening. This situation was getting some attention from Asian Pacific Americans themselves. Ping Chiu's *Chinese Labor in California* detailed the early occupational experiences of Chinese Californians. Published in 1963, Chiu's small book took up the challenge of writing history from the bottom up before doing so became fashionable.

Not waiting around for academic historians to turn their attention to Asian Pacific Americans, Asian Pacific American community members sought to fill in the gaps regarding the trials and contributions of Asian Pacific Americans. Journalist Bill Hosokawa starting writing several lively books reminding readers of all they did not know about Japanese American history. Michi Weglyn did a great deal in the 1970s to publicize the harsh experiences of Japanese Americans interned in concentration camps during World War II.

In the 1980s and 1990s, academic historians began to publish invaluable studies of Asian Pacific Americans. This text cites Ronald Takaki and Sucheng Chan frequently and that is no coincidence since they exemplify the kind of scholarship that makes the writing of this text possible. In the first place, they are deeply knowledgeable about the historical experiences of diverse Asian Pacific American ethnic groups. In the second, they show a profound understanding of how the experiences of Asian Pacific Americans connect to the experiences of other American racial and ethnic groups. In the third, they write well and clearly.

It seems unfair to briefly summarize their extensive scholarly contributions. In *Pau Hana*, Takaki provided many readers with important insights into the experiences of culturally diverse Hawaiian workers, most of whom possessed Asian Pacific ancestry. Takaki's *Strangers from a Different Shore* is considered by many as the standard history Asian Pacific Americans. In 1986, the University of California Press published Sucheng Chan's highly precise study of Chinese agricultural workers in California from 1850 to 1910. Called *This Bittersweet Soil*, Chan's book helped sweep away conventional thinking that Chinese American history is a history of nearly exclusively urban people. She has written two concise surveys--one on Asian Pacific Americans nationally and a second on Asian Pacific Americans in California. And Chan has also found time to engage in several other important projects such as editing the autobiography of a Korean immigrant, Mary Paik Lee, and a book of Hmong American oral history.

A number of other scholars deserve mention as important in reconstructing Asian Pacific American history in the last twenty years. Few historians understand the various strains of Japanese American history better than the late Yuji Ichioka. His book *The Issei* is vital reading for anyone interested in American immigrant history. Gary Okihiro co-authored an informative account of Japanese American agricultural experiences in California's Santa Clara County called *Japanese Legacy*. Moreover, Okihiro's *Cane Fires* paints a convincingly dark picture of Japanese Hawaiian experiences before and during World War II. Since then he has written superb studies focused on Japanese Americans and insightful efforts to link Asian Pacific Americans to American history in general. In *Farming the Home Place*, Valerie J. Matsumoto recreates the historical development of a Japanese American rural community in Central California. The social and family lives of Asian Indian immigrants in California are reconstructed by Karen Leonard in *Making Ethnic Choices*. Yen Le Espiritu has put together a fine oral history collection of Filipino Americans in *Filipino American Lives*. Chris Friday uncovers the roles of Asian Pacific Americans as trade union activists on the American Pacific Coast in *Organizing Asian American Labor*. Judy Yung effectively interweaves race, class, and gender in her studies of Chinese American women in San Francisco, *Unbound Feet* and *Unbound Voices*. The cultural history of Asian Pacific Americans has been illuminated by John Kuo Wei Tchen's *New York Before Chinatown*, Henry Yu's *Thinking Orientals*, and Robert G. Lee's *Orientals*.

None of the studies mentioned in the previous two paragraphs are value-free. They are not uniform in terms of perspective or tone. Yet they are authored by people who believe that racism and nativism have been vital aspects of American society over time and that if we are to combat racism and nativism we need to know as

97

much as we can about their historical roots. They are also authored by people who believe that Asian Pacific Americans have neither been spectators to nor victims of the history made by European American, middle and upper class males. In other words, these studies show that if they are to express a complex and truly objective picture of American history, historians should pay attention to the diverse voices of Asian Pacific Americans and not just to a handful of white males--however important.

CONCLUSION

The study of history is not a science as we conventionally use the term. It does not generate much in the way of unambiguous truths. However, it assumes the existence of an objective reality---Lincoln lived and World War II took place. The interpretation of that objective reality is what often puzzles and frustrates students who want to know that the causes of the Civil War are not subject to disagreement, but are clear and absolute.

Historical interpretations vary and conflict. Thus, how history judges an event will largely depend upon who is writing and teaching that history. When did they live? What were their social characteristics in terms, of race, ethnicity, class, and nationality? What were their ideologies? What were their spiritual beliefs? Historians, like everyone else, have biases. They are not corrupt, then, but only human. They mislead us only when they allow their biases to divert them from asking difficult questions and expressing difficult answers about the past. Much the same can be said of scholars, academic and non-academic, working in other disciplines or crossing disciplines.

Significantly, moreover, historians and other scholars in the social sciences and humanities cannot just focus on what happens to people—their exclusion, exploitation, and even extermination. Ordinary and often oppressed people, as two fine historians such as Herbert Gutman and Judy Yung have shown us, have not just been victims or spectators of history. They have made history in varied and frequently contradictory ways. As humans, they have not always made history well. They have made mistakes. But they have asserted their humanity in difficult and even inhuman conditions by organizing labor movements, writing poetry, maintaining businesses, making movies, running for political office, and playing baseball. They have asserted their sense of agency –of being agents of their own myriad destinies.

REVIEW

1. What is the relationship between the study of history and objectivity?
2. What are the different ways in which objectivity can be defined?
3. Who were George Bancroft and Francis Parkman and what did they contribute to historical scholarship?
4. What do you think were the strengths and weaknesses of scientific history?
5. Who were the progressive historians and how did they contribute to historical scholarship?
6. What kinds of history were written in America during the Cold War?
7. How did historical scholarship change in the late twentieth century? Was it for the better or the worse?
8. How has historical scholarship addressed the experiences of Asian Pacific Americans?

SELECTED BIBLIOGRAPHY

Appleby, Joyce, *et. al. Telling the Truth About History* (1994).
Aptheker, Herbert. *American Negro Slave Revolts.* (1943).
Barth, Gunther. *Bitter Strength.* (1964).
Beard, Charles. *An Economic Interpretation of the Constitution of the United States.* (1913).
Chan, Sucheng. *This Bittersweet Soil.* (1986).
Chiu, Ping. *Chinese Labor in California.* (1963).
Daniels, Roger. *The Politics of Prejudice.* (1962).
Dubois, W.E.B. *Black Reconstruction.* (1935).
Elkins, Stanley. *Slavery.* (1959).
Espiritu, Yen Le. *Filipino American Lives.* (1995).
Franklin, John Hope. *Reconstruction.* (1961).
Friday, Chris. *Organizing Asian American Labor.* (1994).
Gutman, Herbert G. *Power and Culture.* (1987).
Handlin, Oscar. *The Uprooted.* (1951).
Higham, John. *Strangers in the Land.* (1963).
Ichioka, Yuji. *The Issei.* (1988).
Lee, Robert, G. *Orientals.* (1999).

Leonard, Karen Isaksen. *Making Ethnic Choices.* (1992).

McNickle, D'Arcy. *They Came Here First.* (1949).

McWilliams, Carey. *Factories in the Field.* (1939).

_____. *North from Mexico.* (1949).

Matsumoto, Valerie J. *Farming the Home Place.* (1993).

Okihiro, Gary and Lukes, Tim. *Japanese Legacy.* (1985).

Okihiro, Gary. *Cane Fires.* (1992).

_____. *Margins and Mainstreams.* (1994).

_____. *Common Ground.* (2001).

Rosaldo, Renato. *Culture and Truth.* (1989).

Saxton, Alexander. *The Indispensable Enemy.* (1971).

_____. *The Rise and Fall of the White Republic.* (1990).

Stampp, Kenneth M. *The Peculiar Institution.* (1956).

Takaki, Ronald. *Pau Hana* (1983).

_____. *Strangers from a Different Shore.* (1989).

Tchen, John Kuo Wei. *New York Before Chinatown.* (1999).

Yu, Henry. *Thinking Orientals.* (2001).

Yung, Judy. *Unbound Feet.* (1995).

_____. *Unbound Voices.* (1999).

Zinn, Howard. A People's History of the United States. (2003).

PART II
HISTORICAL
EXPERIENCES

V
ASIAN PACIFIC PEOPLE AND AMERICA TO 1865

People of Asian Pacific ancestry have been deeply involved directly and indirectly in American history as early as the outset of European overseas expansion in the late 1400s. Asia, as most of us know, lured Europeans on the rickety wooden ships that "sailed the ocean blue in 1492." What is more the presence of western, central, and eastern Asians as economic, spiritual, and military rivals doubly spurred European monarchs to finance potentially foolhardy transoceanic exhibitions. Subsequently, the diverse lands of the Asian Pacific were perceived by American and European economic, religious, and military wealth as sources of wealth, Christian converts, and power. By the mid-nineteenth, they would also be perceived as sources of inexpensive, reliable, and servile labor that would help enrich agricultural, mining, railroad, and industrial capitalists.

FIFTEENTH AND SIXTEENTH CENTURY ASIAN PACIFIC SOCIETIES AND CULTURES

The stereotype of Asia as the mysterious, unchanging, and historically passive Orient remains quite prevalent. Nevertheless, the fact ought to hit us as obvious that Asia, like Europe, Africa, and the Americas, has been and continues to be populated by people who are at least as culturally distinct from one another as they are similar. Moreover, Asia and Asians were not just spectators to the European movement across the Atlantic to the Americas, but were major stimulants to European expansion.

We will soon examine Marco Polo as representative of the European effort to gain access to the wealth of the "Orient."

Thanks, in part, to Marco Polo's writings, it became clear to thirteenth century European political and economic leaders that Asians were prime players in a geographically expansive economic system that linked East Asia to the Mediterranean Sea and that if Europe did not get into the game soon, Europe's elites would be ruling an economic and military backwater of the world for a very long time. For example, Asia was a key source of wealth producing commodities such as silk and spice. Europe's economic elites wanted these commodities, but European traders had very little that Asian traders wanted. Precious metals such as gold and silver would win favor among Asian traders, but places like England, France, and Spain had very little in the way of precious metals. However, the possibility that gold and silver existed in abundance in the Americas more than tempted European rulers and merchants. These supplies of gold and silver would not only directly enrich the European empire builders, but could be traded to Asian political and economic elites for silk, spice, ceramic goods, and, by the way, gun powder.

Europeans were interested in exploring overland trade routes to western, central, and eastern Asia, but sea routes seemed safer. The reason is that western, central, and eastern Asian traders and armies were so dominant that Europeans feared they could not take advantage of overland trade routes. Thus, they preferred an "end run" across the Atlantic. Indeed, Europeans feared the military threat to their east. Asians such as Genghis Khan had already overrun much of the European continent and there was no guarantee that Asian soldiers might not strike deeply into the heart of the former Roman Empire again. The European search for wealth in the Americas, therefore, was motivated in part by fear of Asian geographic expansion. European lords had to build and maintain impressive armies and navies to protect themselves from the east, as much as from one another.

In China at the time of Columbus's first voyage, we find a society of complex historical processes that clearly defy enduring stereotypes of Chinese people as historically inert. For one thing, Chinese people have historically been enormously mobile. Sucheng Chan writes, "<e>migration as an aspect of Chinese history has frequently been overlooked because historians and the Chinese themselves have tended to view China as an inward-looking agrarian society." For years before Columbus, Chinese and Asian Indians had developed trade routes among Asians and between Asians and non-Asians. Organized and military aggressive Asians had battled into what is now Eastern Europe, creating terror in the minds of non-Eastern Europeans. In other words, we need to revise the image of Asians as "exotics", unchanging, and mysteriously isolated from the rest of the world.

Asian political leaders, as were their counterparts throughout the globe, were clearly people of the world. They often had to deal with populations fragmented from one another by geography, social condition, and religion. Often they developed creative, if not from our perspective, democratic, ways of uniting a vast number of people and a great deal of land under their control.

In India, a caste system organized a largely agricultural society. A caste consisted of kin members, who had to conform to similar customs. These customs might include common food, dress, and rituals. Over time a caste might fracture and if a caste segment emerged, it had to nurture its own customs. A caste segment might also merge with another caste segment. If so, the people involved would also have to find a way to marry their customs. In short, while the caste system was supposedly fixed throughout the time, it proved highly flexible historically.

The Brahmins constituted India's highest caste and were generally capable of dominating Indian society, despite the decentralizing tendencies within India. They developed religious leaders and were India's most powerful legal arbiters. What is more, they were often owners of extensive amounts of land and could call upon the labor services of lesser castes.

India was not isolated. Direct or indirect economic connections between India and Europe existed since before the birth of Christ. Arabs, Persians, and Chinese merchants knew the Indian trade well. Moreover, Indian society was compelled to cope with frequent foreign conquerors over the years. While these conquerors brought political change, their power could not substantially disrupt the "traditional" Indian caste system. Indeed, these conquerors often proved able to accommodate themselves quite nicely to that system.

Like India, China was a site of both change and continuity. It possessed strong economic ties to non-Chinese people. Over one thousand years ago, Arab merchants lived in Canton, a port city in Southeastern China. In the 1400s, Chinese sailors themselves shipped goods as far west as East Africa.

China was a multiethnic region. The Han people dominated in northern parts of China and nurtured an agricultural way of live based on irrigation. As the Han migrated, they either relatively effectively incorporated other ethnic groups or chased them off to more isolated areas. Many of the Hmong and the Mien, for example, found their way into what is now Laos.

The irrigation-based political economy devised by the Han required a more centralized state than those found in other parts of the world. This state assured that large agricultural areas received water. Local or regional governments were supposedly not up to the task.

To administrate this state, a bureaucracy comprised of people known as Mandarins was developed. Unlike the Brahmin, individual Mandarins did not inherit their positions but theoretically earned them by demonstrating scholarly knowledge of the Chinese Classics. But like the Brahmin, the Mandarins held together amazingly well a culturally and geographically diverse population. Furthermore, they withstood political change and with some difficulty a Mongol invasion in the late 1200s A.D.

By the 1400s, Chinese political leaders responded in a significant way to such occurrences as the Mongol invasion and economic contacts with non-Chinese people. Indeed, the Mongol dynasty may have prove matters for China. Despite the historical stereotypes surrounding the Mongolians as simplistically focused on warfare, Jack Weatherford writes:

> General literacy during the Mongol dynasty, and the volume of literary material grew proportionately. In 1269, <Genghiz Khan's grandson> Khubilai Khan established a printing office to make government decisions more widely disseminated throughout the population, and he encouraged widespread printing in general by nongovernmental groups as well.

The Chinese under the Ming dynasty, which had removed the Mongols in 1367, sought to separate China from the outside world as much as seemed practical. The Chinese state decided, therefore, to develop itself internally and leave transoceanic and overland expansion to others, although Ming emperor Yongle sustained substantial overseas expedition commanded by the intrepid Zheng He.

Southeast Asia, comprised of what is now known as Vietnam, Laos, Cambodia, Burma, Thailand, Indonesia, and the Philippines was also largely agricultural. But it also embraced significant cities and economic power. Over time, moreover, it was a terrain over which various influential religions such as Hinduism, Islam, and Buddhism contested for devotees. Indian and Chinese political leaders, as well, competed for domination in Southeast Asia.

Historians have in recent years revised their notions of Japan as geographically closed off from the rest of the world in the 1400s. In 1500, about 16 million people lived in Japan. While Japan had been somewhat subjugated by China in earlier centuries, it had carved out a niche as an economic rival to China by the 1500s. The Japanese engaged in trade with China, Korea, and other parts of Asia. In the mid-1500s, Portuguese traders arrived in Japan, bringing with them guns and Christian missionaries. By the end of the sixteenth century, Japan would increase its economic power by becoming a major producer of precious metal such as silver, copper, and the ever popular, gold. At the same time, Japan was fragmented by civil wars for much of the late fifteenth and sixteenth centuries—civil wars led by military lords or samurai, who were decidedly more impressed with the Portuguese guns than the Portuguese missionaries.

HAWAIIAN ISLANDS BEFORE COOK

During centuries of migration through the western Pacific, Polynesian people made their way toward the Hawaiian Islands between 300 and 700 AD. Hawaiian society before Cook's arrival was highly complex and many scholars are now crediting Native Hawaiians for having histories worth studying. Among the generalizations that seem to apply to Hawaiians before Europeans landed on the islands is that like indigenous people in the Americas and elsewhere they had little use for private ownership of property and individualism. Like many, but not all, people living in the 1700s, their political and economic system was not particularly egalitarian, but substantially interrelated with their religious beliefs.

Before European contact, Native Hawaiians generally experienced an economic and political system that bore some resemblance to European feudalism. Anthropologist Elizabeth Buck writes that the dominant political and economic system among Hawaiians in 1700 "operated under principles of enforced tribute, and surplus appropriation legitimized by principles of divine kingship." In other words, whatever Native Hawaiians produced was subject to appropriation by a monarch whose power was authorized by religious beliefs. Nevertheless, while the monarch was accorded supreme social status and the power to appropriate the fruits of others labor, the group possessed sovereignty over the land. At the same time, something, which Buck refers to as a "communal mode of production", existed among Native Hawaiians. Once apparently dominant among indigenous Hawaiians, a "hierarchical mode of production" had pushed the "communal mode of production" from center stage by the time of European arrival in the late 1770s. This "communal mode of production" meant that agricultural production was based upon reciprocal relations among people who were relatively equal. Thus, egalitarian and hierarchical political and economic systems co-existed at the time of European landfall. Both would seem foreign to representatives of an expanding, global capitalist system.

THE ASIAN PACIFIC AND THE NEW AMERICAN REPUBLIC

The existence of economically tempting Asian Pacific societies, helped inspire European expansion and settlement to the Americas. The French and other Europeans who came to the North America hoped to find a "northwest passage" –a water way linking the Great Lakes to the Pacific Ocean. No such water way was ever found but gaining access to Asian Pacific ports and markets remained important as the British colonies which turned into the infant United States reached out for economic maturity.

Asia's economic link to the British colonies was, of course, symbolized by the Boston Tea Party. In 1773, Parliament passed the Tea Act, which was intended to support the British owned East India Company. The East India Company wanted to dump its tea on the American market and Parliament was all too seemingly happy to help out. Meanwhile, many American merchants had defied British mercantilist laws and smuggled Dutch tea into American ports. These merchants simply did not want to have to compete with East Indian Company tea. Other Americans did not like the idea that the colonies would have to pay a small tax that Parliament attached to the East Indian Company tea. All in all, significant numbers of American colonists rejected British rule over American ports.

In November, 1773, an English ship bearing East Indian tea pulled in to Boston Harbor. When the ship refused the demand made by Bostonians to leave, a group of "patriots" dressed themselves up as "Mohawk" Indians, boarded the ship, and dumped the tea into the harbor. The irritated Parliament passed what came to be known as the "Intolerable Acts," which consisted of four acts aimed at subordinating American colonies to the British government.

Meanwhile, elite Americans such as George Washington and Alexander Hamilton followed the consumption patterns of wealthy Europeans who sought Chinese porcelain and what historian John Kuo Tchen has called "Chinese styled luxuries." The desire for things Chinese inspired the construction of America's first ship to trade with China—the *Empress of China.*

Between China and the United States stood the Hawaiian Islands, unknown among Europeans and European Americans until the late 1770s. A myth of discovery is associated with Hawai'i as in the case of the Americas. This myth tells countless students that an English sea captain, James Cook, discovered Hawai'i just as Columbus discovered the Americas in 1492. There is no denying the importance of Columbus or, for that matter, Cook in human history. They, to borrow from historian Patricia Nelson Limerick, discovered the "Western Hemisphere" and the Hawaiian Islands respectively for Europeans. Limerick writes, "For an experience of discovery, the place involved does not have to be new to everyone; it has to be new to the discoverer. The encounter is, of course, reciprocal; when Columbus discovered the Indians, the Indians had the chance to discover Columbus." Likewise, if Cook discovered Hawaiians, they, in turn, discovered Cook. In other words, overemphasizing European discoveries tends to obscure the existence of those indigenous peoples who were already living in the Americas and the Hawaiian Islands.

European and North American traders and missionaries followed Cook to the Hawaiian Islands. The former introduced the market economy to the islands. Historian Gary Okihiro maintains that "the traders introduced manufactured goods in exchange for natural resources such as sandalwood, supplied arms for warfare, and stimulated the chiefs' accumulation of wealth through additional taxes on <Native Hawaiians'> labor, and income and a monopoly over the provisions and the sandalwood trade." Increasingly, Native Hawaiian labor was focused upon production for a world market. After the emergence of King Kamehameha as the ruler of all the islands in the 1790s, Hawaiian royalty and primarily English commercial interests garnered the profits from this production.

American missionaries began coming to Hawai'i in 1819. They tried to convert Hawaiian Islanders into accepting the wonders of the Puritan Work Ethic and the market place with mixed results. To these missionaries, Native Hawaiians were too fond of leisure, their kin-based economy, and their own traditional religious beliefs. American missionaries also believed Native Hawaiians were too skeptical about working in a cash economy, private property, and Christianity. At the same time, New England-based writer Herman Melville represented Hawaiians and Pacific Islanders in general as quite better off without all that perhaps well-intended attention from Anglo-American missionaries.

The white newcomers successfully pushed for a political system somewhat similar to England—a political system in which the Hawaiian monarch would share power with a hereditary House of Lords and an elected House of Representatives. The next step was transferring as much Hawaiian land as possible into private hands. In 1843, the haoles or whites, allied with Christianized and capitalistic Native Hawaiian aristocrats, achieved privatization and redistribution of land. Called the Great Mahele, this privation and redistribution of land drew foreign investors, many of whom assumed control of large chunks of Hawai'i to develop a sugar trade.

Native Hawaiians did not necessarily accept these changes meekly. In the 1840s, many had urged their king to reject the advances of the haoles. They noted with dismay the changes introduced from the outside to their cherished Hawaiian culture. They also were aware of the European and North American origins of diseases that had claimed the lives of thousands of Native Hawaiians since Cook.

Native Hawaiians labored reluctantly for haoles. Many sugar plantation owners, who were offspring of the early nineteenth century missionaries, complained that their Native Hawaiian laborers were just too lazy. The reality was that Hawaiian workers found laboring almost ceaselessly for eighteen to twenty-four months to bring in a sugar crop unnecessary as long as there were alternatives. Social scientist John Liu argues:

> In the traditional Hawaiian economy, people labored only until they fulfilled their needs and their obligations to the chiefs. The Hawaiians transferred this pattern of economic behavior to the wage system. They frequently quit the plantations and returned to their former modes of living after raising enough money to meet their immediate needs.

To discipline Hawaiian workers, sugar plantation owners pushed the Hawaiian government to enact the Master and Servant

Act in 1850. This act bound laborers to a five-year contract and inflicted imprisonment, fines, and contract extensions on laborers who did not abide by the terms of their contracts. Still, Hawaiian workers did not fully satisfy the haole employers. Thus, non-Hawaiian workers, mainly from Asia were recruited in part to spur on Hawaiian Islander productivity.

Back on the mainland, the first Asian Pacific American community had developed in and around New Orleans. The "Manila Men" were Filipino sailors who labored on Spanish galleons sailing throughout the world in the 1600s and 1700s. Frequently forced to become Spanish sailors, they jumped ship off the coast of Eastern Mexico and made their way into Louisiana, which was then a French colony. These Filipinos intermarried with the "locals" and helped make Louisiana one of the most culturally complex regions of North America. Yet even then the "Manila Men" were probably not the first Asian Pacific people to inhabit North America. That dubious honor probably can be extended to Southern Asians to America as slaves.

Chinese arrived in places like New York City in the early years of the new country. Many of these Chinese were sailors working on American ships. Like the "Manila Men," they probably jumped shipped the first good chance they got and sometimes that first chance was New York City. These men lived in the working class districts of Manhattan and frequently intermarried with the culturally diverse New York City locals. Moreover, a Chinese acrobat troupe was financially stranded in New York City and hunkered down in America's largest city to live out their days.

The most famous ante-bellum American residents of Chinese background were Chang and Eng Bunker, the famous "Siamese Twins." Before the American Civil War, we can see clear stirrings of a developing consumer culture. P.T. Barnum emerged at this time as one of the great American entrepreneurs in the field of commercialized entertainment. His American Museum allowed patrons to see circus performers and bearded ladies. One of Barnum's most popular early exhibits was a Chinese family. These people were not at all bizarre by Chinese standards but Barnum promoted them to American audiences as strange and exotic. More famous were the conjoined twins, Chang and Eng Bunker. Born in what is now Thailand of Chinese ancestry, Chang and Eng Bunker have often been thought of as constituting just one of Barnum's exhibits. But, according to scholar John Kuo Wei Tchen, there association was relatively brief. In the ante-bellum United States, they became independent entrepreneurs who successfully promoted their own appearances as "Oriental" curiosities. Eventually, the two of them were furnished with the status of one U.S. citizenship—not two but one. They retired as plantation owners in the South and slaveholders. They married sisters of a respectable plantation owning family and fathered several children.

IMMIGRATION AND "THE PEOPLE" IN THE UNITED STATES BEFORE THE CIVIL WAR

NATURALIZATION LAW OF 1790

The problem of who were the people in the new United States surfaced when Congress enacted America's first naturalization law. Naturalization refers to who among the non-native born residents is eligible for citizenship in the United States. According to political scientist Rogers Smith, the origins of the term derived from the following: "Once subjectship to the political ruler under whom one was born was believed to be natural—sanctioned by divine will and rationally discoverable natural law. Persons who acquired allegiance to a new ruler were therefore said to be 'naturalized.'" Smith also points out that while many of us might regard such a notion as naturalization as antiquated and just a little ridiculous, the United States. has, nevertheless, retained the term to describe the process by which a foreign born person becomes an American citizen.

In 1790, the new American government sought to encourage the immigration of those it hoped would become productive Americans. Thus, the Naturalization Law of 1790 was relatively liberal in the sense that it allowed only a year of residency in the United States before one could become a citizen and two years of residency if one wanted to hold public office in the United States. However, the U.S. Congress was not desirous of encouraging immigration from just anywhere. Rather, it wanted to restrict naturalization to "free, white persons." America's political leaders believed that only "free, white persons" could contribute in a positive manner to the new republic. The U.S. Congress was clearly concerned about immigrants of African ancestry, who might migrate to the United States from the Caribbean and elsewhere in the Americas. While the waiting period for naturalization would undergo change, the racial restriction written into the 1790 law would remain in effect when Chinese people began to migrate in significant numbers during the late 1840s and 1850s and would endure until 1952. Asian Pacific immigrants, generally defined as non-whites, were, accordingly, ineligible for U.S. citizenship. This meant that for decades the vast majority of Asian Pacific immigrants, unlike European immigrants, lacked much of a political voice in the United States. They could not vote, while lacking the security often attached to citizenship rights.

NATIVISM AND RACISM

Immigrants in general often experienced some form of discrimination in the United States. The Alien and Sedition Acts of 1798 gave the federal government a great deal of power over immigrants. The reigning Federalist Party feared immigrants as a threat to America and, in particular, a threat to it because newcomers to America often joined the rival Republican-Democrat Party. Thus, the Federalists introduced and passed laws calling on immigrants to register with the federal government, wait fourteen years before they were eligible for citizenship, and head off to prison if the government deemed it necessary. When Jefferson's Republican-Democrat Party came to power, the Alien and Sedition Acts were overturned. However, it is important to realize that the targets of that anti-immigrant legislation were white, European immigrants from places like Ireland, France, and England. At the same time, immigrants perceived as non-white typically have suffered the most in American history. And the fact that they were legally seen as ineligible for citizenship did not help matters. Yet while relatively powerless, non-white immigrants were not without the means and will to protest.

By 1850, democracy was no longer the troubling concept that it was sixty years earlier when the Constitution was framed. Democracy had become respectable, but, in order to claim respectability for it, political leaders had to remind themselves and others that only white adult males could vote or hold office. They claimed that the "others," people of color and women, were not responsible enough, industrious enough, or independent enough to expect a voice in the American political and legal system.

However, if only adult white males comprised "the people," some native-born Americans feared that European immigrants such as the Irish and the Germans would achieve too much political power given the substantial numbers of Irish and German-born residents of the United States in the 1840s and 1850s. A strong nativist politics emerged in the United States—a politics that to a significant extent argued that whiteness was insufficiently demarcated by light skin. Whiteness, that is, expressed the Republican qualities of maturity, self-discipline, and manliness—qualities that nativists doubted German and particularly Irish immigrants possessed. This nativist movement won little that was concrete. Nevertheless, nativists helped launch a political party called the American Party that became better known as the Know Nothing Party. This organization, which crossed class lines among native-born Protestant European Americans, gained some political respect in the mid-1850s. The Know Nothing Party called for, among other things, a residency period of twenty years before an immigrant could become a citizen. The Know Nothing Party, however, was not united over the crucial issue of slavery. Northern Know Nothings opposed slavery or at least its western expansion. Southern Know Nothings supported slavery and its western expansion. The Know Nothing Party could not survive these serious differences and disappeared by the end of the 1850s.

Irish and German immigrants had plenty of supporters, however, especially among Democrats who insisted that immigrants from the British Isles or Central Europe were indeed white people and endowed by nature with the capabilities of becoming good Americans. An important part of the appeal that the Democratic Party possessed at this time was its ability to "play the race card." In other words, the Democrats proclaimed to Irish and other working class Americans that they either favored or were indifferent to slavery in the South because otherwise freed African Americans would flood the North demanding jobs, houses, suffrage, and, worst of all, interracial sex. Slavery would protect, many Democrats argued, the ordinary white man's rights to vote, hold a decent job, and the opportunities to economically better himself and his family. Even outside of the South, Democrats called for the racial subordination of African Americans and the ouster of American Indians from their lands in order to protect and advance the aspirations of laboring class and often immigrant white citizens.

SCIENCE AND RACE

Out of response to the growing debate over slavery and the less but still important controversy revolving around immigration, a science of race developed in ante-bellum America. One of the dilemmas facing the emerging science of race was the Biblical interpretation of humanity's origins. That is, if humanity originated with Adam and Eve, then all of humanity was related. The enslaved African's ancestry was not really much different than that of the slave master. Some of the new practitioners of the science of race took on the Bible and argued for the multiple origins of humanity. This could justify racism but it also infuriated those who believed in a literal interpretation of the Bible.

Racial science could and did respond with something of an environmental argument based upon the work of Linnaeus, an eighteenth century European scientist. That is, as humanity dispersed throughout the world, different groups assumed physical, mental, and moral characteristics applicable to their environments—characteristics so deeply embedded that they might as well be inherent.

Individuals of supposedly different racial groups were photographed and their bodies from head to toe explored and measured. Phrenology, the measurement of heads, became a popular science, although somewhat in disrepute among academic scientists. It was based upon the assumption that skulls belonging to groups of Western and Northern European ancestry were the norm. Consequently, a study of skulls belonging to people of non-Western and Northern European ancestry would display their inferiority in some manner. For example, phreonologists pointed out that Asians possessed flat noses. Therefore, Asians possessed "flatness of mind and character by indicating a poor, low organic structure."

A racial hierarchy was fostered and refined. At the top of the hierarchy were Caucasians, white people of European descent. However, not all white groups were considered racially equally. Invariably, people of Northern and Western European ancestry came out better in racial science than people of Eastern and Southern European ancestry. As for Africans and indigenous peoples, they were invariably placed on the bottom of the hierarchy. The racial category of Mongol or Mongolian was reserved for people of Eastern Asian ancestry and was generally considered a category below that of Caucasians.

CHINESE IMMIGRATION TO HAWAI'I AND THE AMERICAN MAINLAND IN THE NINETEENTH CENTURY

The Chinese comprised the first substantial group of Asian Pacific people to enter the United States, emigrating from China in the mid-1800s. Approximately 46,000 Chinese trekked to Hawai'i during the second half of the nineteenth century, while 386,000 came to the American mainland from 1849 to 1930. Most of the early Chinese migrants to Hawai'i and the American mainland came from Guangdong, a province in the Southeastern China. For much of the nineteenth century, this region was devastated by ethnic and class conflict and undermined by economic change and natural disasters.

However, it is important to point out that European imperialism significantly altered the lives of Chinese people living in places like Guangdong. Great Britain, in particular, affected the course of China's development. Long finding it hard to break into the Chinese markets, the British found an alluring way to make money by importing into China a vast amount of opium from India, a British colony. As opium slipped into China, Chinese silver slipped into British pockets. When the Chinese government sought to ban the trade, in part because of opium's addictive influence on its Chinese consumers, the British, supported by the United States which had citizens enriched by an opium trade originating in Turkey, were willing to fight and the result was the first Opium War, which lasted from 1839 to 1842.

The British won this war and forced the Chinese government to pay them an enormous indemnity worth twenty-one million silver dollars. The Chinese government did that which most governments do when short on revenue. They severely taxed the Chinese people. Those Chinese people who were peasants often had to go into debt to pay their taxes and eventually many lost their land. After China lost a second opium war against Britain and France—a war which lasted from 1856 to 1860, further financial burdens were imposed upon peasant and laboring class families.

Natural disasters such as destructive floods and droughts made matters worse for Guangdong peasants. Moreover, there was little relief in urban areas such as Canton, where industry was undermined by British competition. Thanks to the Opium War's outcome the British freely moved their manufactured goods into China and forced Cantonese craftspeople, porters, warehouse workers, and merchants out of work and or out of business.

The growing European presence in Southeastern port cities meant that European and American labor recruiters had free reign to persuade Chinese laborers of the supposed wonders of working abroad. It also meant that European and American missionaries were free to intentionally or unintentionally convince Chinese that migrating to a Christian land would ease their soul's journey toward salvation. Protecting European and European American commerce and missionary work in China was, of course, British and French soldiers.

Consequently, many Chinese young men from Guangdong believed they had little choice but to emigrate to distant lands such as "Sandalwood Islands" (Hawai'i) or "Gold Mountain" (California). They were pulled to Hawai'i by jobs in agricultural labor and they were pulled to the American mainland by initially the California Gold Rush and jobs in railroad, agricultural, and industrial work. In addition to laboring people, Chinese merchants migrated to the United States in search of opportunities for status and wealth denied them in China, where the peasant, however poor, possessed more cultural prestige than the merchant, however well off.

By and large, the early Chinese immigrants to Hawai'i and the American mainland were young men determined to help their families out financially. Because of cultural and financial restraints, relatively few Chinese women migrated abroad. Since the Gold Rush lured thousands of Chinese to the American mainland, many engaged in gold mining.

Many native-born Americans in California and elsewhere inaccurately regarded these Chinese immigrants as coolies. In other words, they were thought of as similar to enslaved African Americans in that they supposedly performed forced labor. And native born Americans widely believed they were like African Americans in their docility in the face of white authority. There were, indeed, Chinese and East Indian coolies laboring in South Africa and South America. The coolie trade was designed during the second third of the nineteenth century to replace the African slave trade that had been outlawed by much of the world. Coolies performed coerced labor. They were often kidnapped or tricked onto ships sailing for South African or South America to take up arduous labor duties in agriculture or mining. But they were able to gain their freedom after a certain amount of years in service and their status as coolies was not inherited by their children. However, the Chinese coming to the American mainland generally arrived as products of the credit ticket system. That is, the typical Chinese heading to the United States during the gold rush could not afford the passage across the Pacific. A shipping company or labor contractor might pay for the immigrant's one way passage to the United States and then the immigrant would have to work off the debt.

Many Chinese labored in California's gold fields, looking for a quick way to help their families out. Individually, a Chinese immigrant could not afford the better claims. But he would pool his limited resources with other Chinese immigrants. Together they might be able to afford a claim that had been worked over a couple of times. Together they would work that claim and share in whatever profits that their hard toil won them. Other Chinese settled in cities and towns geographically and economically linked to the gold fields—places like San Francisco, of course, but also Sacramento, Stockton, Marysville, and San José, from which many Chinese miners walked to get to the gold fields. These "urban" Chinese were occupied as merchants, if they brought with them some capital, or as artisans.

Agriculture stood out as an attractive alternative to gold mining. In part, this was because most of the Chinese immigrants who came to gold rush California were experienced farmers and could use the cultural tool kits they had brought with them as experienced farmers across the Pacific to enhance their prospects as agriculturists in the Golden State. In part, this was also because California's European American population somewhat tolerated Chinese immigrants in agriculture. Some Chinese, as a consequence, took up "truck" farming in and around the gold fields. That is, they grew and sold fresh vegetables to hungry or inadequately nourished gold miners, Chinese and non-Chinese alike. In the process, they made money and furnished what white miners considered a needed service.

Moreover, in places like California's Sacramento-San Joaquin Delta area. Chinese were recruited as farm labor. Before the gold rush, much of this region was swampland. To transform the Delta into what would eventuate as one of America's richest agricultural areas would take a great deal of hard work—much of which was undertaken by Chinese laborers in terms of making the land useful for farming and then doing a significant portion of the farming themselves. Sucheng Chan has written about these laborers often recruited by individual landowners or reclamation companies:

"Chinese tenant farmers and farm laborers were intimately involved in every phase of the Delta's land reclamation and farm-making. In fact, it can be argued that without them the Delta would have taken decades longer to develop into one of the richest agricultural areas in the world."

Fruit growing in Santa Clara Valley was substantially pioneered by Chinese immigrant sharecroppers during the late 1860s and early 1870s. Often miles away from the more urbanized Chinatowns of San Francisco and Sacramento, these Chinese workers fostered communities as well as they could. They would often share tools and whatever savings they had accumulated in order to help each other gain economic independence of European Americans.

For years, Chinese agricultural laborers were at least somewhat tolerated in the Golden State mainly because whites who came to California regarded such labor as beneath them—as the kind of labor fit only for enslaved African Americans. Still, agricultural labor could lead some Chinese immigrants with patience, luck, and skill to independent farming.

In Hawai'i, Chinese agricultural workers were seen as vital to haole and rich Native Hawaiian landowners. There were just not enough Native Hawaiian workers sufficiently willing and healthy to do the kind of work that was needed in order to make the islands a major producer of sugar for the world's market. After Cook's landfall, Chinese merchants had migrated to the Hawaiian Islands in order to facilitate the sandalwood trade between Hawai'i and China. Chinese, moreover, operated a sugar refinery on the islands. When sugar plantation owners needed labor, they increasingly turned to Chinese labor contractors. The Hawaiian need for labor expanded as a result of the American Civil War, which opened up Northern markets to Hawaiian sugar because those markets had been previously supplied by Southern sources. In any event, Hawaiian sugar plantation owners hoped that the Chinese would furnish them with cheap, reliable, and servile labor.

Less attractive to early Chinese immigrants but nevertheless useful was domestic service; that is, furnishing cooking and cleaning services to generally white Californians. Performing such services was very likely not what these Chinese immigrants had in mind when they came to California. However, by doing so, they would escape much of the racist and nativist wrath inflicted upon Chinese miners, make a little money, and perhaps claim eventual self-employment.

By and large, the early American "Argonauts" to California's gold fields were young men harboring the racial and gender ideology prevalent in their communities—that domestic service was fit for enslaved African Americans and women but not for white males. Once in California, they were a half-continent or a continent away from those who did most of the cooking and cleaning for them. Clearly, by performing domestic services for European American men, Chinese men would win respite from anti-Chinese violence, if not, in the short run, respect. Moreover, they would make money and maybe enough money to start their own laundries, restaurants, or other businesses. And in some cases, as Sucheng Chan points out, engage in positive intercultural encounters with European Americans.

One of the more enduring stereotypes of Asian Pacific Americans is that they have been particularly competent in cooking and cleaning, especially for white people. A source of this stereotype was the California Gold Rush. During the Gold Rush, Chinese immigrants most assuredly did not come to the United States in order to cook and clean for European Americans. A significant number of them, however, decided that white antagonism would not allow Chinese immigrants to remain in the gold fields.

The "vice" trade channeled the energies of significant numbers of urban Chinese communities. Gambling halls, opium dens, and houses of prostitution employed many Chinese. Chan has discovered that over thirty percent of Chinese employed in San Francisco in 1860 were either owners of businesses doing trade in recreational vices or probable prostitutes. These businesses helped in capital formation in those communities in which they were common. Yet despite the fact that white ethnic communities subsidized similar kinds of commerce, the anti-Chinese movement would latch on to the vice trade as proof of Chinese corruption. Moreover, the vice trade was, especially in the case of prostitutes, tragically exploitative. The Chinese prostitute, indeed, was about as close to being a slave as anyone else in the Chinese community. While occasionally she had entered the profession with her eyes wide open and consciously made the most out of the existence of sex-starved Chinese and non-Chinese men in Gold Rush California, the Chinese prostitute was generally forced or tricked into the trade. Her parents, furthermore, might have sold her into the trade to make money. With thousands of male Chinese laborers in disparate parts of the world, an international ring in Chinese prostitutes promised wealth to investors and procurers, bribes to legal authorities who looked the other way, and seemingly endless toil, an early death, and little compensation for the prostitutes themselves.

Several different kinds of jobs engaged numerous Chinese during California's early years as a state. Fifteen percent of the employed Chinese in San Francisco in 1860 were fishermen. Chinese fishermen could be found also in the Sacramento-San Joaquin Delta, as well as along the coast of Monterey Bay and San Diego. Meanwhile, Chinese were busy as general merchants, herbalists, tailors, letter writers, fortunetellers, and artisans. In 1860, a railroad company attempting to build a line from San Francisco to San Jose hired Chinese laborers because they were willing to work for a dollar a day.

By the early 1850s, Chinese immigrants had encountered plenty of hostility in California. Much of this hostility related to the perception of Chinese as non-white, culturally inferior people. Much of it, however, also related to the perception of Chinese as economic competition.

In 1850, California passed the Foreign Miner's Tax. This was done at the behest of white miners, who resented the competition offered by Latin American miners and merchants who had primarily trekked into California from Sonora. These Sonorans were often very experienced, skilled, and industrious miners, as well as keen businessmen. It was tough enough for individual prospectors to enrich themselves in the gold fields. It did not help when a certain contingent of miners actually knew what they were doing. And it did not make for happy feelings that these miners were Latin Americans, who, in the eyes of many white Americans, were non-white. The Foreign Miner's Tax, therefore, was passed to protect Anglo economic interests. It stipulated that in order to mine in California, "foreign" prospectors had to pay twenty dollars a month. In order to escape this onerous tax, many Latin American miners relocated to non-mining districts of California or returned to their homes in Mexico, Chile, or Peru.

By 1854, Chinese miners were viewed by many frustrated native- born white miners as unfair and, in any case, unwanted competition. Thus the Foreign Miner's Tax was lowered to three dollars per miner and was enforced exclusively against miners perceived as non-white, which meant Chinese and non-white Latinos. The state of California, as it turned out, was substantially financed by the taxes paid by Chinese miners.

In 1854, as well, the California State Supreme Court delivered a body blow to the state's Chinese population in *People v. Hall*. In this case, a white gambler named George Hall was convicted of murdering a Chinese gambler in San Francisco. The conviction was appealed based on the 1850 law banning the testimony of Native Americans, African Americans, and mulattos in cases involving whites. The California State Supreme Court extended this law to Chinese; thus depriving them of any significant legal standing in the new state. California State Supreme Court Justice Charles J. Murray declared in presenting why he voted to uphold the appeal:

> We have carefully considered all the consequences resulting from a different construction and are satisfied that, even in a doubtful case, we would be impelled to this decision on grounds of public policy. The same rule that would admit them to testify, would admit them to all the equal rights of citizenship, and we might soon see them at the polls, in the jury box, upon the bench and in our legislative halls. This is not a speculation which exists in the excited and overheated imagination of the patriot and statesman, but it is an actual and present danger.

Chinese immigrants resisted what they considered as unjust treatment in pre-Civil War America. In 1855, California's Governor John Bigler became the first major political figure in America to call for the restriction of Chinese immigration. Norman Asing, one of the relatively few naturalized Chinese immigrants in the United states responded forcefully. He replied to Bigler in a letter published in a San Francisco newspaper. In this letter, Asing described himself as "a Chinaman, a republican, and a lover of free institutions <and> much attached to the principles of the government of the United States." He argued furthermore against Bigler's notion that an "aristocracy of color" existed in the United States.

> It is out of your power to say... in what way or to whom the doctrines of the Constitution apply. You have no more right to propose a measure for checking immigration, than you have the right of sending a message to the Legislature on the subject. As regards the color and complexion of our race, we are perfectly aware that our population has been a little more tan than yours.

ASIAN PACIFIC AMERICANS AND THE CIVIL WAR

In the mid-1990s, Chinese American writer Ruthanne Lum McCunn helped shed light on the soldiers of Chinese ancestry who fought in the American Civil War. For example, Edward Day Cahota was the Chinese born adopted son of European Americans living in Massachusetts. During the Civil War, Cahota served in the Union army and saw combat in the Battle of Drury Bluff and the Battle of Cold Harbor. Joseph L. Pierce was another adopted son of European American parents. He fought in the bloody Battle of Antietem in 1862. In 1863, McCunn writes that Pierce "distinguished himself in Gettysburg, where he was among the first to go out on the skirmish line...and volunteered for the critical attack against the Bliss Farm." Generally, those documented cases of soldiers of Chinese ancestry fighting in the Civil War joined the Union's cause. A few, however, fought on the side of the Confederacy.

To a substantial extent, the Civil War encouraged revolutionary changes in the United States. These changes, moreover, affected the course of Asian Pacific immigration to the United States. First, the Civil War made the construction of the Transcontinental Railroad more possible. Southerners had long opposed the central government's involvement in building a Transcontinental Railroad. They believed that states' rights were more important than national economic development. During the Civil War, Lincoln and the Republican Party could push for the building of the Transcontinental Railroad, because Southerners were not in Congress to resist it. In any event, the Transcontinental Railroad eventually employed thousands of Chinese workers, many of whom lingered in the United States after their employment by the Southern Pacific Railroad was done.

Because of the Civil War, the city of San Francisco could no longer easily import manufactured goods from the East Coast. San Francisco's capitalists believed that they would have to develop a homegrown industrial sector. Yet they believed, too, that they had to find a labor force that would work in San Francisco's new factories at relatively low wages. They recruited Chinese immigrants after the war to meet their labor requirements. Indeed, the growth of the Market Economy after the Civil War stimulated a need for immigrant labor in general. On the East Coast, workers of

Irish, German, Slavic, and Italian ancestry were recruited. On the West Coast, workers of Asian Pacific ancestry were called upon.

The Civil War also inspired recruitment of Asian Pacific labor to Hawai'i's sugar plantations. The South had been a key producer of sugar for Northern markets before the Civil War. However, with the Civil War, Northern markets became available to Hawaiian producers. Hawaiian sugar planters in order to meet expanding market requirements also had to expand their quest for labor from China and then Japan.

CONCLUSION

It has been easy for historians to ignore the experiences of Asian Pacific Americans before the Civil War. To be sure, compared to more recent American history, far fewer people of Asian Pacific American ancestry lived on either the Hawaiian Islands before the Civil War or the American mainland. Nevertheless, the experiences of Asian Pacific Americans, ranging from the "Manila Men" to the famous "Siamese Twins" have been well documented and require our attention, as does the Asian Pacific's long shadow cast on early American history.

Unfortunately, the interactions between America and the Asian Pacific, including Asian Pacific people, were not always very positive. By the dawn of the American Civil War, Chinese immigrants faced legalized forms of discrimination in places like California along with racist and nativist violence. In Hawai'i, indigenous people faced exploitation and future demographic destruction at the hands of haoles, many of whom possessed American nationality. Chinese immigrants were, at best, regarded as necessary to the development of the Hawaiian sugar industry. It would be nice to say that such interactions would become more positive after the Civil War—nice but far from the truth.

REVIEW

1. How did Asian Pacific societies influence European expansion to the Americas in the 1500s?
2. What was China like around 1492?
3. What was India like around 1492?
4. What was Southeast Asia like around 1492?
5. What was Japan like around 1492?
6. How did the Asian Pacific influence early American history?

7. What was Hawai'i like in the late 1700s and early 1800s?
8. Who were the "Manila Men"? Why were they important?
9. Outside of California, what kind of people were likely to be Asian Pacific Americans before the Civil War?
10. Who were Cheng and Eng Bunker? Why were they important?
11. What was the Naturalization Law of 1790? Why was it important?
12. What were the Alien and Sedition Acts? Why were they important?
13. How did nativism and racism interact to shape the experiences of immigrants in the United States before the Civil War?
14. What was the role of scientific racism before the American Civil War?
15. Why did Chinese immigrate to the United States and Hawai'i before the American Civil War?
16. Who immigrated from China to the United States and Hawai'I before the American Civil War?
17. What kind of work did Chinese immigrants do in the United States and Hawai' before the American Civil War?
18. Identify and give the significance of the Foreign Miner's Tax?
19. Identify and give the significance of People v. Hall?
20. Who was Norman Asing? Why was he important?

SELECTED BIBLIOGRAPHY

Almaguer, Tomas. *Racial Fault Lines: The Historical Origins of White Supremacy in California.* (1994).

Chan, Sucheng. *Asian Americans: An Interpretive History.* (1991).

_____. *Asian Californians.* (1991).

Hing, Bill Ong. *Making and Remaking Asian America Through Immigration Policy, 1850-1900.* (1993).

Kent, Noel J. *Hawaii: Islands Under the Influence.* (1993).

Lopez, Ian Haney. *White By Law: The Legal Construction of Race.* (1996).

Lum McCunn, Ruthanne. "Chinese in the Civil War: Ten Who Served," *Chinese America: History and Perspectives 1996.*

Ng, Franklin. "Hawai'i and Native Hawaiians," in *New Visions in Asian American Studies: Diversity, Community, Power.* (1994).

Okihiro, Gary Y. *Cane Fires: The Anti-Japanese Movement in Hawaii, 1865-1945.* (1991).

_____. *Margins and Mainstreams: Asians in American History and Culture.* (1994).

Salyer, Lucy E. *Laws Harsh as Tigers: Chinese Immigration and the Shaping of Modern Immigration Law.* (1995).

Takaki, Ronald. *Strangers from a Different Shore: A History of Asian Americans.* (1989).

_____. *A Different Mirror: A History of Multicultural America.* (1993).

Yamato, Alexander. *et. al. Asian Americans in the United States.* Vol. 2. (1993).

Yung, Judy. *Unbound Feet: A Social History of Chinese Women in San Francisco.* (1995).

Zia, Helen. *Asian American Dreams: The Emergence of an American People.* (2000).

VI
ASIAN PACIFIC AMERICANS AND THE "PEOPLE'S CLUB", 1865-1941

While the Civil War did not begin as a struggle to make America more democratic and egalitarian, by its end the war had become a revolutionary struggle against African American enslavement. Nearly 200,000 African American soldiers had joined the union's military to fight to end African American enslavement and to gain access to the People's Club. They were aided by thousands of enslaved African Americans willing to commit acts of espionage and sabotage in the slave south, as well as many white people in and out of the military committed to end African American enslavement.

One of the by-products of this struggle was the Thirteenth Amendment to the U.S. Constitution (1865), which officially ended slavery in the United States. However, supporters of the Thirteenth Amendment frequently understood that freeing enslaved African Americans would not be enough. The United States government would have to guarantee that the freed peoples' right to "life, liberty, and property" would not be denied them by state and local officials.

When it looked like the Southern states would seek to maintain freed African Americans in a state of perpetual fear and peonage, the reigning Republican Party in Congress sought to provide freed people with federal protection. A Civil Rights Law would not do the trick because the Constitution perhaps did not give the federal government the direct power to protect people from state and local officials. Thus, Republican congress members decided to enact the Fourteenth Amendment to the U.S. Constitution (1868).

The first section of the Fourteenth Amendment declares that any one born in the United States or naturalized in the United States is a citizen and deserving of all the rights granted under the Constitution and the Bill of Rights. More to the point:

> No State shall make or enforce any law which shall abridge the privileges or immunities of citizens of the United States; nor shall any State deprive any person of life, liberty, or property, without due process of law; nor deny to any person within its jurisdiction the equal protection of the laws." (U.S. Constitution, Fourteenth Amendment, Section 1)

In other words, the writers of the Fourteenth Amendment asserted that African Americans, born in the United States, possessed all of the rights previously granted to whites by the U.S. Constitution and the Bill of Rights. They also seemed to have wanted to guarantee naturalized immigrants and U.S. born children of immigrants, whether European or non-European, equal rights. Yet the wording of the Fourteenth Amendment could furnish little comfort to Chinese immigrants wishing to become U.S. citizens. As long as the Naturalization Act of 1790 remained in effect, there was little chance of Chinese "aliens" becoming naturalized in the United States. Indeed, before it was passed opponents of the Fourteenth Amendment articulated the racial ideology that the extension of citizenship rights to African Americans should not mean that American Indians and Chinese immigrants deserved citizenship rights. At the same time, the declaration that "any person" living in America deserved protection of "life, liberty, or property" meant that one did not have to be a citizen to have rights that federal, state, and local governments needed to respect. Even immigrants ineligible for citizenship possessed unalienable, natural rights.

Indeed, thanks to Congress's efforts to render the People's club more inclusive, state laws banning non-white testimony in court were eliminated. Accordingly, *People v. Hall* no longer held sway in California's legal system. Congress, moreover, revised America's naturalization laws in 1870. Consequently, "aliens of African nativity and persons of African descent" became eligible for citizenship. At the same time, Congress expressly refused to extend naturalization rights to Chinese immigrants because of their "undesirable qualities."

THE ANTI-ASIAN MOVEMENT IN CALIFORNIA AFTER THE CIVIL WAR

In California, the battle against Chinese immigration grew intense in the decade after the Civil War. The growing presence of Chinese immigrants in California workplaces became a powerful political issue. Significantly, the Democratic Party in California was important in raising the issue of Chinese workers in California as a way to gain votes in the late 1860s. The Civil War, which ended in 1865, seemed to spell doom for the Democrats, because they were widely associated with either support for the rebellious South or a pacifistic policy toward the rebels. Since the North, under Republican Party leadership, won the war, there was good reason for pessimism about the Democratic Party's future.

Northern Democrats played "the race card" effectively to attract voters. They argued that votes for Democrats were votes to preserve white supremacy and that Republican concern for the rights of African Americans in the South and Chinese immigrants in California threatened white jobs, white neighborhoods, and white women. Sadly, people in New York City and San Francisco listened--especially working class, immigrant people who believed themselves endangered somehow by African American and Chinese immigrant occupational and geographical mobility. In the United States, these people had learned they were white and that being white ought to give them some protection against people of color.

With the help of trade unions in the San Francisco Bay Area, the Democratic Party proved instrumental in the formation of organizations called Anti-Coolie Clubs. Falsely associating California's Chinese population with the coolie trade, which in turn was associated with the slave trade, the Anti-Coolie clubs argued much too convincingly that Chinese immigrants possessed the same "unassimilable" characteristics as African Americans.

To be fair, Republicans generally were never quite the allies of people of color that their political opponents portrayed them to be. Indeed, it was the Republican *San Jose Mercury* that compared Chinese immigrants to African "wild bushmen." Clearly, Republicans by the early 1870s were not going to hitch their personal or political ambitions to a platform defending the political and economic rights of people of color. In the early 1870s, a group of politicians became known as Reform Republicans. They disliked the corruption that plagued Republican President Grant's administration and they were what we earlier described as "classical liberals" in that they believed that government's main task was to protect property, which in the 1870s meant encouraging capitalist development. These and other Republicans were more concerned about issues related to economic prosperity than what was happening to Southern African Americans or Chinese Californians.

Meanwhile, Chinese immigrants in California faced less violence than African Americans in the south but they could not rest easily in the Golden State. In 1870, a number of Chinese residents of what is now central Los Angeles were gunned down after European Americans set fire to their homes. That same year, San Jose's Chinatown was "mysteriously" burned down.

The ill-tempered, occasionally homicidal, anti-Chinese movement in California wanted the U.S. government to restrict immigration from China. However, the national government in the late 1860s was not sympathetic to calls for Chinese immigration restriction. The national government's growing obsession with helping capitalism thrive in the United States possessed some useful consequences for Chinese immigrants—at least in the short-run. In 1868, the United States signed the Burlingame Treaty with China. This was supported by national economic interests who wanted to exploit China as a potentially lucrative market for American manufactured goods and investments. Thus, the Burlingame Treaty permitted American commodities into China in an unrestricted fashion. At the same time, many American employers wanted access to China's labor market. Thus, the Burlingame Treaty allowed Chinese immigrants to enter the United States in an unrestricted manner and obligated the American government to protect the rights of Chinese nationals living in the United States.

For several years, the Burlingame Treaty proved painful to white Californians, wishing to halt Chinese immigration. Washington, D.C. and political leaders on the East Coast in general were inclined to consider Californians overly obsessed with Chinese immigrants. In any event, the U.S. government told California it could do nothing to restrict Chinese immigration. In the first place, immigration was the federal government's business. In the second place, the Burlingame Treaty meant that the United States government could not stop Chinese immigration and was obligated to protect the rights of Chinese immigrants.

By this time the Transcontinental Railroad had brought modernizing capitalism in all of its glory and hideousness across the continent to a still very agricultural and pre-industrial California. It also brought Chinese by the thousands to California and the U.S. in general.

Growing racial and ethnic tensions shadowed by class strains was one unfortunate byproduct of the Transcontinental Railroad. The Central Pacific's ability to attract federal land grants depended largely on its ability to lay down as much track as possible. In other words, the more track it constructed through the Sierras and the Rocky Mountains, the more land the Big Four would get from the federal government. The problem was that the Union Pacific was laying down track from Chicago westward and much of the railroad construction undertaken by the Union Pacific was on the Great Plains. The Central Pacific feared that the Union Pacific would gobble up most of the federal land grants. Accordingly, its heads were convinced they needed a large labor force that would not only prove inexpensive but disciplined.

Finding this labor force was not easy. Railroad construction work usually meant low wages, as well as dreary, physically taxing, and often dangerous labor. In the ante-bellum south, slaves were often considered too valuable to perform railroad work. Thus, Irish immigrants were substantially recruited to do the work in the south and the north. As the poorest and most desperate of the white ethnic groups, Irish immigrants were willing, if not eager, to do railroad work. Consequently, the Union Pacific hired generally Irish work teams. And the Central Pacific did the same as the company started to lay track from Sacramento eastward through the treacherous Sierras.

Irish American workers resisted Central Pacific discipline. In other places, they often stood out as the most militant of America's industrial workers. But what aggravated the situation for the Central Pacific were the options available to Irish railroad workers in California. It was not just that they were free to come and go as they pleased but that industrializing San Francisco offered job opportunities as did growing communities throughout the state. They may not have been the best jobs available but they were more than likely safer and more lucrative opportunities than railroad jobs. The Central Pacific, therefore, needed an easier to control labor force.

Chinese immigrants seemed to fit the Central Pacific's labor requirements quite nicely. In the first place, they were widely viewed as docile workers incapable of labor insurrection. Second, they were seen as possessing relatively few rights in the United States. They were not only immigrants but defined by the political-legal system as non-white immigrants with little or no legal immunity from exploitative employers. Third, they were contract laborers. The Central Pacific would pay various Chinese laborer contractors who, in turn, would hire the workers. Consequently, if these workers got fed up with their jobs there was little legally they could do about it until their contracts ended. Indeed, Charles Crocker, who was the most "hands-on" of any of the Big Four, would not have to deal with the Chinese workers personally if he chose not to. Chinese labor contractors could handle distribution of pay, as well as, discipline.

The Central Pacific ultimately recruited thousands of Chinese workers. The Central Pacific paid its Chinese workers thirty dollars a month. White workers would receive the same amount of pay but the company supplied them room and board. The company very happily let Chinese labor contractors take care of housing and feeding Chinese workers. Meanwhile, members of the Big Four such as Charles Crocker expressed general content with Chinese workers.

It is not so clear that Chinese workers were all that content to be working for the likes of Charles Crocker. They performed work that was hard and hazardous. They had to build a railroad line through dangerous, mountainous conditions. Many were buried by snow drifts and killed blowing holes through the mountains. In 1867, several thousand Chinese workers for the Central Pacific went on an ill-fated strike.

When the Transcontinental Railroad was completed, thousands of Chinese workers were discharged. Perhaps, their former employers hoped they would return to China, but many did not have enough money to help their families or help themselves out of debt. Some continued to perform railroad work in California and other parts of the west. Others, however, entered the industrial labor force that had been growing primarily in San Francisco since the Civil War, while others joined the agricultural labor force in places such as California's Santa Clara, Sacramento, and San Joaquin Valleys.

The growing presence of Chinese immigrants in varied sectors of California's economy only seemed to make the state's anti-Chinese movement more desperate—a desperation that expanded during a national economic downturn in 1873—a depression that originated on the East Coast and spread to the west. White run firms that had previously used Chinese workers expressed a willingness to let them go and hire whites as long as those whites muted their wage demands. By this time, the railroad had also brought into California more women and more children. Some San Francisco manufacturers discharged their male adult Chinese workers and replaced them with white women and youth. However, rather than returning to China, the replaced workers found jobs laboring for Chinese employers. The labor market remained glutted and California's economy unstable.

Serious economic problems, growing labor unrest, and political ambitions encouraged the federal government and national political leaders to compromise with the passionate anti-Chinese movement, largely centered in California, and chip away at the Burlingame Treaty. In 1875, the Page Law, named after a California congressman, was enacted. This law denied entry into the United States of Chinese, Japanese, and "Mongolian" contract laborers, prostitutes, and felons. Since many Chinese immigrants had entered the United States as contract laborers, the Page Law seemed, according to the anti-Chinese movement, aimed in the right direction. Moreover, the Page Law's impact upon the entrance of Chinese women into the United States also deserves attention. Historian Judy Yung declares:

> As economic conditions worsened after the 1873 depression, public sentiment continued to mount against the Chinese. In 1875, Congress stepped in and passed the Page Law forbidding the entry of "Oriental" contract laborers, prostitutes, and criminals. The enforcement process, which involved the stringent screening of women in Hong Kong by the American consul, succeeded in reducing not only the number of prostitutes but also the overall number of Chinese women.

While Chinese women entering the United States twenty years earlier might have disproportionately been prostitutes, by 1875 a significant number of Chinese men living in America were sending for their wives and female relatives. However, in the minds of U.S. and California legal authorities a Chinese woman was a Chinese prostitute unless proven otherwise. While determined Chinese women frequently were able to get into the United States, the legal complications and the personal humiliation involved were so great that many other Chinese women intending to come to America probably decided to remain. The Page Law, consequently, made it difficult for Chinese immigrants in the United States to produce a second generation of potential American citizens and voters.

THE LABOR MOVEMENT AND ANTI-CHINESE POLITICS

The late nineteenth century labor movement often strongly advocated and fought for a more democratic vision of America's possibility. However, this vision was just as often diluted by racism, nativism, sexism, and what English historian Eric Hobsbawm described as an "aristocracy of labor" ideology.

Asian Pacific immigrants and children of Asian Pacific immigrants were, then, victimized by white trade unionists in the late 1800s and into the twentieth century. San Francisco became the strongest trade union city in the United States during the late 1800s. Historians such as Alexander Saxton and Michael Kazin have pointed out that San Francisco's trade union movement was strengthened by its ability to organize around the anti-Asian issue. Workers from different ethnic groups and different skill levels in San Francisco might not have had much in common except their general distaste for Asian immigration.

Thus, it was fairly easy for the Workingmen's Party of California, centered in San Francisco, to initiate a popular political movement aimed at Chinese immigrants during the late 1870s. After the Chinese Exclusion Act was passed, European American workers in San Francisco helped launch a statewide boycott against firms employing Chinese workers. At the same time, white boot and shoemakers in San Francisco organized a trade union called the Boot and Shoemakers White Labor League to push out Chinese and then, in the early 1890s, Japanese competition. All of this was done, white workers insisted, to advance democracy and equality in San Francisco.

Nationally, the labor movement generally supported the anti-Asian movement. In 1870, a group of workers in Massachusetts condemned "efforts...to introduce into the manufactories of this state coolie labor form China in order to cheapen, and, if possible, degrade the intelligent educated loyal labor of Massachusetts." During the 1880s, the most powerful national organization of laborers was called the Knights of Labor. Led by the genuinely idealistic Terrence Powderly, the Knights of Labor tried to effectively organize laborers that had often been despised by American trade unionists in the past—including African American and female laborers. However, the egalitarian features of the Knights of Labor did not extend to Chinese workers.

The Workingmen's Party of California (WPC) offers an interesting example of anti-Asian labor politics in the late nineteenth century. The WPC, under the leadership of an Irish teamster named Dennis Kearney, opposed the Republicans as the party that introduced Chinese workers to American shores and as a political party indifferent to the miseries of white working people. The WPC opposed the Democrats as corrupt politicians who cared about nothing except getting votes. The WPC challenged the rich corporate heads of railroads and agribusinesses to hire whites instead of Chinese. Indeed, Kearney demanded that "the Chinese must go!" And significant numbers of California voters—especially working class and lower middle class California voters responded positively to Kearney's rhetoric.

WPC members won political offices throughout the state and gained political control of San Francisco's government. Several WPC members were also elected as delegates to California's second Constitutional Convention held in 1879. This constitution contained passages clearly discriminatory to California's Chinese population. According to scholar Alexander Yamato:

> The California Constitution contained four sections singling out the Chinese, specifically giving cities and towns the right to expel them if bound to be "detrimental to the well-being or peace of the state," denying corporations the right to employ Chinese or Mongolians, prohibiting the employment of Chinese by any local or state government, and, by equating Chinese with coolie labor, directed the legislature to prevent the Chinese from entering the state as well as discourage Chinese immigration.

THE CHINESE EXCLUSION ACT

The "politics of prejudice" in California influenced the national political perspective on Chinese immigrants. Granted, the population of Chinese in other parts of the United States was not great. But the 1870s and 1880s marked a period of rising racism. African Americans and American Indians were victimized perhaps more than ever before by racial discrimination at this time and Chinese immigrants were not going to escape notice, especially since they were ineligible for citizenship and, hence, unlikely to provoke much concern from American politicians ambitious for votes.

One problem was the Burlingame Treaty. In order for the United States to restrict Chinese immigrants, it had to renegotiate with a reluctant Chinese government. However, the American government pressured China into a rewritten treaty in which it would continue to allow American-made goods into its ports, while empowering the United States to stop Chinese immigration.

In 1882, the U.S. Congress enacted the Chinese Exclusion Act. This act denied entry into the United States of Chinese immigrant laborers and declared, if there was any doubt before, that Chinese people were non–white and, hence, ineligible for American citizenship. This act possessed a class bias. Chinese immigrants who could prove they were merchants, scholars, and diplomats were allowed entry into the United States, although they, too, remained ineligible for citizenship. Finally, this act was subject to renewal in ten years time. Ten years later, the U.S. Congress passed the Geary Act, which extended the Chinese Exclusion Act until 1902.

AGENCY AND THE QUEST FOR JUSTICE

Still, people of Chinese ancestry proved capable of resisting discrimination in terms of immigration and naturalization. One strategy they took up involved the American political-legal system, which, in theory, promised equal protection of the laws for all those living in the United States. This promise was reinforced by the Fourteenth Amendment to the U.S. Constitution. Among other things, this amendment guaranteed that anyone born or naturalized within the United States, regardless of race and skill color, would enjoy the same rights as any other citizen of the United States. At the same time, people of Chinese and Asian Pacific Islander ancestry were deeply involved in protesting either whiteness as a prerequisite to citizenship or claiming that they were white and therefore eligible for citizenship.

In 1878, Ah Yup sought American citizenship. A federal district court determined that Ah Yup was ineligible for U.S. citizenship based on "common knowledge" and "scientific evidence." The first justification argued that it was widely known that Chinese people were not white. The court declared, "The words 'white person' ...in this country, at least, have undoubtedly acquired a well settled meaning in common popular speech, and they are constantly used in the sense so acquired in the literature of the country, as well as in common parlance." In other words, according to the existent naturalization law, only immigrants of white and African ancestries were eligible for citizenship. Since Americans commonly considered Chinese as neither white nor black, they were ineligible for American citizenship.

Science, according to the court, backed the denial of Ah Yup's petition for citizenship. *In re Ah Yup*, the court declared:

> In speaking of the various classifications of races, Webster in his dictionary says, "the common classification is that of Blumenbach, who makes five. 1. The Caucasian, or white race, to which belong the greater part of the European nations and those of Western Asia; 2. The Mongolian, or yellow race, occupying Tartary, China, Japan, etc.; 3. The Ethiopian or Negro (black) race, occupying all Africa, except the north; 4. The American, or red race, containing Indians of North and South America; and 5. The Malay, or Brown race, occupying the islands of the Indian Archipelago," etc. This division was adopted from Buffon, with some changes in names, and is founded in the combined characteristics of complexion, hair, and skull....<N>o one includes the white, or Caucasian, with the Mongolian or yellow race

Take that Ah Yup!

Several years later, an ambiguous decision was handed down by the California State Supreme Court in *Tape v. Hurley*. Mamie Tape was a young Chinese American whose parents tried to enroll her in a San Francisco public school. In 1885, the Tapes claimed that there was no public schooling available to San Francisco's Chinese residents and that Mamie and her brother would have to go to school with white children. The Tapes' lawyers argued that the Fourteenth Amendment mandated public school education for Mamie Tape and her brother. Sidestepping the issue of the Fourteenth Amendment, the court actually decided on behalf of the Tapes, claiming that if San Francisco's school district did not wish to educate Chinese American children it should have said so in its by-laws. Of course, doing so would have placed the school district in direct violation of the Fourteenth Amendment. The court, in any event, ordered that Mamie and her brother receive a proper public education in San Francisco. San Francisco's superintendent of schools then convinced the state legislature to provide funding for a segregated Chinese school. It was not until the 1930s that Chinese American children in San Francisco attended integrated elementary schools.

Around the same time, the city of San Francisco was trying to figure out what to do about the Chinese immigrants remaining in the city despite the Chinese Exclusion Law and, in some cases, operated seemingly thriving businesses. In particular, several Chinese San Franciscans engaged in the laundry business. San Francisco's Board of Supervisors decided to pass an ordinance which stipulated that in order to run a laundry in a wooden building the individual or individuals owning the laundry would have to apply for a license from the city.

On the face of it, this ordinance apparently conformed to the need for public safety. Operating a laundry in a wooden building could, indeed, pose a fire hazard. However, this ordinance had been passed largely to deprive Chinese immigrants the opportunity of running laundries in San Francisco, since very few of these immigrants could afford to operate their laundries in buildings constructed out of stone or brick. And once passed white laundry operators found it much easier to get licensed to do business out of wooden buildings than Chinese laundry operators. Basing their legal case on the Fourteenth Amendment, an alarmed Chinese community in San Francisco fought the laundry ordinance. A Chinese laundry operator named Yick Wo was the litigant. The case eventually wound up in the U.S. Supreme Court. In *Yick Wo v. Hopkins*, the nation's highest court decided on behalf of Yick Wo. It claimed that the city of San Francisco had deprived Yick Wo and other Chinese laundry operators of their property rights in violation of the equal protection of the law.

While Chinese immigrants were declared legally ineligible for citizenship, what about American born people of Chinese ancestry? The wording of the Fourteenth Amendment to the contrary, the anti-Chinese movement insisted that a person of Chinese ancestry was ineligible for citizenship regardless of whether that person was born in San Francisco or Canton. The case of Wong Kim Ark brought this matter to a climax before the nineteenth century ended. Born in San Francisco, Wong Kim Ark sought to reenter the United States after a trip to China. Based upon the Chinese Exclusion Law, the American government sought to keep Wong Kim Ark out of the country of his birth. The case of *Wong Kim Ark vs. U.S.* revolved around whether Wong Kim Ark was an American citizen legally empowered to avoid the restrictions imposed upon Chinese immigrants by the Chinese Exclusion Law. The U.S. Supreme Court decided that Wong Kim Ark was, indeed, an American citizen, thanks to the Fourteenth Amendment and, therefore, free to return to his native land.

In 1894, a U.S. circuit court took up the case of a Japanese immigrant living in Massachusetts. In *in re Saito*, this court, basing its decision on the conclusion that Japanese were racially Mongolians and therefore not white, declared Japanese nationals ineligible for U.S. citizenship. Since Chinese immigrants wanting U.S. citizenship ran into the same legal roadblocks, Asian Pacific immigrants in general encountered a powerful obstacle to the People's Club in the late nineteenth century. In other words, one of the biggest European American complaints about Chinese and Japanese immigrants was that they were not interested in becoming good American citizens. However, when Chinese and Japanese immigrants tried to become American citizens the legal system turned against them with widespread backing from white politicians and voters.

PROGRESSIVES AND ASIAN PACIFIC IMMIGRATION

Race, class, and gender influenced national politics when it came to Japanese immigration. The need for labor endured and if the Chinese could not substantially help meet this need, many employers, especially in California and Hawai'i, hoped they could use Japanese immigrants and not arouse much hostility. They were wrong when it came to California. California progressives such as Hiram Johnson and James Phelan were instrumental in proving them wrong.

Like a good number of progressives throughout the country, California progressives were a paradoxical lot. They spoke out enthusiastically for democraticizing California and the United States. They enacted concrete measures that they hoped would weaken the political power of big corporations and political machines. Many of these measures were enacted in other states and, for good or ill, remain a part of the political landscape in much of America.

California progressives tended to believe that out of corruption and/or incompetence, state and local political officials were not adequately responsive to the will of the people. They, therefore, wanted to empower state voters with the ability to pass laws, amend the state constitution, and remove unresponsive elected officials on their own. When progressives acquired state political power under the leadership of Hiram Johnson, they gave California voters the ability to use the initiative, referendum, and recall to democratize California.

By the same token, California progressives found it very easy to oppose Asian Pacific immigration in the name of democracy. In the process, they represented a form of *herrenfolk* democracy. In other words, they feared that democracy was impossible to develop and maintain in a highly heterogeneous society. The citizens of a stable democratic society must, therefore, possess a common culture. Otherwise, democracy would break down into anarchy. The presence of a large population of people of Asian Pacific ancestry would, many progressives were convinced, endanger the stability of America's democratic institutions.

California's progressive politicians, moreover, were convinced in the early 1900s that the growing presence of Japanese immigrants in the state was a potentially powerful vote-getting issue. In particular, raising the danger of Japanese immigration proved a way for California progressive politicians, of typically comfortable, non-working class backgrounds, to connect with California's trade union movement, which generally portrayed all Asian Pacific immigrants as "toiling machines," whose presence would swell unemployment among whites. By the same token, California's progressives could line up support from small-scale white farmers, who did not want to compete with other white farmers with capital enough to hire Asian Pacific immigrants. Nor did these farmers like to compete with independent Asian Pacific immigrant farmers.

In 1905, a group of anti-Asian Pacific Californians organized the Japanese and Korean Exclusion League, which changed its name to the Asiatic Exclusion League in 1907. This league declared what most Americans sadly believed in the early 1900s— that races existed and that the white race in California ought to be empowered to separate and exclude other races. This league supported enthusiastically the effort of San Francisco's elected Board of Education to segregate students of Japanese ancestry from white students by placing Japanese students in educational facilities that had been reserved for Chinese and Asian Indian children.

The Japanese government protested the segregation of Japanese students in San Francisco When the Chinese government had complained about the pernicious treatment given overseas Chinese it was largely ignored because the Chinese government was considered largely impotent in world affairs. This was not the case with the Japanese government, which was rightly considered by people like President Theodore Roosevelt as a rising power in Asia and the Pacific.

Roosevelt, even though generally a white Anglo-Saxon supremacist, did not want to fuel Japanese animosity and tried to get San Francisco's Board of Education to rescind its segregation order. But the Board, backed by the large majority of San Francisco's voters, rejected Roosevelt's appeals. The result of all this was an agreement made in 1907 between the American government and the Japanese government. Called the Gentlemen's Agreement, the American government agreed to battle all discriminatory practices against Japanese immigrants including the segregation of Japanese students in San Francisco. On its part, the Japanese agreed to no longer issue passports to laborers bound for the United States and U.S. territories such as Hawai'i and Alaska. Accordingly, the San Francisco school board rescinded its segregation order.

This Gentlemen's Agreement did not satisfy groups like the Asiatic Exclusion League. People opposed to the Japanese presence in the United States believed U.S. congressional action along the lines of the Chinese Exclusion Act would prove more permanent than an agreement between governments. The Gentlemen's Agreement did not prevent Japanese-born males living in the United States from sending for wives to join them. Nor did it stop Issei from migrating from Hawai'i or Alaska to the continental United States. Finally, little had been done to hamper the economic advancement of Japanese immigrants living in the United States.

Many Japanese women migrated to the United States as a result of the Picture Bride system. However, the anti-Japanese movement sought an end to this practice and some of the economic progress made by Japanese American farmers in California and elsewhere. The picture-bride system was used effectively during the early decades of the twentieth century. Ronald Takaki explains the picture-bride system accordingly:

> The picture-bride system...was based on the established custom of arranged marriage....Marriage in Japanese society was not an individual matter but rather a family concern, and parents utilized go-

betweens...to help them select partners for their daughters. In situations involving families located a far distance from each other, prospective bride and groom would often exchange photographs before the initial customary meeting.

While there were abuses, many of these marriages worked out and through the good and the bad Japanese Americans were better able to effectively forge a second generation on the American mainland than their Chinese American counterparts. The picture bride system, however, provoked hostility from many European Americans who believed that picture-bride marriages proved that the Japanese were "backward" and "unassimilable." Obviously, another reason that the picture bride system bothered European Americans was that it strengthened Japanese American communities. This was particularly the case on the mainland, where Japanese American labor was less needed than in Hawai'i. Indeed, the possibility of the Pacific Coast becoming another Hawai'i frightened many European Americans. The Japanese government, eventually, gave into the fears of white Americans and barred the emigration of picture brides in 1921.

Among the chief vehicles to attain the objectives of the anti-Japanese and anti-Asian Pacific movements were laws passed in various states called Alien Land Laws. In 1913, California's legislature, inspired by progressive Governor Hiram Johnson and undeterred by worried foreign policy makers in Washington, D.C., passed an Alien Land Act. This act did not mention Japanese or any other Asian Pacific people in its wording. It simply stipulated that "aliens ineligible for citizenship" would no longer be allowed to own farm land in California or lease farm land in the state for more than three years. What aliens in California were ineligible for citizenship in 1913 but Asian Pacific immigrants? To be fair to California, similar kinds of legislation were enacted in other states that possessed visible Asian populations.

This act did not accomplish what it set out to do as Japanese-born and other Asian Pacific born farmers in California found interesting ways to get around this legislation. For one thing, an Asian Pacific born farmer might switch ownership to an American born child. An Asian Pacific born farmer might form a corporation with other Asian Pacific born farmers; a corporation in which no single person held a majority stock. Finally, an Asian Pacific born farmer might find a sympathetic citizen or immigrant eligible for citizenship to assume ownership in name, designate that farmer as an employee, and turn over profits to that farmer.

These loopholes in the Alien Land Act angered anti-Japanese Californians. Taking advantage of the supposedly democratic electoral reforms set in motion by California progressives, anti-Japanese Californians supported a proposition to California voters in 1920 that restricted the ability of Asian Pacific born farmers to form corporations and designate children as landowners. This proposition won voter approval easily. Three years later, the California state legislature passed a bill making it difficult, but not impossible, for Asian Pacific born farmers to engage in agreements with citizens or immigrants eligible for citizenship—agreements which would allow the former to receive profits ordinarily going to land owners.

THE WALLS GROW HIGHER, 1916-1924

In the 1910s, the American political system was deeply concerned with immigrants, regardless of origins. Moreover, some politicians, then as now, cynically used immigration as a way to woo votes from native born Americans frightened by the influx of immigrants from Europe, Asia, Mexico, and South America. Political leaders such as progressive Republican Theodore Roosevelt and progressive Democrat Woodrow Wilson dispatched mixed signals on the issue of immigration and ethnicity; thus mirroring and reinforcing the confusion most Americans experienced when it came to immigrants. However, by the onset of World War I something of a consensus had been formed among native-born European Americans—that immigrants of color were "unassimilable." As for other groups such as Southern and Eastern European immigrants and native-born people of color, there was some debate over whether the "melting pot" existed for them and whether they were truly white or not.

In 1917, the US. Congress passed an immigration act that declared a "barred zone" in Asia. Sucheng Chan writes:

> An imaginary line was drawn from the Red to the Mediterranean, Aegean, and Black Seas, through the Caucasus Mountains and the Caspian Sea, along the Ural River, and then through the Ural Mountains. All people living in areas east of the line—which came to

be called the "Barred Zone—were denied entry from then on. Asian Indians were of course among those excluded.

This act was passed during World War I. Racist and nativist organizations such as the Ku Klux Klan grew in importance and political respectability during and after World War II. The Klan maintained a steadfast antagonism toward African Americans and other people of color. However, it also claimed opposition to non-Protestant immigrants and their offspring. The Klan, moreover, gained a substantial amount of respectability in towns and small cities in the Midwest, the South, and even in California. Belonging to the Klan for a store owner, a druggist, and a police officer was a great deal like belonging to the Kiwanis' or the Rotary Club. During the 1924 Democratic Party convention, a proposal condemning the Klan was narrowly defeated. And when the Klan fell off in membership it was not because its ideas had lost appeal but because its leadership had proven corrupt.

CITIZENSHIP AND THE CONSTRUCTION OF RACE

Earlier, we explored the phenomenon of race as a social construction. That this is the case becomes clear when we examine how the American legal-political system defined race in the twentieth century. What else becomes clear is that the American legal-political system has not been free of bias, but has intersected with prevailing racial ideologies.

For the first half of the twentieth century, eligibility for citizenship and race also interrelated. If an immigrant was legally defined as non-white and did not possess African ancestry, she or he was ineligible for citizenship. Thus, many immigrants and immigrant groups found themselves trying to litigate their way to citizenship rights. They found themselves, in short, trying to prove that they were white or that being non-white should not matter.

Some of these would-be citizens had reason for hopefulness. Legal scholar Ian F. Haney Lopez points out that coming up with a clear definition of whiteness was by no means easy in the early twentieth century. He writes:

> Applicants from Hawaii, China, Japan, Burma, and the Philippines, as well as all mixed-race applicants, failed in their arguments. On the other hand, courts

ruled that the applicants from Mexico and Armenia were "white," and on alternative occasions deemed petitioners from Syria, India, and Arabia to be either "white" or not "white." As a taxonomy of Whiteness, these cases are instructive because of the imprecision and contradiction they reveal in the establishment of racial divisions between Whites and non-Whites.

The courts, according to Haney Lopez, used two kinds of proof to justify their decisions. In the first place, they could resort to the science of the day. In the second, they could resist scientific scholarship and refer to "common knowledge." Sometimes, the courts used both scientific scholarship and common knowledge, which meant widely held views about race and racial divisions.

For several years after the Ah Yup and Saito cases, the courts seemed comfortable in using both "common knowledge" and science in rationalizing their decisions on whether an individual possessed the "racial prerequisite" for citizenship. "Common knowledge" and science generally seemed to correspond with one another. By 1909, Haney Lopez points out, "common knowledge" and science began to depart from one another. For example, leading anthropologists were identifying dark-skinned Asian Indians as Caucasians even though there was a huge population of white people who, especially in California, believed fervently that Asian Indians were non-whites. In the early 1920s, the U.S. Supreme Court attempted to resolve the problem in two cases. In doing so, it generally referred to "common knowledge." The first case, *United States v. Ozawa*, involved a Japanese immigrant seeking naturalization rights. The second case, *United States v. Thind*, involved an Asian Indian seeking naturalization rights.

Ozawa's case was fairly easy for the U.S. Supreme Court to handle. The existing scientific evidence pointed out that Japanese people were non-whites and most Americans believed a Japanese person was not a member of a group "popularly known as the Caucasian race." Accordingly, Ozawa was not white and, therefore, ineligible for citizenship. Bhagat Singh Thind's case posed a challenge to the court. Thind hoped that the court's decision in *Ozawa* meant that it equated being Caucasian with being white. If anthropologists believed that Asian Indians were Caucasian, then Thind should have had little trouble becoming eligible for citizenship.

Thind and his legal counsel, however, did not account fully for the power of racial ideology. The court in *Thind* reversed fields and

144

set aside any scientific arguments on Thind's behalf. The court even condemned some of these scientific arguments that included among Caucasians Asian Indians who ranged "in color...from brown to black." It complained "that the average well informed white American would learn with some degree of astonishment that the race to which he belongs is made up of such heterogeneous elements." That "well informed white American" would consider Asian Indians non-whites and therefore ineligible for citizenship.

In trying to resolve the question of "who is white?" American courts perpetuated the notion of race as an ideology. Whiteness or non-whiteness, it seemed, had little to do with objective criteria. Race was a matter of "common knowledge." Sadly, moreover, the court decided in *Thind* to retroactively deny Asian Indians their citizenship. This now meant that Asian Indians were like Chinese, Japanese, and Korean immigrants—"aliens ineligible for citizenship." This now meant as well that Asian Indian immigrants could no longer legally own farm land in California and other states with alien land laws.

NATIONAL ORIGINS ACT OF 1924

In Washington, D.C., politicians heeded and shaped negative public opinion toward immigrants. Immigrants from Southern and Eastern Europe were told they were unwelcome by the National Origins Act of 1924. This act established an immigration quota system based on the 1890 U.S. census. The number of immigrants from Nation A would be allowed entry into the United States equal to two percent of the number of Americans in 1890 born in Nation A. The choice of 1890 as the census year on which to base the quota system proved no accident. At that time, there were relatively few people living in the United States who were born in Southern and Eastern Europe. For prospective Asian immigrants, the National Origins Act of 1924 closed the door to the United States by denying entry to aliens ineligible for citizenship.

Interestingly, one of the groups worried about the anti-immigrant fervor in the United States was agribusiness in places like California and Hawai'i. Large-scale farmers and other businesses which relied upon immigrant labor were concerned that they would lose access to less expensive and, hopefully, more subservient workers. While many native-born European Americans did not like it, Congress authorized no quota for Mexican migrants. Moreover, Filipinos, because they lived in the U.S. Empire, were also free to migrate as U.S. nationals to the continental United States, as well as Alaska and Hawai'i.

The stereotypical image of "stoop labor" emerged to shape European American perceptions of Asian Pacific and Mexican agricultural workers. Only Filipinos or Mexicans, for example, were deemed fit to do the kind of hard, boring, and even dangerous work involved in agricultural labor. According to some arguments, the smallness of Asian Pacific and Mexican bodies put them lower to the ground and made them better pickers than white people. Other arguments went so far as to say that breathing in dirt did not bother Asian Pacific and Mexican workers as much as white workers. In other words, through agricultural labor, people were racialized—given natural characteristics which they did not necessarily harbor.

THE ANTI-FILIPINO MOVEMENT

The Great Depression, starting in the United States in the fall of 1929, eventually created tragic levels of unemployment. European Americans who never would have worked as fruit and vegetable pickers, maids, or dishwashers now claimed an interest in jobs that had been performed, in places like Los Angeles and San Jose, by Filipino or Mexican workers. The agitation against Mexican and Filipino residents often became hysterical in California during the early 1930s. Thus, many governmental officials in California and nationally expressed determination in the early 1930s to repatriate Mexican and Filipino residents.

Repatriation in this context often meant force rather than a reliance upon persuading Mexican or Filipino nationals to return voluntarily to Mexico and the Philippines. Ronald Takaki writes:

> In Santa Barbara, Mexicans were literally shipped out from the Southern Pacific depot....Many of the "repatriates" were children who had been born in the United States. The Los Angeles Chamber of Commerce estimated that 60 percent of the "repatriated" children were American citizens without very much hope of ever coming back into the United States.

Filipinos could not just be packed on trains and dispatched a relatively short way across the border. The places of their birth lay across the Pacific and they held a legal status that afforded them certain rights over other foreign born, but non-citizen, residents. The U.S. Congress, however, eventually came to the aid of those wishing to restrict Filipino immigration and repatriate those Filipinos living in America.

The animosity displayed toward Filipinos was not totally related to economics. When Japanese immigration was cut off, Filipinos were stereotyped by some European Americans as well suited to meet America's labor needs. Filipinos were described as a hard working "little" people, eager to please European Americans. When anti-Filipino sentiments became prominent in the late 1920s and early 1930s, Filipino immigrant males were stereotyped as violent and prone to gambling and substance abuse. Worst of all, they supposedly lusted after white women. To quote a European American businessman: "The Filipinos are hot little rabbits and many of these white women like them for this reason."

In late 1929, an anti-Filipino riot erupted in Watsonville, California. One Filipino was killed and anti-Filipino mayhem spread throughout the Golden State. The anti-Filipino hysteria grew so intense that the California Athletic Commission, which oversaw professional boxing and wrestling in the state, banned Pinoy boxers. The reason was that many Filipino boxers were quite good and quite expert at beating whites. Supposedly white fans would get angry at seeing one of their own brutalized by a non-white and instigate racial violence. Fortunately, cooler heads prevailed and the ban was lifted.

Filipinos, as well as Mexican, workers were not so eager to please those in political power. They organized trade unions and associated, sometimes quite actively, with radical left-wing politics. The Filipino Labor Union, moreover, initiated strikes in key agricultural areas of California, for example. To many of those involved in anti-Filipino politics, the whole argument for bringing Filipinos in to American shores was undercut by the fact that they seemed to think they had rights that demanded protection.

Salividor Roldan was one of these Filipino immigrants who believed he had rights that demanded protection. Filipino immigrants encountered similar problems as other Asian groups in developing families in the United States. They, too, were generally male and too poor to bring their spouses with them if they were married. They, too, expected to return to their native land or make enough money to bring spouses to the United States. They, too, were hemmed in by miscegenation laws which made it difficult for them to legally marry European Americans in the states in which they lived and worked.

There was, however, an interesting twist to the issue of miscegenation laws and Filipinos. Filipinos coming to California in the 1920s and early 1930s were not racially defined in a clear way. Thus, the miscegenation law which plainly restricted Asian-based groups perhaps did not affect Filipinos even though many European Americans considered Filipinos non-whites. In 1933, Roldan, a Filipino living in California, challenged the state's miscegenation law in court. He claimed that the law did not apply to Filipinos and he could marry his white fiancée. The California Court of Appeals agreed with Roldan, but perhaps not in the way that Roldan would have wished. The court defined Roldan racially as a Malay. Since California's miscegenation law did not apply to Malays, then Roldan was free to marry a white woman. The court, however, advised the state legislature to apply California's miscegenation law to Malays. The legislature was already debating the matter and soon it did, indeed, add the "Malay race" to the restricted category.

In 1934, the U.S. Congress passed the Tydings-McDuffie Act. Its message was ambiguous. In the first place, it warmed the hearts of many people who were uncomfortable with the fact that the United States retained colonies. It did so by guaranteeing the Philippines its independence in ten years. In the meantime, the Philippines would be granted a semi-autonomous commonwealth status within the American empire. By the same token, it substantially denied Filipinos further entry into the United States and cut off federal aid to Filipinos then living in the United States. Since the United States was still gripped by the Great Depression, many Filipino immigrants, as well as many other people living in the United States, could use federal aid. Filipino immigrants, accordingly, were advised by the U.S. government to go back to the Philippines. Sugar plantation owners in Hawai'i, however, were prmitted to recruit Filipinos if necessary.

ASIAN PACIFIC AMERICANS AND INSTITUTIONAL RACISM

As the United States headed into World War II, immigrants from places such as China, Japan, Korea, British colonial India, French colonial Indochina, which included Vietnam, Cambodia, and Laos, the Philippines, and the Pacific Islands were not allowed into America. Those that had gotten in before or despite the immigration bans were ineligible for U.S. citizenship. Moreover, such immigration bans had made it difficult for Asian Pacific immigrants to nurture a second generation, born in America, and eligible for citizenship. Thus, while American politicians might not always like the idea of European immigration, they had to recognize that European immigrants could become citizens and, more to the point, voters. Depending upon their class, gender, and religion, European immigrants and their children may not have been powerful members of the People's Club, but they were members. By and large, Asian immigrants and even their American-born children were constantly reminded that they did not belong.

While racial segregation proved most vicious in the South and when aimed at African Americans, Asian Pacific Americans could still feel "Jim Crow's" sting. The great Korean American Olympic diver, Sammy Lee, recalled that when living in Pasadena in the 1930s, he found it hard to practice at the local Brookside Pool. Only on one day a week could people of color swim in the pool—that day was called "International Day." And when it was over the pool's director was ordered by the city to drain the pool's water and provide its white clientele with clean water the next day. The pool director confided in Lee that he did no such thing—that it was too costly and time consuming to obey the city order. But the point is that Sammy Lee, as did many other Asian Pacific Americans in California, lived under the shadow of racial exclusion.

Asian Pacific Americans faced a series of racial barriers. They faced school segregation in San Francisco until the 1930s. They faced housing and employment discrimination. They could not marry a person possessing a different racial identity. If they were working class, it was worse. The right to organize trade unions, extended to factory workers by the New Deal, was not extended to domestic and agricultural workers. Social Security benefits were likewise denied domestic and agricultural workers. On the West Coast and Hawai'i, a significant number of domestic and agricultural workers possessed Asian Pacific ancestry.

THE HAWAIIAN ISLANDS

In 1920, Hawai'i possessed territorial status in the American empire. As such any of its residents born on the islands, even those born on the islands before Hawai'i was officially annexed by the United States in 1900, were American citizens, regardless of race or ethnicity. According to the U.S. census data in 1920, over sixty percent of Hawai'i's population possessed Asian ancestry. By contrast, only three percent of California's population possessed Asian ancestry. And less than one percent of the mainland's population possessed Asian ancestry.

For Asian Pacific Islanders, Hawai'i represented a different experience than did the mainland—not necessarily better in general but certainly different. A great deal depended upon class. If one was a sugar plantation worker, life was tough from the late 1800s up to World War II. And since recruitment as sugar plantation workers was the primary way Asians from China, Japan, Korea, and the Philippines got to Hawai'i, life was tough for a lot of Asian Hawaiians.

Racial and ethnic discrimination clearly existed on the islands even if it was not as consistently virulent as on the mainland. Chinese and Japanese immigration, while initially welcomed by haole plantation owners, aroused resentment from white and indigenous Hawaiians. While independent, Hawai'i sought to suspend immigration from China, for example. After the haole elite removed in 1893 the popular Hawaiian monarch, Queen Liliuokalani, and established an independent republic with the hope of eventual annexation by the United States, many poorer Native Hawaiians were disenfranchised. After Japanese immigrant workers engaged in a series of strikes in the early 1900s, U.S. military intelligence maintained closed surveillance on leading Hawaiian Japanese. And Filipino immigrant males, stigmatized as sexual predators much as African American males were in the south, faced violence and even lynching.

At the same time, the haole elite recognized that even if Asian Pacific immigrants were ineligible for citizenship no matter how long they lived in Hawai'i, their children born on the islands were not only citizens but prospective voters. Overt forms of racial discrimination were not widely favored by Hawaiian public officials.

There were, for example, no anti-miscegenation laws on the islands. Housing and schools were more segregated by class than by race and ethnicity. To be sure, Honolulu had a Chinatown but Chinese Hawaiians could live just about anywhere their income allowed them to live. Their neighbors might possess Japanese, Korean, Filipino, Portuguese, or Spanish ancestry. And while high school age Chinese San Franciscans rarely competed on the high school baseball or football team, secondary schools, public and private, typically had athletic teams featuring Asian Pacific Islanders of all sorts of backgrounds.

However, given the fact that Hawaii's population represented a small chunk of the American Empire's population. And given the fact that Hawai'i, until it became a state, had no impact on who would become the American President and who would serve in Congress, membership in the Hawaiian People's Club may not have been all that important. Nevertheless, because Hawai'i was more racially inclusive than the mainland when it came to Asian Pacific Islanders, it was not unusual to see Hawaiians of color running for and winning public office.

CONCLUSION

On the eve of America's entry into World War II, structural racism was the law of the land. Some bemoaned this situation and were willing to organize on behalf of making America truly more democratic. Others such as President Roosevelt hoped that racism and nativism would fade away as Americans come to their senses and denounce their bigoted political legacy. Others still slept soundly every night convinced that there was no contradiction between a land dedicated to freedom, democracy, and equality and the longstanding American refusal to extend freedom, democracy, and equality across racial and ethnic lines.

The irony of many Americans hailing their country as a generous melting pot struck many thoughtful Asian Pacific Americans. If immigrants, they knew they were fortunate to get into the United States before immigration laws grew harsher and enforcement more thorough. If American-born, they knew that their immigrant parents were not welcomed in the United States. For thousands, their faith in the progress of democracy in America would be severely tested in the coming years.

REVIEW

1. How did Reconstruction impact the People's Club after the Civil War?
2. What was the Fourteenth Amendment? Why has it been important?
3. How did anti-Asian politics get expressed in California after the Civil War?
4. What was the Burlingame Treaty and why was it important?
5. How did the recruitment of Chinese immigrant labor affect the anti-Asian movement?
6. What was the Page Law? Why was it important?
7. How did the labor movement in California and the U.S. impact anti-Chinese politics.
8. What was the Chinese Exclusion Act? Why was it important?
9. How did Asians in America express a sense of agency in the late 1800s?
10. Be able to discuss various court cases such as *in re Ah Yup, Tape v. Hurley, Yick Wo v. Hopkins, Wong Kim Ark v. U.S.,* and *in re Saito?*
11. Who were the Progressives and how did they respond to Asian Pacific immigration?
12. Why might California Progressives agitate against Asian Pacific immigration?
13. What was the Gentlemen's Agreement? Why was it important?
14. What was the Picture Bride system and how did it impact the anti-Asian movement in the United States?
15. What were the Alien Land Laws? Why were they important?
16. What was the "barred zone?" Why was it important?
17. What was the relationship between citizenship and race in the early 1900s?
18. Be able to discuss analytically *United States v. Ozawa* and *United Stats v. Thind.*
19. What was the National Origins Act of 1924 and why was it important?
20. Why and how did an anti-Filipino movement form in the late 1920s and early 1930s?
21. What was the Roldan case in California? Why was it important?
22. What was the Tydings-McDuffie Act and why was it important?

23. How did "Jim Crow" affect Asian Pacific Americans on the mainland?
24. In what ways were Asian Pacific Americans on Hawai'i facing less racial discrimination than on the mainland?

SELECTED BIBLIOGRAPHY

Almaguer, Tomas. *Racial Fault Lines.* (1994).

Chan, Sucheng. *Asian Americans.* (1991).

_____. *Asian Californians.* (1991).

Franks, Joel S. *Crossing Sidelines, Crossing Cultures.* (2000).

Hing, Bill Ong. *Making and Remaking Asian America Through Immigration Policy, 1850-1900.* (1993).

Ichioka, Yuji. *The Issei.* (1988).

Kent, Noel J. *Hawaii: Islands Under the Influence.* (1993).

Lopez, Ian Haney. *White By Law.* (1996).

Ng, Franklin. "Hawai'i and Native Hawaiians," in *New Visions in Asian American Studies: Diversity, Community, Power.* (1994).

Okihiro, Gary Y. *Cane Fires.* (1991).

_____. *Margins and Mainstreams.* (1994).

Ringer, Benjamin. *'We the People' and Others.* (1983).

Salyer, Lucy E. *Laws Harsh as Tigers.* (1995).

Takaki, Ronald. *Strangers from a Different Shore.* (1989).

_____. *A Different Mirror.* (1993).

Yamato, Alexander. *et. al. Asian Americans in the United States.* Vol. 2. (1993).

Yung, Judy. *Unbound Feet.* (1995).

Zia, Helen. *Asian American Dreams.* (2000).

VII
ASIAN PACIFIC AMERICANS AND THE "PEOPLE'S CLUB", 1941-2005

World War II and the Cold War dramatically changed the lives of thousands of Asian Pacific Americans, sometimes for the better and sometimes for the worse. But at the end of the Cold War, one could reasonably argue that more Americans of Asian Pacific Islander ancestry might seriously entertain the possibility that they were indeed members of the People's Club. How influential they were and how close to the exit sign they were standing would be another matter.

WORLD WAR II

In the United States, World War II united Americans perhaps as never before. Deep divisions remained, but for the first time in years there was a great deal of serious soul searching among Americans when it came to race. The enemy sincerely endorsed racism. According to Ronald Takaki, the Japanese government at this time seemed to believe in a "<r>acial ideology that was rooted in <Japanese> mythology and culture." The Japanese people, according to this view, belonged to the superior "Yamato race." "There are superior and inferior races in the world," declared Japanese political leader Chikuhei Nakajima in 1940, "and it is the sacred duty of the leading race to lead and enlighten the inferior ones." Pure-blooded and descended from the gods, he argued, the Japanese were "the sole superior race in the world."

The extent of the murderous racism practiced by Nazi Germany was not well known at the time. The death camps built by Nazis for millions of Jews, as well as gypsies, gays, and other so-called "undesirables" were often considered as rumors that Americans and others believed impossible or simply chose to ignore. But Americans knew that Hitler was enthusiastically racist in his attitude toward Jews, East Europeans, and people of color.

Thus, to Americans who believed it vital to fight the Axis powers it was hypocritical to condemn the enemy's racism and not do something about racial discrimination in the United States. Ignoring racism, moreover, was perceived as not helpful to the war effort. First, many American leaders believed that American unity had to transcend racial divisions if the war effort was to succeed. Second, many American leaders believed that racial divisions made the United States look bad and fed into enemy propaganda machines.

A major challenge to American racial policy came just before the United States entered the war officially. In the months before December 7, 1941, African American trade union leader. A. Philip Randolph, and other African American civil rights activists sought more just treatment of African Americans working in defense-related industries. Inspired by women African American activists, they organized a "March on Washington' in which thousands of African Americans were expected to protest job discrimination while marching in the heart of the nation's capital.

President Roosevelt was very unhappy at the prospect of thousands of African American protesters in Washington, D.C. Roosevelt, because of his desire to keep the support of white Southern Democrats, never really embraced the cause of civil rights for African Americans. Indeed, his eloquent and courageous wife Eleanor Roosevelt spoke out far more forthrightly against racial discrimination. Yet FDR believed that Randolph's proposed march would make the United States look bad to the world. Roosevelt, accordingly, issued Executive Order 8802, which banned racial and religious discrimination in federally funded workplaces such as war plants. EO 8802 also set up the Fair Employment Practices Committee, which sought to investigate discriminatory practices. Randolph and his colleagues, consequently, cancelled the march.

Racial discrimination persisted, of course. But one could argue that African Americans and other people of color experienced economic advancement during the war. The need for workers in defense-related industries lured many African Americans from the South to Detroit, Los Angeles, and Oakland. Mexican Americans also experienced some significant level of upward social and economic mobility.

ASIAN PACIFIC AMERICANS OF NON-JAPANESE ANCESTRY AND WORLD WAR II

Many Asian Pacific Americans made progress against institutional racial discrimination during World War II. The war inspired the federal government to allow Chinese immigrants to become citizens and granted a small quota to Chinese nationals wishing to come to the United States. While doing right by the Chinese was important it was more vital to win the war. By shielding Chinese Exclusion, America handed the Japanese government an excellent propaganda weapon. Thus the ending of Chinese Exclusion may have been a small and tainted victory, but it still knocked the foundations out of the Chinese exclusion laws. Moreover, Filipinos who served in the U.S. armed forces were rewarded by a thankful American government with naturalization rights.

At the same time, other groups were not so lucky during World War II. The U.S. Congress considered, but did not allow naturalization rights to Korean, Asian Indian, or the bulk of Filipino immigrants. Nor were immigration laws changed to permit Korean, Asian Indian, or Filipino nationals into the United States as immigrants. Korean Americans achieved a minuscule, but substantial victory, by getting the American government to recognize them as a category of people separate from the Japanese and Japanese Americans.

Asian Pacific American men and women were also afforded the opportunity to serve in the U.S. armed forces. Many wished to dearly take advantage of this opportunity. One reason why is that many considered themselves proud Americans. Second, many had learned from their elders a distaste for Japanese imperialism. This was especially the case for Korean and Chinese Americans, although after Japan invaded the Philippines, Filipino Americans were eager to join the armed struggle against Japan and its European allies.

There was some hostility toward the recruitment of Asian Pacific Americans into the U.S. armed forces by white military personnel. Initially, Filipino immigrants were not allowed into the U.S. armed forces. Writer Carlos Bulosan recalled going to a recruitment office and being turned down: "As I stood in line waiting for my turn, I thought of a one-legged American revolutionary patriot of whom I had read. But Filipinos were not being accepted."

In February, 1942, however, Franklin Roosevelt announced that the draft laws had been changed and Filipino immigrants were eligible to join the armed forces. An all-Filipino regiment was immediately established and quickly filled. Another regiment was organized and it too was filled. A commander of Filipino troops reported, 'Their enthusiasm and discipline are far superior to any I have seen in my army career."

Koreans and Chinese Americans also served and distinguished themselves in the armed services. Chinese American GIs served in integrated units. Of the 12,000 or more Chinese American GIs, over two hundred died. Chinese American women served as well as men. Maggie Gee served neither as a nurse nor a clerk. Inspired by the famous female flyer of the 1930s, Amelia Earhart, Gee joined the Women's Airforce Service Pilot Program. She wound up flying transport planes and testing damaged planes. Gee, who later became a physicist and political activist, returned to Berkeley "'with a lot more self-confidence."

JAPANESE AMERCAN EXPERIENCES

In terms of immediate benefits, World War II offered a mix bag of good and bad for most Asian Pacific ethnic groups in the United States. For Japanese Americans living on the West Coast of the U.S. mainland, World War II provided a great deal of humiliation, confusion, and disillusionment. To understand those experiences better, we might find it useful to follow the leads of historians Ronald Takaki and Gary Okihiro and compare what happened to Japanese Americans in Hawai'i, where Pearl Harbor is, and what happened to Japanese Americans in California, Washington, Oregon, and Arizona--states that were thousands of miles away from Pearl Harbor. We might also wonder about the experiences of German and Italian Americans.

When Pearl Harbor was attacked, the population of Japanese Hawaiians was about 158,000 or thirty-seven percent of the islands' population. In contrast, there were about 94,000 Japanese Californians or just one percent of California's total population. Gary Okihiro points out that Japanese Hawaiians were not experiencing paradise on the islands. An active anti-Japanese movement had existed in Hawai'i for years. The haole elite did not trust the Japanese population, especially community leaders involved with the Buddhist church, Japanese language schools, and trade unions. Too many Japanese Hawaiians, according to the haole elite, possessed ties to the Japanese government and represented threats to the prevailing economic hierarchy. Consequently, American military intelligence had been gathering information about Japanese Hawaiians for years before the attack on Pearl Harbor.

Nevertheless, Japanese Hawaiians were relatively well integrated into the islands' economy. They had become at least somewhat integrated into Hawaiian social, cultural, and political affairs. They were not isolated in ethnic enclaves, but, according to Takaki, Japanese Hawaiians "had become 'locals', members of the community in Hawaii." On the mainland, according to Takaki, Japanese Americans were "forced to remain 'strangers.'"

When Pearl Harbor was attacked, Washington D.C. expressed perhaps understandable concern about the loyalty of Japanese Hawaiians. Yet Navy Secretary Frank Knox went too far in insisting that Japanese Hawaiians committed widespread acts of sabotage in connection with the bombing. Statements such as Knox's aggravated anti-Japanese feelings on the islands and fueled wild rumors. One of these rumors, Takaki writes, was that "Japanese plantation laborers on Oahu had cut swaths in the sugar cane and pineapple fields to guide Japanese bombers to the military installation."

The military governor of Hawai'i, General Delos Emmons understood the situation better than officials in Washington, D.C., where people like Knox urged the internment of Japanese Hawaiians on December 19, 1941. To follow such a program would prove disastrous to Hawai'i, according to Emmons. As far as he was concerned, Japanese Hawaiians were vital to the islands' economy and defense. Even members of the haole elite were unwilling to see all Japanese Hawaiians interned.

It was more satisfactory to the islands' economic, political, and military leadership to disappoint Washington, D.C. Still, the U.S. interned on the mainland about 1,875 Japanese Hawaiians. Of those interned, more than half were Issei and the rest American citizens. These people were community leaders such as Buddhist priests or people suspected as "haole haters." Meanwhile, the rest of the Japanese Hawaiian population was allowed to generally remain in their homes and their jobs. They were, however, subject to constant surveillance and pressure. Japanese schools were closed down and many Japanese Hawaiians anglicized their names. A notable all-Japanese Hawaiian baseball team called the Asahis changed its name to the Athletics and took on non-

Japanese Hawaiian players from other ethnic groups. Furthermore, the military and employers hoped that the war would keep Japanese Hawaiian workers in line.

As long as Washington, D.C. questioned the loyalty of Japanese Americans, perhaps they were well advised to question the loyalty of the thousands of Americans of German and Italian ancestry living in the United States. One problem with this was that these people were numerous in number and dispersed throughout the continental United States and its territories. They were also citizens or, at least, eligible for citizenship.

Some German Americans and Italian Americans provoked government suspicions. Those who were openly sympathetic with Hitler or Mussolini were bound to catch the eye of the FBI. Indeed, right after December 7, 1941, the FBI chief, J. Edgar Hoover, announced plans to arrest about 857 German and 147 Italian nationals. Nevertheless, generally Americans of German or Italian ancestry did not have to worry about losing their homes and jobs. Americans of Japanese ancestry living on the Pacific Coast of the mainland United States did have to worry.

Upon the attack of Pearl Harbor, the FBI rounded up about 736 people of Japanese ancestry living on the Pacific Coast. These people were largely similar to the Japanese Hawaiians detained after December 7. That is, they were community leaders such as Buddhist or Shinto priests or priestesses as well as newspaper editors. They were arrested without the government specifying the grounds of their arrest. They were then, shipped off to detention centers run by the Immigration and Naturalization Service in New Mexico, Texas, Louisiana, Montana, and North Dakota.

Mas Yasui was one of these people. A long time leader of the Japanese American community in Hood River, Oregon, Yasui was arrested soon after the attack on Pearl Harbor. Later Yasui found out that one of the most important reasons why the American government incarcerated him for the duration of the war was that government agents discovered drawings of the Panama Canal in his home--drawings made by one of his children as a homework assignment.

Meanwhile, Washington, D.C. considered what it should do in regards to the general Japanese American population of the American West Coast. Worried that a mass evacuation might be unconstitutional, the U.S. attorney general sought the advice of legal experts outside of the Justice Department. These experts claimed that unlike German and Italian Americans, Japanese Americans represented a distinct threat. The reason was that "the

Occidental eye cannot rapidly distinguish one Japanese resident from another." Thus, the American government would have to evacuate the entire population of Japanese Americans on the West Coast.

General John L. DeWitt, who was commander of the Western Defense Command headquarters in San Francisco, urged that stringent measures be taken against West Coast Japanese Americans. As far as DeWitt was concerned "A Jap is a Jap....They are a dangerous element, whether loyal or not." Influential organizations on the West Coast such as the American Legion and groups of European American farmers such as the Grower-Shipper Vegetable Association and the California Farm Bureau Federation supported and pressured government officials like DeWitt to evacuate Japanese Americans. In the process, DeWitt and his command ignored government sponsored investigations, including one conducted by J. Edgar Hoover's FBI. Hoover, as a matter of fact, claimed that the evacuation of West Coast Japanese Americans was unjustified in terms of "military necessity." Japanese Americans appeared to Hoover as loyal as any other group in the United States.

The press joined the outcry against Japanese Americans. *Time* magazine's December 22 1941 issue explained to readers how they could tell the Japanese "enemies" from the Chinese "friends."

> HOW TO TELL YOUR FRIENDS FROM THE JAPS. Virtually all Japanese are short. Japanese are likely to be stockier and broader than short Chinese. Japanese are seldom fat; they often are dry and grow lean as they age. Although both have the typical epicanthic fold of the upper eyelid, Japanese eyes are usually set closer together. The Chinese expression is likely to be more placid, kindly, open; the Japanese more positive, dogmatic, arrogant. Japanese are hesitant, nervous in conversation, laugh loudly at the wrong time. Japanese walk stiffly erect, hard heeled. Chinese, more relaxed, have an easy gait, sometimes shuffle.

Getting called "arrogant" was fairly nice compared to what the *Los Angeles Times* said: "A viper is nonetheless a viper wherever the egg is hatched---so a Japanese American, born of Japanese parents--grows up to be a Japanese, not an American." And the *Saturday Evening Post* magazine published a statement by the Grower-Shipper Vegetable Association: "It's a question of whether the white man lives on the Pacific Coast or the brown man. They came...to work and they stayed to take over.... If all the Japs were removed tomorrow, we'd never miss them in two weeks, because the white farmers can take over and produce everything the Jap grows."

West Coast politicians got into the act. California Attorney General Earl Warren urged the federal government to remove Japanese Americans from militarily sensitive areas. He warned that Japanese Californians were "the Achilles heel of the entire civilian defense effort. Unless something is done it may bring about a repetition of Pearl Harbor."

Washington, D.C. did not need much convincing. A few members of FDR's cabinet remained a little worried about the constitutionality of mass Japanese American evacuation. For example, Attorney General Francisco Biddle simply believed that the military situation did not call for the massive evacuation of West Coast Japanese Americans. However, his boss leaned heavily on DeWitt's side of the argument.

On February 19, 1942, accordingly, Roosevelt issued Executive Order 9066, which enabled the Secretary of War to designate military areas "with respect to which the right of any person to enter, remain in, or leave shall be subject to whatever restrictions the Secretary of War or the appropriate Military commandant may impose in his discretion." Pacific Coast Japanese Americans were not mentioned, but clearly they were the executive order's targets. Once issued, the executive order empowered the Secretary of War, Henry Stimson, to designate the Pacific Coast as a war zone and General DeWitt to evacuate Japanese Americans from California, Washington, Oregon, parts of Arizona, and even the territory of Alaska.

First, however, the U.S. military imposed a curfew on West Coast Japanese Americans, now designated as "enemy aliens." The U.S. government also froze the assets of Japanese Americans on the Pacific Coast. Thus, they could not pay bills, mortgages, and rent. Then, on April 30, 1942, West Coast Japanese Americans were informed that they must prepare for evacuation by May 7. This meant that evacuees were to take as much as each could carry in a single suitcase. They had to sell or give away whatever other possessions they had--possessions such as cars and houses.

Once they left their homes, West Coast Japanese Americans were conveyed to local control centers. There, each was registered and each family was given a number. From the control centers, West Coast Japanese Americans were moved to assembly centers.

These assembly centers were generally stockyards, fairgrounds, or horse race tracks. One evacuee recalled, "Suddenly you realized that human beings were being put behind fences just like on the farm where we had horses and pigs in corrals." Soon, however, the evacuees were put on trains which transported them to concentration camps. These camps were placed in relatively isolated regions--Topaz in Utah, Apache in Colorado, Poston and Gila River in Arizona, Minidoka in Idaho, Manzanar and Tule Lake in California, Heart Mountain in Wyoming, and Jerome and Rohwer in Arkansas.

We should note that of the 120,000 or so people of Japanese ancestry forced in the concentration camps, approximately two-thirds were American citizens. The primary reason as stated by the federal government was military necessity. Yet, as Ronald Takaki points out, if military necessity was an appropriate explanation, then why were not thousands of Japanese Hawaiians evacuated? Considering the location of Pearl Harbor, it most certainly makes sense that Japanese Hawaiians would not be subject to government surveillance and pressure alone but would have been relocated in some isolated part of the American mainland. Thus, Ronald Takaki and other scholars doubt that military necessity played such a vital role in the internment of West Coast Japanese Americans. Takaki writes, "The situation was very different from Hawaii's. Economic interests in California did not need Japanese labor, and many white farmers viewed Japanese farmers as competitors. Representing a small, rather than numerically significant racial minority, the Japanese were more vulnerable to xenophobic attacks."

A good number of modern students wonder why Japanese Americans on the West Coast did not protest their evacuation and internment. Some scholars of the Japanese American experiences point out that people of Japanese ancestry tended to believe that there was no point in fighting what cannot be helped; that one must suffer injustice with dignity and patience. A more practical perspective is that massive resistance to internment would provoke even greater oppression and would reinforce in the minds of an already very jumpy and racist nation that Japanese Americans were disloyal. This essentially was the position of the Japanese American Citizens League, which believed that internment was wrong but that protest would only make a bad situation worse. In other words Japanese Americans should show their patriotism by going quietly to the camps. Yet Japanese Americans did protest. Some used the legal system to gain justice. Others used peaceful civil disobedience as a way to protest. And a few others still used more provocative, even violent, forms of protest.

Min Yasui was a lawyer and one of the sons of the previously mentioned Mas Yasui. After Pearl Harbor, Yasui tried to enlist in the army but was turned down several times. When curfew was imposed upon West Coast Japanese Americans, Yasui sought to test the constitutionality of this curfew by walking around the streets of Portland, Oregon, late at night. He, however, could not get arrested. So, he dropped in on the Portland police and demanded his arrest. Eventually, Yasui was arrested, charged, and convicted. The judge in the case agreed that the curfew order was unconstitutional if applied to U.S. citizens. But he maintained that Yasui had surrendered his citizenship when he went to work for the Japanese consulate before the war. Yasui appealed his case up to the US Supreme Court, which condemned the lower court for deciding that Yasui surrendered his American citizenship. However, the court agreed with the U.S government that because of the wartime circumstances it had a right to impose a curfew on Japanese Americans.

Gordon Hirabayashi was a University of Washington student and a pacifist. He took the curfew order and the evacuation order to court. He was convicted for refusing to obey both orders and was sentenced to serve concurrent terms. When his case reached the United States Supreme Court, it supported the constitutionality of the curfew law, but refused to decide on the constitutionality of the evacuation order given the fact that Hirabayashi had already served his sentence for curfew violation.

Fred Korematsu was a welder from San Leandro, California. He tried to enlist in the Navy after Pearl Harbor was attacked and then tried to stay in San Leandro after the evacuation order. Korematsu even changed his name and submitted to plastic surgery to remain with his non-Japanese American girl friend. He was eventually caught and arrested for violating the evacuation order. The U.S. Supreme Court subsequently upheld Korematsu's conviction.

Mitsuye Endo was a clerk for California's Department of Motor Vehicles before December 7, 1941. She was fired after Pearl Harbor was bombed and subsequently evacuated to Tule Lake. Endo challenged legally the right of the U.S. government to detain her. The U.S. Supreme Court agreed with Endo's complaint that the federal government could not detain loyal citizens--even during wartime. This was done in the fall of 1944 by which time a great deal of damage had already been done and the unconstitutionality of the evacuation order remained undecided.

In 1943, the federal government began to require that all internees answer loyalty questionnaires. Question 27 asked draft age male internees: "Are you willing to serve in the armed forces of the United States on combat duty, wherever ordered?" The next question asked all internees: "Will you swear unqualified allegiance to the United States of' America and faithfully defend the United States from any or all attack by foreign or domestic forces, and forswear any form of allegiance or obedience to the Japanese emperor, or any other foreign government, power or organization?"

About 22 percent of the Nisei male internees eligible for the draft answered with a no, qualified their answer, or refused to answer. Some became "no, no boys." That is, they answered no to both Questions 27 and 28. One explanation was that they refused to join the armed forces while their families lived behind barbed-wire fences. If the government thought they were good enough Americans to fight, then the government should have considered them and their families good enough Americans to stay out of concentration camps. Other "no, no boys" were willing to fight in the U.S. armed forces, but were insulted by Question 28. That is, they were Americans. Why would they have to foreswear allegiance to some other country?

The Issei were reluctant to answer yes to these questions as well. At least as Japanese nationals they possessed some kind of citizenship status even if affiliated with an enemy government. To foreswear loyalty to Japan meant that technically they were a people without a country since the United States did not allow Issei citizenship rights.

Many of the "no, no boys" wound up in the Tule Lake Camp, which generally housed people considered as troublemakers or potential troublemakers. At the Heart Mountain camp, a group of men organized a Fair Play Committee and declared that they would resist the draft as long as they and their families' rights remained unrespected. Some of the leaders of Heart Mountain's Fair Play Committee were sentenced to four years in the federal prison in Leavenworth, Kansas.

Collective protest flared in some concentration camps. At the Manzanar Camp, several hundred internees demonstrated against the arrest of presumed disloyal internees. Soldiers fired tear gas and bullets into the crowd. They killed two internees and wounded ten. Later some protesters took out their anger out on other internees by beating them up as suspected government informers.

To protest the internment seems understandable. Other Japanese Americans responded by doing whatever they could to prove their loyalty to the United States. This meant, in many cases, joining the armed forces. Indeed, about 25,000 Japanese Americans served in the military during World War II. Some served as translators. Many, however, engaged in active combat in the European theater of war.

Hawaiian Japanese composed the 100th Battalion, otherwise known as the "Rainbow Brigade." The 442nd Regimental Combat Team consisted of Japanese American mainlanders, generally recruited from the concentration camps. The Hawaiians and mainlanders trained together and merged into the 442nd in Italy. The 442nd time and again proved its valor as it became the most decorated unit of its size during the war. Nearly 18,000 served in the 442nd. Over half of these men were either wounded or killed—a sadly high casualty rate by any standards.

IMMIGRATION REFORM DURING AND AFTER WORLD WAR II

World War II marked a major turning point in America's racial history. The United States and its allies fought against countries whose governments were clearly inspired by racist doctrines. As mentioned previously, many Americans across racial and ethnic divisions were convinced that if they were going to fight against racist governments in Germany, Italy, and Japan, then they must also fight against racist legal and political institutions in the United States. Hawaiians of different racial and ethnic backgrounds shared this belief. Many Japanese Hawaiians fought bravely in World War II. Daniel Inouye was a Japanese Hawaiian who lost an arm in combat. People like Inouye were not going to return home and remain second-class citizens or worse. They allied with multi-racial and multi-ethnic trade unions and got involved in local and territorial politics largely through the Democratic Party. They helped shift political power from a haole dominated Republican Party to a multi-racial and multi-ethnic Democratic Party.

While World War II and the subsequent Cold War inspired the worst in American society, they also inspired the best in American society. The struggles for liberalized immigration reform and racial justice became more powerful than ever. During World War II and its immediate aftermath, we can see some of these struggles bearing fruit. For example, in 1943, the Chinese Exclusion Act was eliminated. In 1945, the U.S. Congress passed the War Brides Act, which permitted American war veterans to bring home wives from China and the Philippines. In 1946, Koreans, Southern Asians, and Filipinos were allowed to come into the United States in small numbers and were granted naturalization rights. Admittedly, this all may seem very limited. But the door was opened a bit to further immigration reform and the eventual overturning of the Naturalization Law of 1790. Asian American Studies scholar Tim Fung has written that the liberalization of Asian immigration:

> resulted in a rapid and dramatic shift in the historic gender imbalance of <Chinese and Filipino> groups. For example, between 1945 and 1952, nine out of ten (89.9 percent) Chinese immigrants were female, and 20,000 Chinese American babies were born by the mid-1950s. Similarly, between 1951 and 1960 seven out of ten (71 percent) Filipino immigrants were female.

As of 1950, the one Asian group that was left out of these reforms was the Japanese. The World War II struggle against Japan retarded immigration reform for the Japanese. However, by the early 1950s, the international scene had changed. Japan was considered an ally of the United States in its struggle against communism and immigration reform for Japanese people was in the wind.

In 1952, the U.S. Congress passed the McCarran-Walter Act. This act permitted Japanese immigrants to become American citizens and allowed more Japanese to migrate to America. Accordingly, race was no longer considered a legal bar either to citizenship or entrance into the U.S. Nevertheless, the quota for immigrants from Asian countries remained only one hundred people a year.

The McCarran-Walter Act and all of the previous acts that liberalized immigration and naturalization policies from Asian countries were not just the consequences of the U.S. government becoming generous or concerned about winning propaganda wars against Nazis and then Communists. Asian Pacific American groups pushed hard and long for these changes. The Japanese American Citizens League considered the McCarran-Walter Act a vital victory.

THE CIVIL RIGHTS STRUGGLE AND POLITICAL CHANGE

Americans of diverse racial and ethnic backgrounds struggled for racial justice long before World War II. However, the post-World War II years witnessed powerful and relatively effective campaigns to eliminate institutionalized racism in the United States. We should keep in mind that in 1900, the U.S. government and most state and local governments had given their blessings to the racial segregation of public facilities. Through World War II many Asian Pacific Americans and other people of color had to deal with racially segregated schools, housing, and recreational facilities.

While generally considered a white vs. black struggle it is important to note that other people of color, including Asian Pacific Americans, had long been fighting for inclusion in the People's Club. What else could Wong Kim Ark have been but a late nineteenth century civil rights activist? Moreover, the victories achieved by civil rights activists did not just benefit African Americans, but other people who had faced historical discrimination based on race, ethnicity, and sex.

IMMIGRATION REFORM

Both the Civil Rights movement and the Cold War inspired immigration reform in the 1960s. As the Civil Rights movement called upon America to end racial discrimination, it did not seem fair to many Americans that immigration practices remained discriminatory. President John F. Kennedy reminded Americans that they lived in a "nation of immigrants" and that immigration exclusion based upon national origins was both un-American and bad international politics. Kennedy and other immigration reformers were ever mindful that if the United States was going to win Asians to the American side of the Cold War, it could not afford to keep them from coming to the U.S. simply because they were Asians. Immigration reformers were also mindful that liberalization of immigration laws could conceivably strengthen the

United States by allowing into the country hard working, creative, and skilled people.

While the Kennedy administration helped initiate immigration reform, Lyndon B. Johnson signed the Immigration and Nationality Act in 1965. This act intended to abolish the restrictive national origins quotas of 1924. There were two primary requirements to gain legal admission into the United States. First, one should have an occupation that was needed in America. Second, one should have family members already in the United States. The people who wrote and supported this bill generally expected its passage would boost European immigration. However, it actually significantly increased immigration from Latin American and Asian Pacific countries. For example, from 1961-1970, 33.8% of America's legal immigrants came from Europe, 12.9% from Asia, and 38.6% from Latin America. From 1971-1980, 17.8% of America's legal immigrants came from Europe, 35.3% from Asia, and 40.3% from Latin America.

In the mid-1970s, the American economy soured and its anti-immigrant politics became more visible. In 1976, the U.S. Congress enacted a bill that restricted the number of professionals and other workers from coming into the United States. Another bill, the Health Professions Educational Assistance Act, also restricted immigration by making it more difficult for non-English speakers to enter the health professions. Sucheng Chang writes, "Since Asians comprised a large percentage of the health professionals admitted before 1977, this law has curtailed their chances of getting an immigrant visa on the basis of their professional training."

While this was going on, however, a substantial number of refugees from Southeast Asia were allowed to enter the United States. As South Vietnam was conquered by communism early in 1975, President Gerald Ford authorized the admission of 130,000 Vietnamese refugees. In order to help pay for the resettlement of these refugees in American communities, the U.S. Congress passed the Indochina Migration and Refugee Assistance Act in 1975. To deal with the second wave of refugees from Southeast Asia, the U.S. Congress passed the 1980 Refugee Act. In both the 1975 and 1980 acts, the American government assumed much of the financial burden of admitting and resettling thousands of refugees. The various states, however, supplied much of the bureaucracy overseeing resettlement.

The 1980s witnessed continued controversy over U.S. immigration and refugee policies. In the Congress, Republican

Senator Alan Simpson and Democratic House member Romano Mazzoli, led an attack on illegal immigration. They were significantly backed by Ronald Reagan who claimed that the United States needed to take greater control of its borders.

Both Latin American and Asian Pacific American civil rights groups expressed concern. In particular, Mexican American activists worried that laws aimed at "illegals" would wind up penalizing legal immigrants and U.S. citizens of Mexican ancestry. Based upon past history, their concerns were understandable. Moreover, they argued, illegal immigrants were not really criminals but hard working people who looked to America to fulfill their hopes. In fairness, they maintained, employers who knowingly hired illegal immigrants should also face legal penalties. Indeed, agribusinesses in the Southwest worried that Congress would cut them off from their largely Mexican immigrant work forces. Yet while much of the focus on illegal immigration was cast on Latin Americans, Asian "illegals" were scarcely non-existent.

In 1986, the U.S. Congress passed the Immigration Reform and Control Act (IRCA). It called for stricter controls over American borders. IRCA also imposed criminal and civil penalties on employers who knowingly hired illegal immigrants. It permitted a temporary residency status to illegal immigrants who had been in the United States since before 1982 and also provided for a temporary worker program to make agribusiness interests happy.

By the early 1990s, it became increasingly apparent that illegal immigration had become a hot political issue. The continued stagnation of the American economy also helped keep the issue of illegal immigration alive and well, as did the fact that in the public's mind the illegal immigrant was inevitably a person of color. In California, concerns about illegal immigrants led to the writing of Proposition 187, which was placed on the November, 1994, ballot.

Proposition 187's backers hoped that its passage would deny state services to illegal immigrants and their children. Such services included health care and education. A key backer of the proposition was California Republican Governor Pete Wilson, who had formerly achieved a reputation as a relative liberal when it came to immigration policies. Accordingly, many critics of the act claimed that Wilson was less concerned about illegal immigration than reviving his wavering political popularity in the Golden State and boosting his dim prospects as a Republican candidate for President.

California voters supported Proposition 187 by a wide margin. Opponents, however, took the proposition's constitutionality to court and key court decisions generally favored the proposition's opponents. One constitutional problem, for example, was Proposition 187's denial of state financed public services to children of illegal immigrants. If these children were born in the United States, then they were American citizens. On this matter, the Fourteenth Amendment to the U.S. Constitution seems clear. All U.S. citizens have the right to equal protection under the law. If the children of U.S. citizens are eligible for state financed public services, then the American born children of illegal immigrants are also eligible. The one way people who believe in the objectives of Proposition 187 can deal with court challenges was to propose an appropriate constitutional amendment. Republican House members tried, without much success, to gain support for such an amendment in the late 1990s, but they have persisted into the early 2000s.

The generally good economic times of the late 1990s largely stilled the calls for immigration restriction, but those calls were revived after September 11, 2001. Although immigrants of Middle Eastern ancestry were mostly targeted, immigrants from other parts of the world faced the pressure as well. After the attack on the Twin Towers and the Pentagon, Congress enacted the USA Patriot Act, which broadened the American government's law enforcement agencies' powers to conduct searches, engage in surveillance, and detain suspected terrorists. Critics feared that such powers were too extensive and would lead to oppressive measures towards people of Middle Eastern ancestry and wrongly perceived Middle Eastern ancestry, especially people of Pakastani and East Indian backgrounds.

By 2005, many Americans, generally led by conservative voices, called for stricter control of the American border. The fear of illegal immigration had not quite reached fever pitch, but certainly it was coming close as private citizens organized into vigilante border patrols in the southwest. Illegal immigrants, some conservative commentators claimed, were criminals, however hard working and self-sacrificing. Moreover, they harbored in their midst drug pushers and worse, international terrorists.

On the other side, a significant number of Americans declare that immigrants have not caused America's problems and that to the extent that they have been hard working, law-abiding, and socially responsible, they have helped keep those problems from getting worse. Even illegal immigrants require respect, some declare, because such immigrants come to the United States to do work that no one else wants to do. In the process, they pay taxes without getting nearly the benefits from those taxes that American citizens or legal U.S. residents get. Moreover, according to these Americans, the attack upon illegal immigrants is a waste of money and time. If people want to come into the U.S. badly enough they will. The money spent on border guards and INS sweeps could better be used on hiring more police officers, fire fighters, and teachers.

What complicates this debate is that good people of culturally diverse backgrounds and even political perspectives have lined up on different sides. In the wake of 9/11, what makes this debate truly explosive is that most recent immigrants, legal or illegal, are usually defined as non-white, non-European and in many cases non-Christian. Thus, the issue of race, ethnicity and religion has taken front and center stage when it comes to the issue of immigration.

POLITICS OF ENGLISH ONLY

Clearly, resentment against immigrants has not just been directed at "illegals." The presence of significant numbers of legal immigrants has also provoked widespread concern among native born Americans. One outburst of this concern has been the English Only movement. In 1983, an organization called U.S. English was formed by a Michigan ophthalmologist named John Tanton and California's Republican senator of Japanese ancestry, S I. Hayakawa. The impetus behind this organization's ability to attract national support was the belief entertained by many Americans that bilingual education and multiculturalism were ruinous to American society. A common culture, undergirded by a common language--English--was U.S. English's overall demand. In particular, however, it called for amendments to the U.S. and various state constitutions that would make English the official language of the United States. U.S. English also sought to eliminate multilingual election ballots and restrict bilingual education. While many supporters expressed no hostility toward liberal legal immigration policies, Tanton himself believed in restricting legal immigration to the U.S.

Since 1983, U.S. English has spawned Official English movements wherever a large population of immigrants lived. According to sociologist John Horton, the leaders of Official English movements have had anti-immigrant tendencies: "In unraveling the politics of Official English, we need to separate national and local leaders from their supporters. The leaders were clearly xenophobic. Their message was about unity, but the subtext implied the need to control the immigrant masses of Latino and Asian newcomers who wanted to keep their own cultures and would not learn English."

In places like Monterey Park, California in the 1980s, the English Only movement stirred delight and anger. Situated near Los Angeles, Monterey Park became a multiracial, multiethnic city, possessing a significant number of immigrants, primarily of Chinese background by the late twentieth century. In 1960, for example, over 85% of Monterey Park's population consisted of people of European American ancestry. In 1990, 11.7% of Monterey Park's population consisted of people of European American ancestry. Latinos comprised 31% of Monterey Park's population, while about 56% were Asians.

This is a substantial demographic change in a relatively short period of time. Looking at it from the perspective of Monterey Park's long time native-born residents, not all of whom were white, this change could simultaneously be exciting and frustrating. Many of the immigrants helped energize Monterey Park economically. On the other hand, native-born European Americans, Mexican Americans, and Japanese Americans noted the disappearance of favorite stores and restaurants that were replaced by mini-malls with signs in languages they did not understand.

The Official English movement tapped into this frustration and fear that immigrants were taking over. In Monterey Park, a serious campaign was undertaken to make English the city's official language. The effort was defeated, but many people inside and outside of Monterey Park agreed with the sentiments expressed by one of the campaign's leaders: "We have no handle on the destiny of America....<T>here's no stopping the Asians for one. There's no stopping the Latinos for another....We cannot close the gates, because once we've allowed half of Taiwan to empty onto our shores and a good third of Mexico and Central America, are we going to say no to the continent of Africa or the Russians?"

In the 1990s, the politics of English only became a theme in Presidential politics. In the 1996 campaign Republican candidates Robert Dole and Pat Buchanan supported efforts to make English the official language of the United States. They both, moreover, passionately rejected the need for bilingual education. They argued that a command of the English language should become vital to those wishing to participate as citizens and voters in the United States. Unity not diversity should, therefore, be America's goal.

Chicano artist Guillermo Gomez-Pena argued, on the other hand, that the changes feared by many Americans need not lead to hostile and permanent divisions within American society. He argued that such changes could lead to greater democratic participation in American society. For people like Dole and Buchanan, there seemed to be only one way to become a "full citizen" of the United States. For people like Gomez-Pena, there were a "multiplication of...criteria" for people to get "validated...as full citizens."

Nevertheless, the debate over bilingualism and English Only continues into the twentieth-first century. In 1998, opponents of bilingual education won a great victory in California when a ballot measure seeking to eliminate bilingual education in the state's public garnered voter approval. Six years later, supporters and opponents of that ballot measure still dispute the consequences of its victory.

POLITICS OF AFFIRMATIVE ACTION

As the United States headed into the twenty-first century, there were few hotter political potatoes than affirmative action. One major problem was that many Americans simply did not agree upon a single definition of affirmative action nor did many understand the origins and historical development of affirmative action programs. As we passed into the twenty-first century American ignorance on affirmative action continued to burgeon.

We can find the legal foundation of affirmative action in the Civil Rights Law of 1964. Title VII of that law banned discrimination based on race, creed, color, national origins, and sex. It also established the Equal Employment Opportunity Commission (EEOC) to investigate complaints and ask the U.S. Department of Justice to prosecute violators. As a way of supplementing Title VII, President Johnson issued Executive Order 11246, which mandated that employers, labor unions, colleges and universities had to create affirmative action plans to show how they would correct the under representation of people of color and women in their institutions.

Given the Republican Party's general animosity toward affirmative action today, we should note that the issue of quotas came up during the Republican Nixon administration. At that time, the Nixon administration created the "Philadelphia Plan," which stipulated that contractors doing business with the federal government establish numerical goals to inspire the relatively quick hiring of people of color. These numerical goals became known as "racial quotas." One example of the way this would work was that the state of Alabama in the early 1970s was required to hire one black state trooper for each white hired. Alabama would have to continue to do this until African Americans comprised one-fourth of the entire force.

In the 1970s, a number of individuals challenged the constitutionality of affirmative action programs. These challenges argued that affirmative action programs discriminated against innocent whites, who were made to suffer for past, unjust policies. In other words, these challenges condemned affirmative action programs for practicing "reverse discrimination."

One of the most important legal challenges was *Allan Bakke v. Regents of the University of California* (1978). Bakke had been denied entrance to the University of California, Davis's medical school. Bakke complained that he had been discriminated against because of his white skin. The university had set aside sixteen of the one hundred available slots for "economically and/or educationally disadvantaged persons." In other words, according to Bakke, sixteen slots had been set aside for people of color. The university defended its practices by saying that it had merely sought to increase the number of students from underrepresented groups.

The U.S. Supreme Court ruled in Bakke's favor. However, it hedged in denouncing affirmative action programs as completely unconstitutional. The court stated that such factors as race and ethnicity could be considered in determining a university's admission policies. Clearly, however, the court declared that race and ethnicity could not be the sole factors in determining admission or hiring policies. In 1979, the U.S. Supreme Court ruled in *Weber v. Kaiser Aluminum* and *Chemical Corporation* that voluntary goals and timetables for hiring people of color were constitutionally acceptable.

With the emergence of the Reagan years, attacks upon affirmative action became fiercer. And even though contemporary conservatives were able to get sympathetic justices appointed to state and federal court systems, affirmative action programs remained constitutional into the 1990s and beyond. Of course, there was and remains a relationship between the legal and political attacks on affirmative action. Republicans made affirmative action an important political issue in many parts of the

United States during the 1990s. In California, Governor Pete Wilson actively campaigned against the University of California using affirmative action as a component of its admission policies. Consequently, the university's board of regents voted to end affirmative action admission policies. Wilson also supported the anti-affirmative action California Civil Rights Initiative on which Californians voted in November, 1996. Winning easily, this initiative banned state funded institutions from using race, ethnicity, and sex as factors in determining recruitment practices.

Democrats have generally shied away from enthusiastic support for affirmative action programs. One major reason has been that voters in places like California oppose, in particular, racial quotas in hiring and school admission policies. President Bill Clinton seemed to represent the prevailing attitude toward affirmative action by Democratic Party leaders. Clinton claimed that affirmative action programs needed to be investigated and potentially reformed. They did not, however, require complete dismantling.

Not all Republicans, moreover, agreed that affirmative action was a good issue to stress. Leaders such as House Speaker, Newt Gingrich, and the then Texan governor, George W. Bush, might have opposed affirmative actions programs. However, they believed that by harping on the evils of affirmative action programs, Republicans would lose the support of people of color, women, and white male moderates, who considered high taxes a bigger problem than affirmative action programs. Indeed, the relatively poor showing of Republicans in California since 1996 indicates that voters in that key state believed that the party had become too actively hostile to immigrants, people of color, and women. And the fact that now President Bush has not put opposition to affirmative action center stage in his victorious election campaigns suggest that Republicans do not need to attack affirmative action to win.

The people who oppose affirmative action programs generally argue that merit should reign as the sole consideration in employment and school admission policies. They believe that affirmative action programs have meant that lesser qualified people have been hired or admitted simply because they were black or women. The more qualified have, in such cases, been punished simply because they were European American and male. Of course, most opponents agree, past injustices have been done to people of color and women. But it remains unjust and unconstitutional to punish the innocent for the sins of others and dead others at that.

Some critics such as Nathan Glazer and Shelby Steele have argued that affirmative action actually counters the spirit of the Civil Rights movement. The Civil Rights Movement, they declare, sought a truly color blind society. Martin Luther King, Jr., in his famous March on Washington speech is often quoted as saying that people want to be judged by the "content of their character" and not by their skin color. To use race as a consideration in hiring or school admissions would defy the struggle for a colorblind America.

Another argument is that affirmative action programs are costly and promote unnecessary bureaucratic burdens on businesses and schools. Glazer maintained that government has gone about as far as it can go in eliminating institutional racism. Now, the argument continues, it is up to individuals to personally learn to live with one another.

A fourth argument is that affirmative action winds up hurting the crusade against racial and gender discrimination more than helping it. In the first place, affirmative action stigmatizes those who get jobs and admission to schools under its auspices. They and their colleagues or, classmates, will always wonder if they were qualified enough to earn their way into those good jobs or good universities without the help of affirmative action programs. In the second place, affirmative action breeds hostility from otherwise decent and generous white males. It, therefore, promotes racial and sexual bigotry. Finally, it punishes highly qualified Asian Pacific Americans with straight A's and high SAT scores—Asian Pacific Americans that would otherwise substantially fill first year classes from the University of California, Berkeley, to Harvard.

A final, qualified argument comes from scholars such as William J. Wilson. Wilson has maintained that affirmative action has benefited middle class people of color. The real problem however, is the group Wilson and others have identified as the "underclass." Largely because of changes in capitalist development, according to Wilson, the people in this group are disproportionately non-white and generally incapable of finding meaningful work that will push them and their families above the poverty line. Thus, Wilson believes that affirmative action programs divert funding, time and, indeed, society's attention from eliminating this permanent underclass.

Proponents of affirmative action have argued that it can improve the quality of a workforce or a student body. Of course, they point out, if one assesses quality in terms of standardized examinations and grade point averages, then a good many people of color and women will not get the best jobs and get into the best universities. Yet should standardized examinations and grade point averages be the predominant way we assess who is qualified in American society? Many thoughtful experts point out that standardized examinations possess cultural biases. As for grade point averages, we all know that a B in one school might be an A in another. Thus, these proponents argue we should remember that there never has been nor ever will be a fool proof, scientific way to determine merit. People have been hired or admitted to schools for all sorts of subjective reasons in the past. She dresses neatly. He likes golf. Her mother gives lots of money to the school. He's going to be an All American basketball player. Thus, what is so wrong about a boss or a university board saying "We need more women and people of color around here? We need to get the perspectives of diverse groups of people so we can grow as a place of work or as a place of learning."

Most proponents of affirmative action try not to dismiss the frustration of Americans who might feel themselves frozen out of their dreams by affirmative action. However, like Ronald Takaki, they do not believe that racism or sexism has been significantly eliminated. They often, moreover, propose that instead of fighting over crumbs women and men of different racial and ethnic groups should work harder and work together for a society that creates more meaningful jobs and more good schools and universities.

Supporters of affirmative action frequently argue that such programs are neither unconstitutional nor go against the spirit of the Civil Rights Movement. They maintain that the Fourteenth amendment to the Constitution guarantees "equal protection" under the law for all persons living in the United States. Given that racism and sexism remain prevalent, proponents declare, affirmative action programs also remain necessary.

Proponents of affirmative action programs often tend to wonder why people like conservative Republicans agree with Glazer and Steele. Conservative Republicans did not generally support the Civil Rights movement in the first place and now they curiously embrace the Civil Rights movement as a way of fighting affirmative action programs. In any event, affirmative action supporters answer people like Glazer and Steele, that affirmative action programs have been moved by the same objective that sustained the Civil Rights movement--to end inequality. By attempting to make sure qualified people of color and women can get good jobs and quality education affirmative action programs fight racial and gender inequality in the spirit of Martin Luther King and Rosa Parks.

As mentioned earlier, affirmative action supporters such as Ronald Takaki insist that institutionalized discrimination against people of color is not a thing of the past--that being white and a male still gives one privileges unavailable to other Americans. In any event, the consequences of historical racial and sexual discrimination have not disappeared. Supporters of affirmative action, accordingly, agree with the argument made by economist Lester Thurow who has written that outlawing discrimination is only a first step in any society that truly values equality. It would be like removing handicaps from some runners in a race without beginning the race over with everyone starting from scratch and without their handicaps. That is, those runners who started the race without any handicaps would still lead the race.

Affirmative action supporters deny the importance of the "stigma" criticism. They generally argue that affirmative action programs do not benefit unqualified people, but qualified people who at an earlier time would have been systematically denied opportunities because of their race or sex. The people who get jobs and into schools because of affirmative action programs might well understand that they are stigmatized in the eyes of some Americans and, in particular, European American males. But they also understand that they have been stigmatized historically because of their race and sex and that one of the best ways to fight that stigma is to take advantage of the opportunities provided them by affirmative action programs. European Americans, writes Richard Delgado have been "beneficiaries of history's largest affirmative action program." And if the kinds of people who have benefited from racial and sexual discrimination in the past feel insulted and become more bigoted, people of color and women should not have to suffer for the character flaws of too many white men.

As for Wilson's argument that economic changes and not race cause the most problems for people of color, proponents of affirmative action frequently charge that Wilson needs to pay attention to the continued importance of race in American life. The fate of the middle class and poor people of color cannot be separated. For example, Omi and Winant claim in terms of African Americans: "Government workers, educators, and other tertiary sector worker...may have achieved middle-class status and incomes, but their employment relates directly to the management, marketing, and servicing of the black community as a whole."

OPPOSITION TO AFFIRMATIVE ACTION FROM THE LEFT

Richard Delgado is a legal scholar, who in the late 1990s agreed with affirmative action proponents that racism remained an important problem in American fife. However, he took a very interesting, critical stance toward affirmative action programs. Delgado argued, in the first place, that affirmative action programs represented little threat to the prevailing racial and sexual hierarchy in the United States. He wrote that affirmative action "assur<ed> that only a small number of women and people of color are hired or promoted. Not too many, for that would be terrifying, not too few, for that would be destabilizing. Just the right number, generally those of us who need it least, are moved ahead."

One of the major problems with affirmative action programs, according to Delgado, has been the "role model argument." We did not explore this argument previously, but, according to Delgado, a number of affirmative action supporters considered it "unassailable." It proposed that one of the great things about affirmative action is that it promotes and illuminates individual role models for young people of color and women. As a person of color Delgado did not want to be an affirmative action "cover boy."

> A white-dominated institution hires you not because you are entitled to or deserve the job. Nor is the institution seeking to set things straight because your ancestors and others of your heritage were systematically excluded from such jobs. Not at all. You're hired if you speak politely, have a neat haircut, and, above all, can be trusted not because of your accomplishments, but because of what others think you will do for them. If they hire you now, and you are a role model, things will be better in the next generation.

Delgado's words are tough. We may not find them agreeable. However, he helps to remind us that affirmative action may be even more complicated and controversial than many of us think.

THE MODEL MINORITY THESIS

Asian Pacific Americans have been linked to these often heated debates concerning poverty, immigration laws, and affirmative action. In other words, they have been linked to the debates as to who truly belongs in the ranks of the People. One of the most important connections between Asian Pacific Americans and American social policy is the model minority thesis. The model minority thesis surfaced around 1965. The timing was no coincidence. Since the mid-1950s, the Civil Rights Movement had tried to eliminate institutional racial discrimination in the United States. By the mid-1960s, more and more African American activists had become convinced that only a radical transformation of American society would empower black people. Eloquent black nationalists emerged in greater numbers to call on African Americans to create a separate black nation within the American nation. Influential groups such as the Black Panthers blended a severe critique of white racism and capitalism to come to roughly the conclusion that African Americans could not achieve justice as long as European Americans possessed such immense power over Black lives. Martin Luther King, while remaining loyal to non-violence and racial integration, was developing something of a socialist analysis of the American capitalist system. Moreover, by the late 1960s, Latino/as and American Indians also called for militant political action and radical transformations of American society.

All of this was quite troubling to those Americans, who declared little sympathy for racism but believed that there was nothing inherently unjust about America's political and economic institutions. Consequently, these people found a great deal of comfort in the model minority thesis, which essentially has argued that Asian Pacific Americans, even though faced with significant racial prejudice, have overcome all barriers and have made it in American society. They have been welcomed into the ranks of the People. Asian Pacific Americans have succeeded, according to the thesis, because they have valued individual initiative, hard work, and education. They have not complained about mistreatment from whites. They have not cried out for welfare. They have not needed affirmative action programs. They have not needed assistance in finding jobs or passing math classes. They have, instead, quietly pulled themselves up by their own bootstraps. And since Asian Pacific Americans have succeeded without resorting to militancy, the thesis has pointed out, then African Americans, Mexican Americans, Puerto Rican Americans, and American Indians can and ought to do the same. In short, American political and economic institutions have become colorblind. If certain groups or individuals do not rise up the socio-economic ladder in America and if they do not achieve political equality, they have only themselves to blame.

Scholars such as William Peterson and Thomas Sowell have supported the model minority thesis. Journalist Charles Murray has elegantly backed the thesis as well. Among politicians, former President Ronald Reagan enthusiastically cheered the notion of Asian Pacific Americans as a model minority.

Many Asian Pacific Americans have also considered themselves members of a model minority group. This is quite understandable. People find it gratifying to hear that they belong to a racial and/or ethnic group that rates high marks from popular presidents and notable scholars and intellectuals. They want to know that the hardships they endured and the sacrifices made by their ancestors and themselves have not been in vain.

Nevertheless, a number of Asian Pacific American scholars and community activists have questioned the model minority thesis's validity and intentions. These people do not question that Asian Pacific Americans have worked hard and accomplished a great deal in the face of enormous obstacles. They do not doubt that there is significant statistical evidence available demonstrating that people of Asian Pacific ancestry do better in terms of income and education than the national average. But generally they agree with David O'Brien and Stephen Fugita, who argue that the model minority thesis is little more than a stereotype.

> Many third and fourth generation Japanese Americans find this "model minority" image offensive, so do persons in other minority groups to whom the Japanese have been compared. In their view, it paints an oversimplified picture of Japanese Americans and, more generally, Asian Pacific American success. Since this group is "successful" no resources need to be allocated to deal with unique problems. Moreover, if one accepts the model minority logic then presumably any group can be successful in America through perseverance and hard work.

Another scholar, Deborah Woo, points out that we need to bear in mind class and gender variations in comparing Asian Pacific Americans to other racial and ethnic groups. She asserts that the liberalization of immigration laws in the 1960s brought to the United States people of Asian Pacific ancestry who possessed middle and upper class backgrounds and were relatively well educated. These people found it relatively easy to succeed in a market-oriented, technically advanced American society. For example, she states that in the late 1980s over two-thirds of the Asian Pacific Americans with doctoral degrees were trained and educated abroad. Woo writes, moreover, that "Asian American women with a college education are concentrated in narrow and select, usually less prestigious, rungs of the 'professional-managerial' class."

The model minority thesis attempts to homogenize diverse and often contradictory experiences. Numerous people of Asian Pacific ancestry living in the United States have received and continue to receive public assistance in order to survive. Numerous Asian Pacific Americans have, as Helen Zia asserts, supported affirmative action programs. Numerous people of Asian Pacific ancestry living in the United States have not done well in school. Numerous people of Asian Pacific ancestry have engaged in criminal activities, on the one hand, and courageous political protest, on the other. Numerous people of Asian Pacific ancestry would rather shoot hoops than sit behind a computer. Numerous people of Asian Pacific ancestry do not believe they are welcomed in the People's Club.

STRANGERS STILL?

In the early 1990s, Sucheng Chan put the issue of the model minority thesis in perspective when she described its purpose as ideological. It related not to an "objective reality," but to how different sides of public policy issues have perceived American social, political, and economic realities. For a number of American political and intellectual leaders, the model minority thesis has proven that the United States does not need affirmative action or welfare programs because Asian Pacific Americans have not needed affirmative action or welfare programs. Some supporters of liberal immigration policies have used the model minority thesis to argue that, at least, Asian Pacific immigrants have contributed greatly to the United States. On the other hand, some supporters of restrictive immigration policies use the model minority thesis to argue that Asian Pacific immigrants "are taking over." Whatever side a person ultimately takes on these and other important social policy problems facing Americans, one might hope that the millions of Americans of Asian Pacific ancestry do not have to continue to play the role of a political football getting kicked around by ambitious politicians and policy makers.

Clearly, the "people's domain" has grown in America since 1790. Sometimes, this was because of wise political leadership that recognized that enlarging the "people's domain" was the right or, at least, the smart thing to do. But often it was because culturally diverse social movements pushed effectively for a more democratic American society.

The growth of the "people's domain" has, however, not been linear nor is there any guarantee that it will not be "downsized" in the future. From the varied perspectives of historically subaltern people, American political history has not been one grand achievement piled on another grand achievement. Rather, it has been a history of desperately hard earned victories and tragic lapses into corruption, greed, and indifference to institutionalized injustice.

Today, Americans can boast that racial and ethnic identity does not bar an individual from immigrating into the United States. However, Americans could have made a similar boast in 1790. One hundred years later, Chinese immigrants were legally barred from entering America. In other words, if we value the steps that have been made toward making America a more democratic, free, and egalitarian society, we need to recognize that social progress cannot only be halted, it can and has been forced into retreat.

Perhaps, moreover, the "people's domain" in America may not be as large as many of us would like to think. Many intellectuals and activists have argued that institutional forms of discrimination remain a vital part of American society. And Asian Pacific Americans have been targeted along with others people of color, women, gays and lesbians.

Over twenty years ago, a Chinese American named Vincent Chin was murdered in Michigan by white men, who got off with relatively light sentences. This case inspired Asian Pacific Americans to unite across racial lines against what they condemned as a double standard in the American justice system. The killers were auto workers disturbed by the economic downturn facing their community. They also blamed the Japanese auto industry for this downturn and mistook Chin for a person of

Japanese ancestry. While no doubt facing difficult times, these men were still murderers and the fact that their victim was non-white, according to Asian Pacific American activists, seemed to be the only "mitigating" circumstance freeing them from the full consequences of their crime.

In 1989, the U.S. Supreme Court delivered what Helen Zia calls a "landmark decision" in *Wards Cove Packing Company v. Antonio*. An Alaskan firm, Wards Cove Packing Company was accused by Filipino and Native Alaskan workers of engaging in a long time pattern of racial discrimination. Based on a previous court decision, the workers' attorneys believed they needed to prove statistically that a pattern of racial discrimination existed in order to win the case. However, that previous court decision was rendered by a court largely appointed by Democratic presidents and sympathetic to civil and workers' rights cases. By 1989, conservative Republicans, more sympathetic to employers than workers, had filled court vacancies. In 1989, the court claimed that the rules had changed. The litigants needed to prove overt and specific cases of racial discrimination, which they did not do to the court's satisfaction. Wards Cove Packing Company won and the U.S. Supreme Court, Helen Zia writes, struck a severe blow to racial and workplace justice.

The case of Wen Ho Lee, according to Helen Zia, proves that the legal-political system in the United States. remains substantially aligned against people of color. The Taiwan born Wen Ho Lee worked as a scientist at Los Alamos National Laboratory. In 1999, he was accused of espionage and subsequently imprisoned. Charges of racism were hurled at the U.S. government, which refused to back down. While Lee admitted to a security violation in downloading codes, he also claimed that other scientists did the same. Convinced that the U.S. government's evidence against Lee was fallacious, the federal judge hearing his case apologized to Lee "for the unfair manner you were held in custody by the executive branch" and ordered the scientist's release.

ASIAN PACIFIC AMERICANS AND COMMUNITY POLITICS

Perhaps, other ethnic groups may have used the American political system to achieve membership in the People's club more effectively than Asian Pacific Americans. However given the history of structural discrimination against them and their relative lack of numbers outside of Hawai'i, Asian Pacific Americans made important political gains in post-World War II America.

The political empowerment of Asian Pacific American communities, however, has proven more difficult on the American. mainland than in Hawai'i. We should keep in mind that the dynamics in Hawai'i have been different for Asian Pacific Americans than on the mainland. There have proportionately been more U.S. citizens of Asian ancestry in Hawai'i than on the mainland. Asian Hawaiian U.S. citizens have voted and engaged in electoral politics since before World War II. By the same token, before World War II Asian Pacific American ethnic communities were more integrated into the larger Hawaiian society than Asian American ethnic communities on the mainland. Thus, for many Asian Hawaiians being a "local" became an important aspect of their political identity. Native Hawaiian scholar Haumani-Kay Trask refers to "locals" as "both <native> Hawaiian and non-<native> Hawaiian long-time residents of Hawai'i." "Locals", therefore, have established a sense of community that crosses ethnic and racial lines and Japanese American "locals" might well consider Chinese American or Native Hawaiian politicians as equally quite capable of representing them and their "local" communities.

The post-World War H era witnessed a blossoming of Asian Hawaiian political activism aimed, in part, at integrating Asian Hawaiians into Hawai'i's political mainstream. For many of these politically engaged Asian Hawaiians, the Democratic Party proved the means through which they could gain political power. The Republican Party was considered the party of the haoles while the Democratic Party, largely because of Franklin D. Roosevelt, was seen as more receptive to the political aspirations of middle and working class people of color.

Aided by Hawaiian trade union activists such as those affiliated with the International Longshoreman and Warehousemen's Union, a significant number of Asian Hawaiian Democrats such as Daniel Inouye, Spark Matsunaga, and Patsy Mink achieved growing political influence and won elections. Inouye became the first U.S. house member from Hawai'i when it became a state in 1959. In 1962, Inouye became a U.S. senator. Matsunaga and Patsy Mink also became house members. Indeed, the empowerment of Asian Hawaiians caused some concern on the part of white mainland politicians, whose racial prejudice slowed the process of allowing Hawai'i statehood.

On the mainland, Asian Pacific American political efforts took longer to take flight. Dalip Singh Saund, an Asian Indian, became the first Asian Pacific American house member when he was elected from a district in California's central valley. Saund's election won national attention in 1956. However, in order to get elected Saund had to appeal to large numbers of non-Asian Pacific Americans.

Other Asian Californians won support for their electoral campaigns, but, like Saund, they could not win if they simply counted on Asian Pacific American support. Norm Mineta is a Japanese American, who first gained attention when he was elected as Mayor of San Jose in the early 1970s. In 1974, Mineta was elected as a Democrat to the U.S. House of Representatives from a district encompassing San Jose's Japantown--a community where he grew up. However, Mineta's district mostly consisted of non-Asian Pacific Americans. In 1976, the controversial SI. Hayakawa became the first Asian Pacific American senator from the mainland. A conservative Republican from California, Hayakawa gained considerable support from middle and upper class whites. In 1978, Democrat Robert Matsui joined Mineta in the U.S. House of Representatives. A Sacramento resident, Matsui had plenty of support from Japanese Americans in the Sacramento area, but his victory counted on plenty of support from non-Japanese Americans.

In summarizing the political activities of Asian Californians, Sucheng Chan writes:

> By 1989, California boasted not only two Asian American members of congress, but also several federal judges, an immensely popular Chinese American female secretary of state, March Fong Eu, over a hundred county and municipal officials, school board members, municipal and county superior court judges, and dozens of appointees in various state and local agencies. It was an impressive record of achievement considering how recently Asian Americans had entered the political arena.

Moreover, in the 1990s and early 2000s Asian Pacific Americans have continued their political involvement on the local, state, and national levels. In the process, they have given the lie to the stereotype of Asian Pacific peoples as politically apathetic. Since 1965, women of Asian Pacific American ancestry have achieved some measure of political gains. For example, in the 1970s there were four women of Asian Pacific ancestry holding public office in the United States. March Fong Eu served in the California state assembly. Patsy Takemoto Mink served as a House member from Hawai'i, while Jean Sedako King and Patricia Saiki were in Hawai'i's state senate. Within fifteen years, however, there were forty women of Asian Pacific ancestry elected to public office in the United States. They all lived in Western states. Twenty lived in California, while seventeen, two, and one lived in Hawaii, Oregon, and Washington respectively. Yet, there was no woman U.S. Senator of Asian Pacific ancestry and only one woman House member of Asian Pacific ancestry. Nor was any Governor of a state a woman of Asian Pacific ancestry. However, Jean Sedako King was elected Lieutenant Governor of Hawai'i, while March Fong Eu was elected Secretary of State of California for several terms.

Since the 1980s, change has been accomplished, but this change lacks the depth that many would prefer. If women political leaders in general have been marginalized, this has been even more the case for Asian Pacific American women, although they have run for and gotten elected to local and state public offices in Washington, California, and Hawai'i. Indeed, Republican Elaine Chao became the first Asian Pacific American woman named to a presidential cabinet position when she was appointed by George W. Bush after the 2000 election. Meanwhile, Hmong American Mee Moua became the first person of her ethnic background to achieve elected office when she was elected state senator in Minnesota in the early 2000s. At the same time, Swati Dandekar became the first Asian Indian American elected as an Iowa state representative.

Males elected to major public office have included the first Filipino American governor, Ben Cayetano, who served two terms as Hawai'i's state leader. In 1996, Chinese American Gary Locke became the first mainland American of Asian Pacific ancestry to become governor. In 2005, Locke completed his two terms as governor of Washington. Daniel Akaka joined Daniel Inouye as a U.S. senator from Hawai'i. In congress, David Wu represents an Oregon district and Michael Honda serves the same constituency that sent Norm Mineta to Washington, D.C. Asian Pacific American men become city and town mayors such as Michael Chang in Cupertino, California. In local government, Michael Woo was a prominent city council member in Los Angeles. Woo ran unsuccessfully for mayor in 1993.

As to whether each and every one of these elected and appointed officials have well represented the concerns of Asian

Pacific American communities is, of course, subject to interpretation. However, many have certainly tried to maintain and reinforce connections to Asian Pacific American communities. For example, while most of his constituents were non-Japanese Americans, Norm Mineta, who resigned from the House in 1995, consistently sought to represent Japanese American concerns. His voice in Congress was vital in getting enacted in the late 1980s, a bill admitting the U.S. blundered in placing Japanese Americans in concentration camps during World War II and paying $20,000 to each survivor of the concentration camps as reparations for the wrongs done to him or her. In the late 1990s, Mineta became the first Asian Pacific American selected for a cabinet position when Bill Clinton appointed him. After George W. Bush became president in 2000, he kept Mineta in the presidential cabinet in the crucial position of Secretary of Transportation.

VOTING

Asian Pacific American political empowerment has largely been dependent upon the ability of Asian Pacific immigrants to become informed citizens and voters. For years, as we know, immigration exclusion and the denial of citizenship rights to immigrants, limited the number of Asian Pacific American voters outside of Hawai'i. Since the 1965 immigration act and the Vietnam War's creation of thousands of Southeast Asian refugees, the number of American residents of Asian Pacific ancestry have risen. However, Asian Pacific American involvement in politics has widely been seen as deficient.

Pundits have articulated several reasons why Asian Pacific Americans do not get involved politically as much as other major groups. One reason is that a substantial number of Asian Pacific Americans are immigrants or refugees who, for a variety of reasons, have not seen the wisdom of becoming naturalized citizens. A second reason is that even if they have become citizens, Asian Pacific immigrants and refugees lack the experience and cultural tools to participate effectively in the American political process. A third reason is that many Asian Pacific immigrants and refugees retain an abiding and understandable distrust of political involvement since they associate politicians with the corrupt and authoritarian practices in their homelands. And a fourth reason is that Asian Pacific cultures teach passivity rather than activism.

However, as the U.S. entered the twenty-first century, it has become clear to scholars such as Paul Ong and Don Nakanishi that Asian Pacific immigrants are certainly not restrained from any eternal cultural prohibitions from becoming active American citizens or at least as active as most Americans. Moreover, they have also noted the greater number of Asian Pacific immigrants seeking elected positions on the local level. Indeed, naturalized Asian Pacific citizens have in places like Orange County and Santa Clara County in California run for and gained election to numerous local school boards and city councils—a sign that Asian Pacific Americans are serious about their membership in America's People's Club.

CONCLUSION

While perhaps not totally satisfying to Asian Pacific American political activists, the greater participation of Asian Pacific Americans in the political process signals that the People's Club has become more inclusive. But before Americans pat themselves on the back, we need to bear in mind the relatively recent controversy over Asian Pacific American political involvement.

In 1996, the Democratic National Committee (DNC) was accused by Republicans of accepting millions of dollars of contributions from foreign Asians. A key player in all of this was John Huang, a Chinese American who served as vice chair of the DNC's Finance Committee. Huang was charged with arranging for these foreign donations which helped Clinton and the Democrats to stave off a concerted Republican challenge.

Huang's involvement was troubling. The money raised was illegal and the idea of foreign capitalists trying to influence an American election should have disturbed Americans across party lines. However, instead of taking a serious look at political reform in general, Republican critics focused on the "race card." In airing complaints about the "Bamboo Network" and "The Asian Connection," Republicans diverted attention from even more serious breaches of election laws involving much more money than that raised by Huang and going to candidates of both major parties. Moreover, Huang also raised legal contributions from countless ordinary, law-abiding Asian Pacific Americans who simply wanted to participate in the American political system. The focus on Huang, moreover, not only prevented politicians in both parties from seriously confronting how money has corrupted

American democracy but sent a chilling message to ordinary Asian Pacific Americans—"You are not American enough to be full-fledged members of the People's Club."

REVIEW

1. How did World War II affect race relations in general in the United States?
2. How did World War II change the experiences of Asian Pacific Americans?
3. How did World War II change the experiences of Japanese Americans, in particular?
4. How did Japanese Americans experiences vary between the Hawaiian Islands and the West Coast of the U.S. mainland?
5. How did Asian Pacific American experiences with the American political-legal system change after World War II?
6. What was the McCarran-Walter Act? Why was it important?
7. How did the Civil Rights movement change Asian Pacific American experiences with the American political-legal system?
8. What was the Immigration and Nationality Act of 1965? Why was it important?
9. What was the Health Professions Educational Assistance Act? Why was it important?
10. How did the war in Southeast Asia affect the migration of Asian people to the United States?
11. What was the Immigration Reform and Control Act? Why was it important?
12. What was California Proposition 187? Why was it important?
13. How did the 9/11 tragedy affect America's attitude toward immigration?
14. What has been the politics of "English Only"? Why has the "English Only" movement been important?
15. What is Affirmative Action? Why has it been an important source of debate in American political life?
16. What are the various arguments for and against Affirmative Action?
17. What is the Model Minority Thesis? Why has it been important?
18. Are Asian Pacific Americans "strangers still"?

19. How have Asian Pacific Americans become involved in electoral politics in the United States?
20. What do controversies such as the one surrounding John Huang suggest?

SELECTED BIBLIOGRAPHY

Ancheta, Angelo N. *Race, Rights, and the Asian American Experience.* (2000).

Chang, Sucheng. *Asian Americans: An Interpretive History.* (1991).

Chu, Judy. "Asian Pacific American Women in Mainstream Politics, 'in *Making Waves.* Asian Women United of California. (eds.) (1989).

Daniels, Roger. *Coming to America.* (1994).

Fong, Timothy and Shinagawa, Larry H., (eds.) *Asian Americans.* (2000).

Hing, Bill Ong. *Making and Remaking Asian American Through Immigration Policy, 1850-1990.* (1993).

_____. *To Be An American.* (1997).

Horton, John, *et. al. The Politics of Diversity.* (1995).

Kivisto, Peter. *Americans All.* (1995).

Lipsitz, George. *The Possessive Investment in Whiteness.* (1998).

Lopez, Ian Haney. *White By Law.* (1998).

Matsuda, Mari J. *Where Is Your Body? And Other Essays on Race, Gender and the Law.* (1996).

O'Brien, David J. and Fugita, Stephen S. *The Japanese American Experience.* (1991).

Omi, Michael and Winant, Howard. *Racial Formation in the United States: From the 1960s to the 1990s.* (1994).

Steele, Shelby. *The Content of Our Character.* (1990).

Takaki, Ronald. "Reflections on Racial Patterns in America, "in *From Different Shores.* Ronald Takaki. (ed.) (1987).

_____. *Strangers From A Different Shore.* (1989)

Thurow, Lester, C. *The Zero-Sum Society.* (1980).

Wilson, William J. *The Truly Disadvantaged.* (1987).

Winant, Howard. *The World is a Ghettol. (2001).*

Woo, Deborah. "The Gap Between Striving and Achieving: The Case of Asian American Women," in *Making Waves: An Anthology of Writings By and About Asian American Women,* Asian Women United of California, (eds.) (1989).

Wu, Frank H. *Yellow..* (2002).
Zia, Helen. *Asian American Dreams.* (2000).

VIII
ASIAN PACIFIC AMERICAN SPORTING EXPERIENCES

For well over a century, sports have formed an indelible part of the American experience. Americans, especially American males, have assessed one's fitness in American society based upon how much a person loves sports that Americans have long and often improperly claimed as their national property—baseball, basketball, as well as, of course, America's own variety of football. Since at least the Civil War, many Americans have claimed that such sports can reveal the best in the American character—competitiveness, fair play, team work, physical and mental toughness, and an appreciation for a "level playing field." Indeed, the latter phrase should remind us how sports have penetrated American English. Words and terms such as "huddle," "score," "Monday Morning Quarterback," and "dunk shot" have been commonly used when Americans meet one another in a wide variety of social and business settings. Thus, to many non-Asian Pacific Americans who watch big-time sports on television and in-person, the relative absence of Asian Pacific Americans on the playing fields and courts signals that people of Asian Pacific Islander ancestry are "strangers from a different shore." But appearances can, of course, deceive. Americans of Asian Pacific ancestry have engaged in a variety of sports for decades and not just sports stereotypically associated with Asians such as the martial arts, but sports such as American football, soccer, baseball, basketball, prize fighting, wrestling, golf, tennis, and volleyball. They have found through sports a source of real joy. They have found through sports the ability to assert a sense of agency. They have found through sports a way to reinforce a sense of community with people who share their ethnicity. They have found through sports the means to build cultural bridges to people who do not share their ethnicity. Some have even found through sports a path to celebrity status and wealth. However, as Asian Pacific Americans cross the sidelines and foul lines to break up double plays and hit jump shots, their journeys have been shadowed by individual and structural efforts to distinguish them from other Americans—to intentionally and unintentionally mark them as "strangers", as unfit for membership in America's People's Club.

SPORTS AND COMMUNITY

Historians of Asian Pacific American experiences have noted that just as other racial and ethnic groups in the United States, Asian Pacific American ethnic groups needed to develop durable community ties if they were going to sustain themselves in a land that for years was institutionally biased against them. Many of these community institutions furnished meaningful spiritual, economic, political, and cultural support for community members.

However, by the twentieth century, Asian Pacific Americans began to develop sports organizations as a way of linking mainly young men frequently cut off from their loved ones by thousands of miles. Community leaders frequently supported these efforts because sports might well divert these young men from disreputable recreational activities such as gambling, substance abuse, and prostitution as well as criminal activity and radical political militancy. Some of these community sport organizations might have venerable roots in the native lands of Asian Pacific immigrants. For example, Japanese immigrants on the Hawaiian Islands rather quickly formed sumo organizations.

Other community sports organizations might reflect the globalization of more modern athletic competition. Japanese immigrants in Hawai'i, as well as on the American mainland, relatively quickly formed baseball teams. In part, this was because baseball had been introduced to Japan by the 1870s and had become popular among college educated males. (Sumo, by the way, had a working class and peasant following.) As Issei laborers made their way to the Hawaiian Islands and the American mainland, they were accompanied by a cadre of professionals, who either played or watched baseball at their colleges. For example, an Issei Christian preacher named Takie Okumura founded the first Japanese Hawaiian baseball team before the turn-of-the-twentieth century. Concerned about how young, working class Issei men and boys spent their free time, Okumura established a baseball team in Honolulu called the Excelsiors to lure them away from trouble.

Baseball did not necessarily need a strong connection to the homeland to appeal to immigrants. It did not need expensive equipment and could be played in relatively confined places. Indeed, because it was widely popular in late nineteenth century America, baseball gathered apostles among Chinese immigrants. In San Francisco, Chicago, and New York City--Chinese immigrants who formed baseball teams.

During the early 1900s, the Hawaiian Islands became a hotbed of ethnic-based baseball teams. Reflecting the cultural diversity of Hawai'i, island baseball teams represented Hawaiians of Portuguese, indigenous, Chinese, Japanese, Korean, and Filipino ancestries by the 1910s. As the two largest Asian Pacific Islander ethnic groups on the islands, Japanese and Chinese Hawaiians fervently organized teams and leagues.

In 1912, the economic elite of Honolulu's Chinatown helped to sponsor a team entirely comprised of talented ballplayers possessing Chinese ancestry. Six thousand dollars was raised in and out of Honolulu's Chinatown to send this team across the Pacific to tour the American mainland. This team would represent not only Chinese Hawaiians but Hawai'i in general in order to promote mainland tourism and investment. Yet it did more than that as it won a majority of over 100 games against mainland college and semi-professional teams, stunning mainland spectators and sports reporters who could not believe that "Orientals" played America's National Pastime so well.

Disingenuously promoted on the mainland as representing a non-existent Chinese University of Hawai'i in order to schedule games against colleges and universities such as Stanford and Texas University, the team was known on the islands by variously names. Originally, they were the All-Chinese. As the team became more ethnically diverse in order to remain competitive, it became known as the Hawaiian or Chinese Travelers. Though 1916, the team made annual tours of several months of the American mainland, playing some games in Canada and Cuba as well. They continued to play colleges and semi-professional nines, winning a large percentage of the games. They also played and held their own against white and African American professional teams. By the end of their last tour, the Travelers were scarcely All-Chinese. However, nearly all of the players possessed either Chinese, Japanese, or indigenous Hawaiian backgrounds. And even if they no longer truly represented Honolulu's Chinatown, they represented Hawaii's emerging local culture that in turn represented a multicultural community of Hawaiians transcending fixed racial and ethnic divisions.

Evolving out of the Excelsiors, the Asahis comprised another prominent Honolulu baseball team. Consisting of Japanese Hawaiians, the Asahis competed in various Honolulu leagues in the 1910s. The team also traveled to Japan in 1915 and held its own against elite Japanese nines. Over the years, the Asahis became a fixture in the Honolulu-based Hawaii Baseball League, the islands' strongest league. They won more than their share of championships against ethnic based teams such as the Portuguese Braves, the Chinese Tigers, the All-Hawaiis, and a haole team known as the Wanderers. During World War II, however, the prejudice against Japanese Americans in Hawai'i, while not as pronounced as on the West Coast, still was troubling. One of the more harmless but still telling examples of this was that the Asahis' team name was changed to the Athletics. More non-Japanese Hawaiians played on the team and whites ran it. After World War II, the team returned to Japanese Hawaiian management and was more often referred to publicly as the Asahis.

On the American mainland, Asian Pacific Americans organized community baseball teams. The Los Angeles Chinese nine was one of the best semi-professional teams in urban Southern California Angeles during the 1920s. In the East Bay, a Chinese American nine representing the Wah Sung Organization in Oakland also won plenty of games. Lee Gum Hong, the ace pitcher, competed professionally in the Pacific Coast League as we will examine later in the chapter. Moreover, Filipino Americans assembled baseball teams in the San Francisco Bay Area and Los Angeles.

However, on the mainland Japanese American community teams thrived wherever there were Japanese Americans. Other teams called the Asahis were established in the 1910s in Seattle and San Jose. Both teams were comprised of talented Japanese American athletes and traveled to Japan to play that nation's leading nines.

World War II generated a substantial disruption of Japanese American communities on the West Coast. It did not end Japanese American involvement in baseball. Baseball teams and leagues were organized for all age groups of Japanese American males. A delightful children's book about the experience of baseball in the camps is called *Baseball Saved Us*, which reflects the viewpoint of at least many males who were interned during World War II.

In recent years, Japanese American and Korean American communities have been excited by the performances of Japanese and Korean professionals in Major League Baseball (MLB). When Masanouri Murakami pitched competently for a year for the San Francisco Giants in the mid-1960s, Japanese Americans expressed pride. However, it was not until the appearance of Hideo Nomo in a Los Angeles Dodger uniform thirty years later could Japanese and other Asian Pacific Americans confidently assert what most knew all along--that people of Asian Pacific background could excel in the MLB. "Nomomania" swept Southern California and other regions containing large populations of Japanese and Asian Pacific Americans. A skilled and charismatic pitcher, Nomo never became a superstar but he pitched usually well for a number of teams in both the National and the American Leagues.

Joining Nomo on the Dodger roster in the 1990s was a Korean fireballer, Chan Ho Park. Los Angeles's large Korean American population rallied around Park. Korean American businesses reportedly closed down when Park took the mound. However, Park claimed he felt too much pressure; even his private life was too closely scrutinized by the local Korean American community. Thus, he might have felt some relief when he headed for the Texas Rangers, for whom he pitched for several years.

While several fine Japanese nationals have appeared on MLB rosters since 2000, none has had the impact of Ichiro Suzuki, a dynamic outfielder and hitting machine for the Seattle Mariners. His exploits have also encouraged pride among Japanese Americans as have Hideki Matsui's rise to stardom with the New York Yankees in the 2003 and 2004 seasons.

More open to females than its ancestor, baseball, softball attracted considerable ethnic community support on the Hawaiian Islands and the American mainland. Before World War II, several Japanese American female teams thrived in and around Los Angeles. During World War II, Jane "No Hit" Ota starred in women's softball at a concentration camp in Jerome, Arkansas.

One of baseball ancestors, cricket has garnered community support from Americans of South Asian ancestry. As the British colonized places like India, they brought with them their recreational passions, one of which was cricket. Doing so not only comforted the English, so very far home, but the colonizers believed that by teaching cricket to middle and upper class Indian males they would gain Indian consent to British rule. As it turned out, cricket proved more popular in India than the British. And over time Indian, Pakistani, and Sri Lankan cricket teams not only became quite good but competitive with elite English teams.

As South Asians immigrated to the United States in significant numbers after World War II, they brought with them their passion for cricket. The televising of matches between Indian and Pakistani cricket teams became important community events in places like Fremont, California, which housed a substantial population of Americans of South Asian ancestry. Moreover, Americans of South Asian ancestry have assembled cricket teams and leagues, including youth leagues organized somewhat along the Little League model.

Basketball has been another team sport closely tied to Asian Pacific American communities. Like baseball, basketball did not require extensive equipment or space. However, it needed at least a semblance of a playground or an indoor gymnasium. Because the sport before World War II relied more heavily on speed, ball handling, and guile than on size many Asian Pacific American community squads were able to compete effectively against non-Asian Pacific American teams.

As early as the 1910s, Japanese American community teams emerged in places like San Francisco. Indeed, San Francisco's Japantown turned into a hotbed of community basketball between World War I and World War II. In San Jose, a Japanese American male team called the Zebras became a source of community pride similar to the Asahis. In Stockton, a female team called the Busy Bees was so good it barnstormed California and won dozens of games in a row.

While perhaps not as important in keeping a sense of community going in the camps and certainly not as well publicized, basketball nevertheless was played by both male and female internees. Not only were basketball leagues organized in the camps, but camp teams met local high school and other fives during World War II.

After World War II, Japanese American community teams continued to bloom. In Hawai'i, Americans of Japanese Ancestry (AJA) organized basketball teams and leagues. There were so many excellent Japanese Hawaiian basketball players that the AJA assembled two all-star teams—one to tour the American mainland and the other to tour Japan after the war. On the mainland, the Zebras remained a Japanese American powerhouse, but Los Angeles, Sacramento, Seattle, Salt Lake City, and Chicago were also represented by talented Japanese American teams. Fifty years later, Japanese Americans still find meaning in community basketball. In the Santa Clara County, Japanese Americans support teams representing San Jose's Community Youth Service, Palo Alto Youth Service, and Mountain View's Buddhist Church.

Chinese Americans began to organize teams on the mainland as early as the 1910s. However, the depression witnessed an outpouring of Chinese American teams for both sexes. In San Francisco, Chinese American youth teams won playground tournaments. And by 1940, sports-minded Chinese Americans, of which there were more than a few, called San Francisco's Chinatown a Mecca of community basketball. Indeed, out of San Francisco's Chinatown emerged a traveling professional team known as Hong Wah Ques.

Before World War II, professional basketball was not nearly as well organized as it is today. There were professional teams and leagues but they existed mostly on the East Coast and they rarely thrived. Teams that wanted to make money usually had to barnstorm—travel around from town to town playing local teams much as the All-Chinese baseball team did in the 1910s. Some of the more famous of these traveling teams were African American fives such as the Harlem Renaissance and then the Harlem Globetrotters, who were actually based in Chicago rather than New York's Harlem district. Other notable traveling teams were the Original Celtics and the Jewish American Philadelphia Sphas (South Philadelphia Hebrew Association). In fact, Buck Lai, a Chinese Hawaiian athlete who played for the All-Chinese team, led a team called Buck Lai's Hawaiian All-Stars. Supposedly all-Hawaiian, these mostly haole players donned hula skirts and wore leis during the first few minutes of a game.

Because they were often seen as exotic in places like Sioux City Iowa, ethnic-based teams could be marketable in the 1930s and 1940s. And because pre-World War II basketball found height an advantage rather than a necessity, teams with quick defenders and good ball handlers and outside shooters could usually hold their own. Thus, a white promoter organized a Chinese American team of talented San Franciscans, the tallest of whom was 5 ft. 10 and included high school legend Robert "Egg Foo" Lum.

The team boarded a station wagon and headed to the Midwest in 1940 and 1941. The players were paid $250 a month, which was good money for a young Chinese American at the time, and were told by their employer not to speak English whenever they played. Indeed, the promoter wanted them to perform before white Americans who most likely had never seen in person anyone of Asian ancestry, let alone a skilled Asian basketball player. In the process, the promoter wanted to market the San Franciscans as exotic Orientals and thus adorned them with silk warm ups to reinforce their "Celestial" image.

The Hong Wah Ques were more than just a novelty act, however. They played well against teams such as the Harlem Globetrotters. Robert Lum, for example, dazzled observers with his ball handling and shooting skills. The players were often insulted by spectators with terms such as "Chink." Yet since they could not speak English while playing, some took delight in cussing out spectators in Cantonese.

In the 1940s, St. Mary's Catholic Church in San Francisco's Chinatown served as a major sponsor of community teams. The male team became known as the San Francisco Chinese Saints. Competing against presumably amateur community and commercial fives in the San Francisco Bay Area, the Saints usually won. One of the team stars was five foot three inch Willie "Woo Woo" Wong. St. Mary's also sponsored female teams. Led by a great all around athlete and Willie Wong's sister, Helen Wong, these teams ranked among the best Chinese American female fives in the nation.

Meanwhile, Seattle and San Jose hosted the Oriental Invitational Basketball Tournament in the late 1940s. The San Jose Zebras were invited, as were the Chinese Saints and the AJA all-star team from Honolulu. Several other teams came from all over the nation, as well as Canada. A Filipino American squad from San Francisco also competed. In San Jose, packed crowds watched the championship game at San José State's Spartan Gym and local standouts such as the Zebras' T-Bone Akizuki in action.

Over fifty years later, Chinese and Filipino Americans assemble community teams and tournaments for both sexes. Moreover, Chinese American communities, especially those situated in National Basketball Association (NBA) cities, have been excited by the emergence of Yao Ming, a seven foot six inch Chinese National team star who has become one of the best centers in the NBA for the Houston Rockets, as well as a multi-media darling in the United States.

American football has historically received less support from Asian Pacific American communities on the mainland. In part, this was because an American football team requires more players, more costly equipment, and a sizable chunk of land for a field. This does not mean Asian Pacific American community teams failed to develop. Chinese American communities in California, for example, prominently organized American football teams before World War II. One of the best Chinese American elevens in the 1930s was called the Unknown Packers and played out of San Francisco. Moreover, for many years in the 1930s, a Rice Bowl game was held between Chinese American all-stars from the San Francisco Bay Area and Los Angeles. The game was held as a benefit for China then under siege by Japan.

Japanese Americans formed football teams, as well. Teams such as the Berkeley Nisei played other Japanese American teams, as well as Chinese American squads. Given the tensions between China and Japan during the 1930s, community games between Japanese American and Chinese American squads could be quite bitter. During World War II, male camp internees set up American football leagues and teams.

Asian Pacific American communities have long supported individual Asian Pacific Americans who have starred in American football. When Japanese Hawaiian Wally Yonamine joined the San Francisco 49ers in 1947, he was a source of satisfaction to Nikkei on both the mainland and the Hawaiian Islands. Likewise, Dat Nguyen's recent exploits as an All American linebacker turned pro for the Dallas Cowboys have excited community support from Vietnamese Americans.

Other sports such as bowling, tennis, golf, and volleyball have attracted community backing from Asian Pacific American communities. Bowling, for example, proved popular in many Asian Pacific American communities on the mainland and the Hawaiian Islands. Unfortunately, the two most important bowling organizations in the U.S., the American Bowling Congress (ABC) and the Women's International Bowling Congress (WIBC) excluded non-whites for many years. Thus, community-based teams could not compete in ABC or WIBC sanctioned tournaments. This clearly rankled many Asian Pacific American bowlers who wondered why America fought a war against fascism if racism continued to permeate American sports and why Asian Pacific Americans died in that war. Indeed, veterans of the 442nd were important leaders in the fight against racial exclusion in bowling, while a group of Chinese American women bowlers in Southern California protested racial exclusion by pointing out that their husbands had fought for the United States in World War II.

By the early 1950s, the ABC and the WIBC succumbed to the pressure brought on by anti-racist activists and ended their Jim Crow policy. Asian Pacific American community bowling teams and leagues proliferated to an even greater extent as a result. And for many years, bowling has been one of the most popular forms of community-based recreation largely because it appeals to people of nearly all age groups, both sexes, as well as across social and economic barriers.

Because it was largely associated with middle and upper class whites, tennis's appeal to Asian Pacific American communities was relatively slow to materialize. When a tennis court was built in San Francisco's Chinatown in the 1920s, old timers thought it was a waste of good space—who would have the time to play the game? However, even before World War II, Chinese American community members in San Francisco became notable advocates of recreational tennis. Eventually, the community sponsored an annual tennis tournament.

Golf, too, historically attracted more elite, white participation. However, before and after World War II, all sorts of Asian Pacific American golf clubs were formed on the American mainland and the Hawaiian Islands. Wishing to keep a lid on racial animosity, pre-World War II Japanese Americans in California were known to get up early in order to make it to the golf course before whites teed off in significant numbers.

Volleyball, a team sport with a long history on the Hawaiian Islands, found substantial support among Filipino agricultural workers. Before World War II, these workers were often too poor to participate substantially in other recreational sports and the companies they worked for were often unwilling to provide them with the space for baseball. Thus, Filipinos took part enthusiastically in volleyball on the Islands and pioneered "The Manila Bomb," which subsequently became known in the sport as the spike. Filipino Americans on the mainland also supported volleyball teams and tournaments.

Asian Pacific American communities did not neglect sports associated with traditional Asian Pacific cultures. For example, sumo was integrated into Nikkei community activities in Hawai'i and the American mainland. When Japanese Hawaiian workers celebrated the Emperor's birthday in the late nineteenth century, they often staged sumo matches as part of the festivities. In San Jose in the early twentieth century, a sumo league was organized. And in the camps, some Issei wanted the Nisei to take part in sumo rather than more Americanized sports such as baseball, basketball, and football.

CROSSING CULTURES

For decades, athletes of Asian Pacific American ancestry have crossed cultural borderlands to compete with and against non-Asian Pacific Americans. This has been truer of Hawai'i than the American mainland, because social stigmas were more associated with class on the islands than they were on the more race conscious mainland. In recent years, wherever Asian Pacific Americans have lived in significant numbers, one can find their presence on Little League baseball teams and high school tennis squads.

Even before the twentieth century, Hawaiian baseball teams were comprised of haole, indigenous Hawaiian, and Asian athletes. And down through the years, Hawaiian baseball has been highlighted by the participation of culturally diverse Asian Hawaiian ballplayers. Chinito Moriyama was a clever second baseman, who played not only for the Asahis but also the Travelers. Moriyama used the pseudonym of J. Chin so he would seem Chinese to American mainlanders. Possessing both Chinese and Native Hawaiian ancestry Albert and Lang Akana played for the Travelers but also "All-Hawaiian" teams. Other Hawaiians of indigenous and Chinese ancestry, Tommy Kaulukukui and John Kea Kerr played in the 1930s and 1940s for the Chinese Tigers as well as several multi-ethnic nines. However no Hawaiian competed with so many different kinds of teams than Filipino American Crispin Mancao. A clever left handed pitcher, Mancao pitched for the Chinese Tigers and the pre-dominantly Japanese American Rural Red Sox as well as commercial and all sorts of Hawaii Baseball League teams from the 1930s to the 1970s.

Hawaiian high school and college baseball and softball teams have long fielded multi-ethnic, multi-racial teams. In the late 1940s, for example, Tommy Kaulukukui's brother, Sal, played on a University of Hawai'i team with a standout Japanese American athlete, Jyun Hirota. In the 1990s, a Hawaiian of Filipino ancestry, Ben Agbayani, starred in the outfield for Hawaii Pacific University.

Hawaii has also dispatched Hawaiian athletes to the American mainland to compete for college teams. Ninety years ago, William Achi played for Stanford and the University of Chicago. After World War II, Bill Nishita starred as a pitcher for Santa Rosa Junior College and then the University of California. In recent years, Shane Komine was an All-American pitcher for the University of Nebraska, while catcher Kurt Suzuki led California State

University, Fullerton, to a NCAA championship. In softball, Lovie Jung starred for Fresno State before joining the gold medal winning U.S. Olympic team in 2004.

In terms of coaching, Bill Kajikawa and Les Murakami merit mention. Kajikawa was a true pioneer as an Asian Pacific American coach. Born in California, he was raised in Arizona. In the mid-1930s, he starred as an all around athlete at Arizona State Teachers' College, now Arizona State University. Upon graduation, he coached the school's baseball team. And after he returned home from fighting in the 442nd during World War II, he headed the college's baseball team for many years. Hawaiian Les Murakami coached the University of Hawai'i's baseball team for twenty-nine years, leading that program into national respectability.

As early as the 1910s, Asian Pacific Americans on the mainland played ball with non-Asian Pacific Americans. A young man surnamed Sangi competed with Los Angeles High School, while another surnamed Tokio played for a Lodi semi-pro team. In the 1920s, East Bay athlete Lee Gum Hong pitched for Oakland High School, while Earl Tanaka played for and captained the Occidental College nine. In the 1930s, Russ Hinaga captained the Milpitas nine, as well as played with the San Jose Asahis. His sister Alice Hinaga starred as a pitcher in San Jose's Night Ball League. Night Ball, which was operated for both men and women, featured a ball which was larger than the traditional hard ball but smaller than the softball. In Los Angeles during World War II, one of the best high school players was a Filipino American from San Pedro named Bobby Balcena. Starting her athletic career in Denver in the 1940s, Nancy Ito became one of the most prominent softball players in the country. She also competed in a women's baseball league in New York City in the early 1950s. In 1996, Vietnamese immigrant Kim Maher Ly played for the U.S. Olympic champion softball team.

Basketball has drawn Asian Pacific American athletes across cultural barriers. Japanese American Fred Koba suited up for Stanford in the early 1920s. Ten years later, Ted Obashi played forward for the University of California. Hawaiian Al Chang played guard for Redlands College in Southern California toward the end of the decade. After World War II, Willie "Woo Woo" Wong competed in varsity basketball for the University of San Francisco.

In Hawai'i, meanwhile, college, high school, and commercial teams typically possessed more than a few players of Asian Pacific Islander ancestry. Three of the greatest players and coaches of the 1930s and 1940s were Ah Chew Goo, Art Kim, and Bert Chan Wa.

The University of Hawai'i's basketball team after World War II included standouts such as Japanese Hawaiian Fred Furukawa and Chinese Hawaiian as William Lee.

In recent years, male college basketball has included players of Asian Pacific Islander ancestry such as Alika Smith, a talented point guard for the University of Hawai'i in the late 1990s. Stanford's backcourt has been helped by Julius Barnes, an athlete of Samoan ancestry, and Ryan Haas, a point guard possessing Korean ancestry. Hawaiian Derek Low did a fine job as a freshman point guard for Washington State during the 2004-2005 college season.

Asian Pacific Islander female basketball players have surfaced on Hawaiian and American mainland courts. Helen Wong starred on her Star of the Sea high school team after World War I. Cambodian immigrant Da Houl was *Los Angeles Times'* player of the year in 1983 when she competed for Brea Olinda High School. Houl, subsequently, moved on to the University of Hawai'i where she starred as a point guard. In the 1990s, Filipino American Jennifer Omana starred for Haverford College and B.J. Itoman for the University of Hawai'i. At Stanford, Lindsay Yamasaki excited the program's legions of basketball fans in the San Francisco Bay Area. In recent years, Michelle Tom played varsity basketball for Arizona State, Kristin Iwanaga for Cal, Natalie Nakase for UCLA, and flashy point guard Corrie Mizusawa for St. Mary's and then Oregon.

Basketball coaches of Asian Pacific Islander ancestry have become increasingly numerous. We have already mentioned that Bert Chan Wa and Ah Chew Goo were pioneering Hawaiian coaches in the 1930s and 1940s. After World War II, Bill Kajikawa took over the Arizona State basketball program for a number of years. At the same time, Dan Fukushima began a long career of coaching by assuming the reins of the East Contra Costa College Junior College five. Fukushima, subsequently, headed down to San Jose, where he coached basketball and taught English for years at James Lick High School. In women's basketball, Coleen Matsuhara coached for several years on the staffs of Long Beach State, Notre Dame, UCLA, and the University of Texas. In the mid-1990s, she coached the University of California, Irvine to a conference title and then became an assistant for the Los Angeles Sparks of the Women's National Basketball Association (WNBA). And at the University of Hawai'i, Vince Goo, Ah Chew's son, coached women's basketball successfully for years.

Football, American, soccer, or rugby, has been a major inspiration of Asian Pacific Islander cultural border crossings. In 1916, Andy Yamashiro, a great all around Hawaiian athlete, played guard on the mainland for Temple of Philadelphia. A few years later, Chinese American Son Kai Kee played end for the University of California. In the 1920s, Art Matsu was a standout quarterback for William and Mary. The next decade witnessed the emergence of Tommy Kaulukukui, a Hawaiian of indigenous and Chinese ancestry. A halfback for the University of Hawai'i, Kaulukukui stunned the American football world when he ran back a kick off for over 100 yards against UCLA at the famed Los Angeles Coliseum. Kaulukukui, subsequently, became a small college All-American. Speaking of UCLA, by World War II, the school suited up two Hawaiian brothers who played in the backfield—Conkling and Francis Wai. Meanwhile, the ubiquitous Bill Kajikawa was an all-league standout for Arizona State.

All sorts of Asian Pacific Islanders competed in high school American football in the early decades of the twentieth century. In Hawai'i, of course, it was impossible to put together a high school team without young men of Asian Pacific Islander ancestry. On the American mainland, high schools in San Francisco, Sacramento, Santa Clara County, and Los Angeles frequently suited up players of Asian Pacific Islander ancestry.

During and after World War II, several Asian Pacific Islander athletes competed for American football teams in Hawai'i and the American mainland. Filipino American Bobby Balcena starred as an end for San Pedro High School during World War II. Korean American Sam Kim played for the University of San Francisco. Frank Miyaki was a "triple threat Nisei" for Washington State. Jack Yoshihara suited up for Oregon State, while Joe Nagata quarterbacked for Louisiana State. In the late 1940s and 1950s, George Fong was a solid running back for Cal, Joe Tom was a quarterback for Oregon University, and Abe Dung led Santa Clara to a Sugar Bowl victory. Johnny Naumu, who possessed Hawaiian and Japanese ancestry, was an exciting broken field runner for USC. Harold Kan'e starred as a fullback for Dayton University in Ohio. San Jose State College suited up a number of Asian Pacific Islander football players in the late 1940s and into the 1950s, including a scintillating passer and ball carrier from Los Angeles, Babe Nomura. Meanwhile, coached by Tommy Kaulukukui, the University of Hawai'i gridiron team included Tommy's brother, Sal, Harold Kahuanui, Jyun Hirota, Dick Asato, and dozens of fine football players of Asian Pacific Islander ancestry.

An interesting phenomenon in post-World War II American football has been the presence of players of Pacific Islander ancestry, particularly Samoan. For example, Packard Harrington, who possessed Samoan and Irish ancestry, starred in Honolulu high school football before World War II. After, he headed for St. Mary's where he was a good enough linebacker to get drafted by the Cleveland Browns. A few years later, his brother Al played halfback for Stanford.

After World War II, Hawaiian barefoot leagues began to disappear. One of the more interesting chapters in American football history, Hawaiian football leagues were organized as early as the 1920. These leagues featured, unsurprisingly, athletes performing in often makeshift helmets and pads but definitely without cleats. The leagues were divided up into weight divisions and teams usually represented neighborhoods rather than ethnic groups. Generally, the teams were comprised of players from all the major Hawaiian ethnic groups but they mostly appealed to young men of working class and lower middle class backgrounds, who were disproportionately Asian Pacific Islander. The games were highlighted by speed and finesse. Reflecting the Hawaiian communal spirit pervading the islands' local culture, a successful offensive play often consisted of a number of laterals.

Since 1960, several players of Asian Pacific Islander ancestry have stood out on the college teams. In the 1960s, Michigan State University suited up several Hawaiians of Asian Pacific Islander ancestry thanks, in part, to the fact that Tommy Kaulukukui served as an assistant coach in East Lansing. Among the Hawaiians recruited was Charley Wedemeyer, whose older brother, Herman, was an All-American for St. Mary's in the 1940s before going pro. Wedemeyer possessed indigenous Hawaiian and Chinese ancestry and was a very good player for Duffy Daugherty's Spartans. In the late 1970s, Daryl Wong was an excellent quarterback for Lowell High School in San Francisco. He then moved on to Dartmouth. And in the early 2000s, Timmy Chang was one of the best passers in the nation while quarterbacking the University of Hawai'i's high powered offense.

As yet, no Division I college football team has seen fit to hire a coach of Asian Pacific Islander ancestry. Hawaiian raised Norm Chow has been on some short lists but has not taken over a big time college program. A former college lineman and Canadian pro football performer, Chow became offensive coordinator for Brigham Young University (BYU), where he mentored great quarterbacks such as Jim McMahon and Steve Young. When he was passed over for BYU's head coaching job, Chow headed to North Carolina State where he helped turn quarterback Philip Rivers into a pro football prospect. Chow then moved across the continent to become USC's offensive coordinator. Once again, he bred success and great college quarterbacks such as Carson Palmer and Matt Leinert. Chow was supposedly a top candidate for Stanford, but he was passed over once again. In 2005, Chow headed for the pros and an offensive coordinator position with the Tennessee Titans.

Asian Pacific Islander Americans have played soccer with fervor and skill. Women's college soccer has been graced by the Fair twins. Raised in Santa Clara County, Lorrie and Ronnie Fair possess Chinese ancestry. Lorrie starred for the powerful University of North Carolina team and subsequently became a defender for the U.S. world cup team in the late 1990s. Ronnie was good, too, as she illuminated Stanford's soccer team. Possessing Filipino descent, Tiffany Roberts also stood out for North Carolina.

Volleyball is another team sport which has attracted athletic Asian Pacific Islander Americans. The University of Hawai'i Rainbow Wahines have been a perennial power in Division I women's volleyball. Coached by Dave Shoji, the team has been sparked over the years by talented Asian Pacific Islander Americans such as Robyn Ah Mow, a clever setter who also played for the U.S. Olympic team. Logan Tom, who possesses Hawaiian ancestry, emerged as a powerful spiker for another perennial power—Stanford. Tom, too, played for the U.S. Olympic team. Hawaiian Eric Wong starred for the UCLA men's volleyball team before representing the United States in the Olympics in beach volleyball.

PIONEERS AND STARS

Americans of Asian Pacific ancestry have pioneered difficult cultural borderlands to achieve recognition in professional and amateur sports. They have also used sports to gain at least a modicum of celebrityhood, as well as occasionally good money. Athletes such as Tiger Woods, Nancy Kwan, Kristi Yamaguchi, and Michelle Wie have become major national and international celebrities. Yet other, not so well known or forgotten athletes of Asia Pacific ancestry, such as Vicki Manalo, Bobby Balcena, Buck Lai, Wally Yonamine, and Jacki Pung also merit attention as pioneers in American sport history.

Prize fighting is a sport which has historically attracted working class, young men of color. In the 1920s, the Philippine

Islands were a part of the American Empire and Filipino experiences in sport were American experiences in sport. In that decade, dozens of Filipino young men began to risk their bodies and brain matter to box professionally in the United States. None was more honored than a prize fighter who performed as Young Pancho Villa. Coming to the United States in the early 1920s, Young Pancho Villa fought his way to the World Flyweight championship and held the title until an abcess tooth combined with boxing injuries led to his premature death in 1924. Several years later, Filipino American Dado Marino became the first Hawaiian to win a world championship.

Professional wrestling has not been much of a true sport for a long time. Nevertheless, professional wrestlers have proven themselves superb athletes and often very effective entertainers. Before World War II, several Americans of Asian Pacific background wrestled professionally. A Hawaiian of Chinese ancestry, Walter Achieu was a former professional football who performed in the Midwest in the 1930s. After World War II, Japanese Americans appeared as prominent wrestling villains, evoking several nasty, World War II stereotypes about the Japanese. Born in Utah, Kenji Shibuya spent many years as an all around athlete in Los Angeles and Hawai'i. As a professional wrestler, Shibuya adopted the persona of the sly and vicious Japanese male. Shibuya appeared to raucous audiences in places like San Jose's Civic Auditorium as a thug capable of doing anything to beat the "Yankee Dogs."

Teammates on the Hawaiian Travelers, Vernon Ayau, Andy Yamashiro, and Buck Lai were Asian Pacific American pioneers in professional baseball. A slick fielding shortstop, Ayau became the first ballplayer of Chinese ancestry to play professionally on the mainland when he competed briefly for Seattle of the Pacific Northwest League in 1917. While his appearance in a Seattle uniform aroused opposition from those who wanted to keep Organized Baseball in America "lilly white," Ayau's inability to hit professional pitching seemed to doom his chances at a professional career. Playing under the name of Andy Yim, Yamashiro joined a minor league team in Gettysburg, Pennsylvania in 1917. The next year, Yamashiro played for Bridgeport of the Eastern League. In 1919, Yamashiro competed in a few games for New Haven of the Eastern League and then departed from mainland professional baseball.

Early in 1915, Buck Lai and a Hawaiian Traveler teammate, Lang Akana, were set for tryouts with the major league Chicago

White Sox and the Pacific Coast League Portland Beavers respectively. Neither played high level professional baseball on the American mainland. Akana clearly was victimized by racial opposition. Lai was rumored to be victimized by racism as well.

In 1918, Lai had another chance to play major league baseball. The Philadelphia Phillies invited the Hawaiian to spring training camp in Florida and seemed to have given him a fair chance to make the squad. By this time, Lai had fallen in love with a white woman on the East Coast and stayed there for most of the rest of his life. In 1917, Lai played semi-professional baseball in Pennsylvania and New York. Lai did not make the Phillies and after leaving the Philadelphia franchise, wound up playing along with Andy Yamashiro on the Bridgeport nine. For four years, Lai patrolled third base for Bridgeport and then left the Eastern League to compete in semi-professional ball for nines such as the then famed Brooklyn Bushwicks.

In 1928, Lai was invited to tryout for the New York Giants, one of the most notable franchises in major league baseball. Once again, Lai was cut and his full time professional baseball career was ended at thirty-two. For the next several years, Lai played for the Bushwicks and operated a barnstorming basketball team called the Hawaiian All-Stars, although only Lai was really Hawaiian.

The short-lived basketball team might have given Lai the idea to organize a truly Hawaiian baseball team, which toured North America from 1935 through 1938. The team consisted of some of the best Asian Pacific Islander athletes on the islands and took on semi-professional and African American professional teams throughout the continent.

Buck Lai's son, William T. Lai, Jr., played on the Hawaiian touring team. In the late 1930s, he went to Long Island University, where he played first base and outfield for the varsity nine. After serving in World War II, Buck Lai, Jr., returned to Long Island University where he became an assistant basketball and baseball coach. In the 1950s, he revived LIU's basketball program, which had faced extinction because of a gambling scandal. Lai also served as the university's athletic director and provost. Meanwhile, Lai was employed by the Brooklyn Dodgers as a scout and instructor. He even wrote two well read instructional books on baseball and basketball.

Bobby Balcena was the first Filipino American to play major league baseball. A son of Filipino immigrants, Balcena grew up in San Pedro, California, where he starred in high school football and baseball. After World War II, the St. Louis Browns signed him to a contract. However, he lingered in the minor leagues for years, playing in places such as Mexicali, Wichita, San Antonio, Kansas City, Buffalo, Vancouver, and Honolulu. In Seattle, Balcena became a fan favorite, particularly of that city's relatively large Filipino population. He also attracted the attention of the Cincinnati Redlegs' franchise, which called him up at the end of the 1956 season. Balcena got what ballplayers call a "cup of coffee" in the big leagues. After a few at bats and insertions as a pinch runner, Balcena's brief big league career was over. Perhaps he was too small at five feet seven to deserve a shot. Perhaps he was not good enough. Perhaps he was too Filipino.

In the late twentieth century, a few professionals of Asian Pacific ancestry carved out solid American major league careers. Mike Lum was a hard hitting Hawaiian of Japanese ancestry and Chinese Hawaiian step parents. He played for teams such as the Atlanta Braves and Cincinnati Redlegs. After starring for the University of Nebraska baseball team, Japanese Hawaiian pitcher, Ryan Kurosaki, got into a few games for the St. Louis Cardinals. In the 1980s, Lenn Sakata became the first Nikkei to play in the American World Series, when he was a valuable utility infielder for the Baltimore Orioles. Hapa Atlee Hammaker had a few good seasons pitching for the San Francisco Giants. And Benny Agbayani, a Hawaiian of Filipino and Samoan background, proved a dependable hitter for the New York Mets in the early 2000s.

Today, Johnny Damon stands out as potentially the first Hall of Famer of Asian Pacific American ancestry. A son of an American military father and Thai mother, Damon helped the Boston Red Sox achieve their first World Series victory since 1916. A dynamic lead off hitter and outfielder, Damon has emerged as one of baseball's most charismatic and popular players.

Pioneering the difficult terrain of post-World War II Japanese big league ball was Hawaiian Nisei, Wally Yonamine. Indeed, Yonamine's stands out as a double pioneer. A son of plantation workers, Yonamine's gained notoriety first as a marvelous high school football player on Maui and then for Honolulu's Farrington High School. Touring the mainland with a Hawaiian all-star football team, Yonamine's dazzling skills as a ball carrier attracted a scholarship offer from Ohio State and contract offers from the New York Yankees and the San Francisco 49ers of the All American Football Conference. In 1947, Yonamine became the first full-blooded Asian Pacific American to play professional football when he joined the 49ers.

Yonamine's stay with the 49ers was not long or seemingly all that happy. Some say it was because he was not used to playing in front of big crowds and was too nervous to do well. Yonamine himself contended that he was concerned about anti-Japanese hostility in the San Francisco Bay Area. Moreover, Yonamine's injured an arm while playing baseball on the islands and found it harder than normal to do the things that football players need to do like block, catch, tackle, and hold on to the ball.

Yonamine tried playing minor league professional football in the Pacific Coast Football League. But he was lured by the money that could be made in professional baseball. He tried out for the San Francisco Seals in 1950. He did not make the Pacific Coast League team but manager Lefty O'Doul was impressed enough to sign him to a Seal contract and farm him out to Salt Lake City, where he batted well over .300.

However, O'Doul was convinced that Yonamine could not make it to the big leagues and persuaded him to consider a career in the Japanese major leagues. The Tokyo Giants, the most powerful franchise in the Japanese major leagues, wanted Yonamine and offered him a signing bonus to play in Japan in 1951. Yonamine accepted the Giants offer and became the first prominent American to play professionally in Japan since the end of World War II.

Possessing Japanese ancestry did not shield Yonamine from Japanese fans who resented him as a foreigner—a *gaishin*. They threw things at him and gangsters even threatened to beat him up. What made matters more tense is that Yonamine played baseball aggressively. He did things which Japanese professionals were not supposed to do—beat out bunts and break up double plays. Yet his aggressiveness also won fan support and the respect of players, many of whom copied his pugnacious style of play. Moreover, Yonamine made friends because the friendly and generous Hawaiian was anything but pugnacious off the baseball diamond. He also made friends because he was very good at what he did—batting consistently over .300 and helping the Giants to remain a Japanese powerhouse in the 1950s. In the early 1990s, Yonamine was elected to the Japanese Baseball Hall of Fame after years of playing, coaching, scouting, and managing in Japan.

Yonamine was the best of Japanese Americans to play in the Japanese big leagues but he was not the only one. Hawaiian "Bozo" Wakabayashi was a successful pitcher in Japan before World War II. After World War II, Hawaiian Jyun Hirota and Californian Fibber Hirayama also played well for the Giants and the Hiroshima Carps respectively.

Herman Wedemeyer was Yonamine's Hawaiian contemporary. Possessing a Chinese and Hawaiian background, Herman Wedemeyer surfaced as one of the most exciting players in college football while suiting up for St. Mary's of Moraga in the mid-1940s. Wedemeyer tried professional football in the late 1940s, but because of injuries and/or lack of enthusiasm for the game, did not do as well. His younger brother Charley also played big time football for Michigan State before taking up a career in high school coaching in Los Gatos, California. Sadly, Charley Wedemeyer came down with ALS (Lou Gehrig's disease). Happily, he fought the disease for years, earning a place as one of American sports great role models.

There have been other formidable professional gridders of Asian Pacific Islander ancestry After World War II, Charley Ane, a large Hawaiian of indigenous and Chinese descent, starred as a lineman for USC in the late 1940s and early 1950s before becoming an all-pro for the Detroit Lions. A son of a Filipino immigrant worker, Roman Gabriel was an All-American quarterback at North Carolina State before notching several fine seasons in the NFL with the Los Angeles Rams and Philadelphia Eagles in the 1960s and early 1970s. Hawaiian Mel Tom was a top defender for San Jose State before moving on to the Chicago Bears and Philadelphia Eagles. Samoan American Junior Seau became one of the NFL's most fearsome linebackers in the 1990s. USC grad Johnny Morton is a *hapa* of Japanese ancestry. In the 1990s and early 2000s, he became one of the best pass receivers in the NFL. Meanwhile, Hines Ward, who has a Korean born mother, has developed into another fine NFL receiver. A son of Vietnamese immigrants, Dat Nguyen was an All-American linebacker at Texas A&M and then became a regular linebacker for the Dallas Cowboys in the early 2000s.

The first American basketball player of Asian Pacific ancestry to play big league professional basketball was Wat Misaka. A native of Utah, Misaka was known as a defensive wizard for the University of Utah when it copped the NCAA and National Invitational Tournament (NIT) titles in the mid-1940s. The NIT tournament, held in New York City, was at the time more prestigious than its NCAA counterpart. When Misaka took the court with Utah five against well established basketball powers such as the University of Kentucky he immediately became a fan favorite, due to his hustle and intensity. Thus, it was not all that surprising that the New York Knicks would sign Misaka for the 1947-1948 season. Misaka managed to get into a few games for the New York five, which was then in its professional basketball infancy. However, he was eventually released, although Misaka remained convinced that a prejudiced Coach Joe Lapchick did not give him a fair chance.

In later years, a few basketball players of Asian Pacific ancestry competed professionally in the United States. Hailing from San Jose, Raymond Townsend starred as a guard for the legendary UCLA five. Townsend's mother was a Filipino American, who was also quite active as a community basketball player in the 1950s. After leaving UCLA, Townsend was drafted by the Golden State Warriors in the late 1970s and began a respectable NBA career. Hapa Rex Walters learned his basketball while playing for the San Jose Zebras. He became a top contributor to the University of Kansas' success in the late 1980s. From Kansas, Walters headed to the NBA, where he played several seasons, generally in a utility role. Another *hapa* Corey Gaines suited up for the New York Knicks in the 1990s. After the turn-of-the century, Stanford's Lindsay Yamasaki showed up in the WNBA.

Professional golf has inspired the participation of marvelously talented Asian Pacific American stars. Tiger Woods, of course, is celebrated as an icon of multicultural America. Possessing African, Indigenous American, Thai, and Chinese descent Woods has arguably golfed better in the late 1990s and early 2000s than anyone has before and anyone might in the near future. Female professional golfers Jean Park, Christine Kim, and Dorothy Delasin have emerged from America's Korean and Filipino American communities respectively to win their share of Ladies Professional Golf Association (LPGA) tournaments. And as this is written, youthful Korean Hawaiian Michelle Wie is conjuring up speculation that she can be just as dominant in the LPGA as Tiger Woods has been in the Professional Golf Association. (PGA) The six foot tall Wie has even held her own in men's tournaments.

Americans of Asian Pacific Islander ancestry have won more than their share of Olympic medals. In 1912, the celebrated Duke Kahanamoku became the first Native Hawaiian to win Olympic gold. Kahanamoku, subsequently, aided greatly the global popularity of Hawaiian sport of surfing. In 1948, Korean American Sammy Lee became the first Asian Pacific American to win the Olympic gold in diving, winning both the platform and the springboard championships. Lee's skills as a diver were so widely respected that South Korea's leader Syghman Rhee asked him to represent South Korea in the 1952 Olympiad. Lee thought about it but decided to dive for the United States again and was able to take home two more gold medals, as a consequence. In 1953, Lee became the first Asian Pacific American to win the prestigious Sullivan Award as America's best amateur athlete. After retiring from competitive diving, Lee, who was also a physician, coached his beloved sport. The magnificent Greg Louganis, who possesses Samoan ancestry, was one of his pupils.

Vicki Manalo was born in San Francisco in 1924. Her father was a Filipino immigrant and her mother was an English immigrant. Growing up in a working class neighborhood, the athletic Manalo wanted to take up diving on a serious basis. However, San Francisco's leading swimming and diving teams typically practiced in pools that excluded non-whites. She, therefore, changed her last name to Taylor, her mother's maiden name, and launched her career in competitive diving. As a teenager, Manalo blossomed into one of the best divers in a nation. Moreover, by the mid-1940s, she began to dive using her real last name. Heading into the 1948 Summer Olympiad, Manalo's coach was her husband Lyle Draves and with his help dived past other more famous American competitors to win the Olympic gold in platform and springboard diving. As a consequence, Vicki Manalo became the first American woman of Asian Pacific ancestry to win Olympic gold.

In swimming, Japanese Hawaiians did well in the post-World War II Olympics. Ford Konno and Yosh Oyakawa won Olympic gold medals in the 1950s. And Evelyn Kawamoto was another world class swimmer. Kawamoto, moreover, married Konno. Sadly, one of the greatest Japanese Hawaiian swimmers of all, Keo Nakama, was never able to medal in the Olympics mainly because his peak years occurred in the midst of World War II.

Several Hawaiians of Asian Pacific ancestry performed well in weightlifting after World War II. One of these was Hal Sakata, who later gained more fame as an actor playing Odd Job in a James Bond movie. Another was Tommy Kono, who took up weightlifting while in the concentration camps. It became more than merely a way to pass time, as Kono became arguably the most versatile weightlifter of the 1950s, winning world and Olympic titles in more than one weight division.

In more recent years, Asian Pacific American ice skaters have gained attention as prominent Olympic competitors. In 1992, Kristi Yamaguchi skated to Olympic gold. Since then, America's greatest ice skater has been Southern California's Nancy Kwan. However, while she has won many international titles the Olympic gold has escaped her. Once she took second to Tara Lipinsky. MSNBC's website announced, consequently, that an "American" had defeated Kwan, prompting protests from Asian Pacific Americans and a belated and not very satisfactory response from the network.

CONCLUSION

A growing literature of Asian Pacific American historical scholarship has pointed us in the right direction when it comes to discovering Asian Pacific American agency. This scholarship will show us that Asian Pacific Americans have protested injustice, edited newspapers, written magnificent poetry, directed important movies, designed beautiful buildings and moving monuments, raised families, and endured hardships. Yet relatively little of that scholarship acknowledges the importance of sports for Asian Pacific Americans historically.

Through sports Asian Pacific Americans could assert a sense of community and agency under often harsh conditions. Through sports, they could cross cultural barriers in order to play with and against non-Asian Pacific Americans. Through sports, they could achieve at least a semblance of fame and, in the case of Tiger Woods, an obscene amount of money. Through sports they could express a conviction that they, too, belonged in the American People's Club. Perhaps most of all, they could have fun, when, at times, fun was hard to find. However, through sports, they encountered bigotry, sometimes intentional and sometimes not. They recognized that "racism's traveling eye," to quote scholar Elaine Kim, remains observant on even baseball diamonds and basketball courts.

REVIEW

1. How have sports helped Asian Pacific Americans achieve a sense of community?
2. How have sports helped Asian Pacific Americans to cross cultural barriers?
3. Who have been Asian Pacific American pioneers and stars in American sports?
4. What kind of discrimination have Asian Pacific Americans faced in American sports?

SELECTED BIBLIOGRAPHY

Cisco, Dan. *Hawai'i Sports.* (1999).

Franks, Joel S. *Crossing Sidelines: Crossing Cultures.* (2000).

_____ . *Whose Baseball?* (2001).

_____ . *Hawaiian Sports in the Twentieth Century.* (2002).

Nagata, Yoichi. "The First All-Asian Pitching Duel in Organized Baseball: Japan vs. China in the PCL," *Baseball Research Journal.* No. 21., 1992.

Regalado, Sam. "Sport and Community in California's Japanese American 'Yamato Colony,' 1930-1945," *Journal of Sport History.* 19 (Summer 1992).

INDEX